TROUBLE SHOOTER

Jitendra Dixit is a Mumbai-based journalist with a career spanning nearly three decades, specializing in crime, conflict and political reportage. He was part of the founding team of Star News in 2003 and served as the editor (West) at ABP Network India until 2023. He is currently the executive editor at NDTV in Mumbai.

Jitendra began his television career with Aaj Tak in 1999 and has reported on major national and international events including the Gujarat riots (2002), the Mumbai serial blasts trials (2007), the 26/11 terrorist attacks (2008), the Japan tsunami (2011) and the Kedarnath tragedy (2013). In 2015, he received the prestigious RedInk Award for his documentary on the Kashmir elections.

He is also the author of several books exploring Mumbai's contemporary history, crime and politics.

TROUBLE SHOOTER

The Untold Encounters
of IPS Officer
K.P. RAGHUVANSHI

JITENDRA DIXIT

PAN

First published 2025 by Pan
an imprint of Pan Macmillan Publishing India Private Limited
707 Kailash Building
26 K. G. Marg, New Delhi 110001
www.panmacmillan.co.in

Pan Macmillan, The Smithson, 6 Briset Street, Farringdon,
London EC1M 5NR
Associated companies throughout the world
www.panmacmillan.com

ISBN 978-93-6113-341-1

1 3 5 7 9 8 6 4 2

Typeset in ITC Galliard Pro by R. Ajith Kumar, New Delhi
Printed and bound in India by Thomson Press India Ltd.

MIX
Paper | Supporting responsible forestry
FSC www.fsc.org FSC® C010615

To the resilient Adivasis of Dandakaranya
and those commandos of C-60 who made the
ultimate sacrifice in the line of duty

CONTENTS

FOREWORD

I have known Jitendra Dixit since 2000, when I was heading a Special Task Force (STF) to implement the recommendations of the Srikrishna Commission, which had investigated the Bombay riots of 1992–3. At the time, Jitendra was an emerging journalist in TV news and often visited me for exclusive stories. These informal sessions continued over the years, particularly during my time at the helm of the Anti-Terrorism Squad (ATS) and state railway police. Over tea, I would share learnings and experiences – both positive and challenging – from my various postings. Even after I retired, Jitendra maintained contact and frequently met with me to hear anecdotes from my policing career. He was especially intrigued by my tenure in Gadchiroli and as head of the STF. He urged me to write about my journey as a police officer, but I always laughed off the idea, believing my life wasn't extraordinary enough to be chronicled.

Then, one afternoon in June 2022, Jitendra surprised me at my office in the Hindustan Petroleum building in Churchgate. Now six years post-retirement, I had been working there as a consultant. To my astonishment, Jitendra presented a thick stack of notebooks in which he had been meticulously documenting our conversations over the years. He informed me of his plan to write a book about my life and sought my cooperation to verify certain facts and gather additional information about my family. Jitendra insisted that the book would be invaluable not only for aspiring police officers but also for those in uniform combating the Maoist insurgency. My story would demonstrate the efforts and sacrifices of the Maharashtra Police in countering crime and corruption in the state. Despite my Reluctance, I eventually yielded to Jitendra's persistence.

Reading this book has been a nostalgic journey, allowing me to relive the thirty-five years I served with the Maharashtra Police. Reflecting on my past, I feel content knowing I served with integrity, dedication and enthusiasm. Despite obstacles and setbacks, my passion for policing and the support of my colleagues and family helped me navigate difficult times. This book also reveals that a police officer's most formidable adversary may not be a Naxal, terrorist or gangster, but someone within his own ranks. Although initially wary of including my unpleasant encounters with politicians, I recognized that ultimately, this is Jitendra's book. As a journalist, he had the freedom to bring such stories to light.

I am grateful to Jitendra Dixit for writing *Troubleshooter* and congratulate him on this commendable endeavour. His illustrious reportage and storytelling skills are evident throughout. It was a pleasant surprise to note the extensive legwork and independent research Jitendra has done for the book. Rather than rely solely on my narration, he travelled to Gadchiroli several times, met people who worked during my tenure and visited the locations mentioned by me to ensure accuracy and credibility. I believe this book will prove valuable for readers.

K. P. Raghuvanshi
Indian Police Service (Retired)
15 July 2025, Mumbai

PREFACE

'In Mumbai, gangsters hide from the police. In Gadchiroli, the police hide from Naxals.'

Hearing these shocking words from the mouth of an 'encounter specialist' germinated the idea of this book in my mind. It was an afternoon in 2012 and I was at an Udipi restaurant outside Dadar Railway Station in Mumbai. Seated before me was my friend, Ravindranath Angre, who had gained notoriety for 'encountering' over fifty gangsters in Mumbai and Thane in the nineties. He was arrested on charges of extortion but later acquitted and posted in the Naxal-infested district of Gadchiroli, considered a punishment posting in the force.[1] Moreover, he was posted in the control room, away from the field and all the action.

During our hour-long meeting over tea, Angre explained how dangerous it was to be a policeman in Gadchiroli. Cops were often abducted and butchered by Naxalites, he said, 'But the only devil these beasts fear is C-60! If they kill a policeman, C-60 will make sure to avenge the murder. They are not your regular policemen.'

He clarified that C-60 was an elite force of the Gadchiroli Police, established to tackle Naxalism in the area. The force had effectively checked many dreaded Naxals and most of its commandos were local tribal youths.

Before meeting Angre, I knew little about C-60. I was born and brought up in the South Mumbai locality of Masjid Bunder, once infamous for communal clashes and gang-related violence. I grew up listening to underworld stories narrated by my elders at home. This birthed my interest in crime reporting, a calling that led me to start my career as a TV journalist in 1999. At the time, gang wars and other underworld activities were at their peak in Mumbai. As a crime beat reporter, my brief was to focus on organized crime syndicates in the city and later, on terrorist organizations like Lashkar-e-Taiba (LeT) and Indian Mujahideen, which had executed some of the deadliest attacks in India.

My conversation with Angre triggered a desire in me to dig up more information on C-60. I soon realized that the force was founded by Indian Police Service (IPS) officer, Krishipal Raghuvanshi, whom I met in 2000 when he was heading an STF to prosecute those who had been indicted for the Bombay riots of 1992–3.

Raghuvanshi deliberately maintained a low profile, but he was compelled to interact with journalists to some extent because of the significant positions he held. After delving deeper into the history of C-60, I started meeting him frequently and urged him to share interesting anecdotes about the formation of the unit and his policing career.

I diligently noted everything he had told me after our meetings, never revealing that I was thinking of collecting them in a book. I kept in touch with Raghuvanshi across his roles as inspector general (Konkan Range), additional director general (Railway Police) and chief of the ATS. He retired in 2015 as one of Maharashtra's most senior policemen.

In 2018, a major encounter between C-60 commandos and Naxalites occurred in Gadchiroli. Faced with no alternative, the police had killed several insurgents in what was claimed to be the biggest crackdown against Maoist violence in India. Coincidentally, my employer that time (ABP News) asked me to produce a short documentary on C-60. This offered me an opportunity to visit Gadchiroli and interact with the commandos. They gave a demo of their training, and I also went with a team to trek in the jungle. My interactions with the commandos and the then superintendent of police (SP) of Gadchiroli, Dr Abhinav Deshmukh, provided valuable insight into Maoist violence in the area and their efforts to contain it.

In June 2022, I met Raghuvanshi in Mumbai and revealed to him that I was writing a book about him and the C-60. He responded, 'Why do you want to glorify me? What I did in Gadchiroli was part of my job.' To convince him, I said that the book would help not only those researching left-wing extremism in India but also cops who might serve in the region. Still, Raghuvanshi was not very keen and met with me regarding the book at long intervals.

I then discussed the project with my friend and literary agent Anish Chandy. While Anish was pondering over whether to represent my book, Raghuvanshi informed me that he was visiting Delhi in December 2022. I arranged a meeting for him with Anish at a coffee shop in Greater Kailash. This proved to be a turning point. Anish realized that there is much more to Raghuvanshi's story – action-packed as it is – than his raising the C-60 commando force. 'The book should be about you, sir, not C-60,' Anish advised. His words convinced me, too, to rethink the heart of the book. It metamorphosed into a biography of Raghuvanshi – the man who had been a troubleshooter for the Maharashtra government on multiple occasions.

Apart from chronicling the highlights of K. P. Raghuvanshi's career – the C-60 squad, countering Naxalism in Gadchiroli and terrorist attacks in Mumbai – this book also delves into the real life of a policeman; the human behind the khaki uniform. Raghuvanshi didn't just speak to me of his laurels but also the mistakes he committed, the actions which made him feel guilty. He has endured his share of controversies, after all.

In a world where cop stories are told through action-packed masala movies and gory television shows, this book hopes to provide a well-rounded view of police work through the lens of Raghuvanshi's high-intensity stints in urban, rural and forest zones. Over the years, he's been pitted against Naxals, terrorists, gangsters and politicians alike.

I have also delved briefly into the impact of the Naxal

movement on the tribal villages of Gadchiroli. The Naxals who were initially seen as emancipators of the Adivasis ultimately transformed into extortionists and murderers. Numerous youths have been killed by Naxals for not toeing the line or on suspicion of being police informers. The already impoverished tribal communities have been exploited financially.

It is important to mention here that I have reimagined certain incidents and conversations based on the inputs of relevant people. However, even while taking some liberty for the sake of readability and flow, I have adhered to the facts. Since a large portion of the book details incidents that happened thirty to forty years ago, I have tried to visualize that era in my own words. I have changed the names of accused individuals who were still under trial while the book was being written, or convicts whose appeals are pending in the higher courts. I have interchangeably referred to insurgents in Gadchiroli as Maoists, Naxals and Naxalites, and the forest dwellers of Gadchiroli as Adivasis and tribals. I have used the name Bombay while narrating events that happened in the city before 1996 and Mumbai post that.

I have written this book in my individual capacity, and the news organisation I am employed with is not associated with it.

Jitendra Dixit
15 July 2025, Mumbai

1

A GUNFIGHT IN THE FOREST

No birds chirped in Dandakaranya forest on the morning of 22 April 2018. Instead, the rising sun was accompanied by the sounds of relentless gunfire, cries, curses and explosions. The lifting fog carried the scent of gunpowder. Wild birds scattered in search of safety. Splashes were heard as men in military attire jumped into the nearby Indravati river to escape the conflict.

'Jai Hind, sir. The information we received is correct. The enemy is located at the given coordinates. When we attempted to enter their camp, the sentries opened fire on us. We have begun retaliating and have already eliminated six Naxalites.'

SP Abhinav Deshmukh dreaded early morning phone calls. They usually carried unwelcome news of failed operations or the deaths of police personnel. When his phone rang in the early hours of 22 April, he couldn't help but feel a surge of tension. However, hearing these encouraging words from his junior colleague brought a smile to his face. Finally, his efforts to curb insurgency in the region were paying off. Abhinav informed the commander that he would send reinforcements and make his way to the scene as soon as possible.

Originally from Osmanabad, a young Abhinav had pursued a career in medicine until he realized that the world of stethoscopes and thermometres was not for him. He became an IPS officer in 2009 and was designated SP of Gadchiroli district in 2017. The post is viewed as both a punishment and the most important post in the Maharashtra Police. The SP is responsible for the government's battle against Naxalism and must ensure safe elections, implement the administration's schemes and protect its reputation.

Prior to commencing his posting, Abhinav familiarized himself with the lifestyle of the tribal community – their livelihood, customs and traditions – and the history of the Maoist movement in the district. He also gathered information about dangerous Naxals who had terrorized Gadchiroli and killed many policemen.

One of the most important and turbulent times in Gadchiroli is the plucking season for tendu leaves, which starts in May and lasts for over twenty-five days. This activity is crucial for the region's economy, as tendu leaves are used to make beedis. A beedi is made by rolling tobacco in a tendu leaf. In India, a total of 371,000 tons of tendu leaves are produced each year, valued at ₹950 crore. Gadchiroli is the largest producer in the country, accounting for 46,000 tons worth ₹115 crore.[1]

The Naxals entered the tendu leaf trade because they believed that contractors and the government were exploiting the tribals and paying them unfair wages. As a result, they began abducting and killing tendu contractors, as well as burning their vehicles and storehouses. The Naxals issued ultimatums to contractors who won the auction to buy the tendu leaves, demanding a significant amount of money during the plucking season in order to avoid their wrath. Every year, before the season began, the Naxals would secretly meet with the contractors to determine the sum of money to be extorted. The amount was based on the contract they had received – the bigger the contract, the more money was to be paid. The contractors didn't have much say in deciding the amount; the Naxals had the final word. This system had been in place for decades.

Abhinav knew that this gathering was the perfect opportunity to apprehend the Naxals. They would set up a camp for the meeting, where they would eat and sleep. However, such an operation would not be easy. The Naxals carefully chose meeting locations that were difficult for the police to reach and that they could easily escape in case the police did find them, as the Naxals were familiar with the area. The nearby villagers were threatened and forced to provide food for the camp, and sentries were deployed around the area to alert their comrades of any danger.

On 20 April 2018, the Gadchiroli Police received information from their Intelligence Cell that Naxal commanders were planning to hold a meeting with tendu contractors near Tadgaon in Laheri. This was confirmed by the Technical Cell of the police, through human intelligence gathered from retired police officers, officers who had infiltrated Naxal groups at great risk to their own lives as well as surrendered Naxals.

That night, two teams of C-60 commandos and Battalion-9 of the Central Reserve Police Force (CRPF) departed from their respective headquarters for the designated location. They travelled around 150 kilometres under the cover of night, leaving their vehicles a few kilometres away from the spot. They then proceeded on foot through the jungle until they reached their destination, taking care to hide among the bushes. The camp was allegedly located at the border of the Bijapur district of Chhattisgarh, on the opposite bank of the Indravati river, surrounded by hills on three sides. Since both states considered the Maoists to be a common enemy, jurisdictional boundaries were often crossed during operations.

The riverbanks were under constant surveillance, sharp eyes watching for any sign of disturbance. The commandos had to move silently and cautiously to avoid detection by the residents of Kasansur, a small village nearby. They feared that there might be Maoist sympathizers among the villagers who could expose the mission and lead to its failure. By 21 April, there had been no activity observed at the suspected Maoist gathering spot. This left the commando team perplexed and filled with uncertainty.

Despite their growing frustration, the commandos remained vigilant. They continued strategizing on how to storm the camp, searching for the best route to cross the river and pathways that would lead them to the hilltops. Amidst their planning, an informant alerted the team that the Maoists might be holding the meeting in Bhamragarh instead, 90 kilometres away from their current location. After careful consideration, Abhinav decided to send the two C-60 teams to Bhamragarh and instructed a small group of CRPF commandos to maintain their position.

With dusk setting in, the C-60 teams – led by commanders Madhukar Naitam and Vasudev Madavi – departed for Bhamragarh. They had covered half of the distance when they received yet another intelligence report: the Maoists had reached the previous location and set up camp in the darkness. This confirmed the accuracy of the original information. The police often contend with false flags and conflicting information when working with multiple informants. Surprised that the Maoists had chosen such a tactically absurd place for their camp, Abhinav instructed both teams that had left for Bhamragarh to return via a wireless message.

To attack the camp, the commandos had to cross the Indravati river. They parked their multi-purpose vehicles (MPV) 12 kilometres away from the camp and proceeded on foot. The jungle walk was riddled with danger. Dandakaranya was home to a variety of venomous snakes and animals. Bears in the area were known to attack humans, and patrolling cops often had close encounters with them. However, the greatest threat was posed by the abundance of mosquitoes that had multiplied after the recent unseasonable rainfall.

After hacking through dry grass for approximately two hours, both teams reached the bank of the Indravati. As locals, the C-60 commandos were familiar with suitable spots for crossing the river, taking into account its current, the depth of the water and numerous rocks for tying ropes. At around 2:30 a.m., the commandos began stealthily crossing the river. Commander Madavi's team led the way, followed by Commander Netam's. Crossing the river under the cover of darkness presented a challenge – to ensure their weapons and ammunition did not get wet. The river's width was a little over 100 metres. The commandos moved forward, balancing their belongings on their heads and holding onto ropes secured to rocks. River crossing was part of their training and within an hour and a half, all the commandos successfully reached the other side. The Naxals had stationed sentries to guard the riverbanks. During the day, a sentry's watch would extend up to approximately 500 metres, but in the darkness of night, this range was limited unless they possessed night-vision binoculars. The commandos swiftly took their positions on the hillocks that surrounded the camp from three sides and by 5 a.m., were ready to launch their attack.

According to intelligence reports, one of the dreaded Naxals attending the meeting was Dolesh Atram, also known as Sainath. He had joined the Naxal movement as a teenager in 2004 and quickly proved to be a demon for the police force.[2] He was known for abducting and killing policemen, particularly those who were on leave. He and his accomplices would seize their victims from marketplaces, buses or bus depots and brutally murder them. Some were stoned to death, while others had their throats slit. Among his victims were officers going home to care for their elderly and ill parents or meet their newborn children for the first time; those attending family functions or newly married officers taking their first leave. Sainath showed no mercy towards anyone. With seventy-five serious offenses registered against him, a reward of ₹16 lakh had been placed on Sainath's head.[3] Top Maoist leaders in the area, impressed with his performance, appointed Sainath the commander of the Permili dalam. Not long before he had been inducted into the Divisional Committee of the CPI (Maoist).[4]

Their weapons loaded, the commandos waited for dawn with their index fingers on the triggers. The plan was to surround the Naxals from all sides and make an announcement once the first ray of sunlight appeared, giving them no avenue of escape. The aim was to capture the Naxalites alive – they held valuable information that could aid in further operations and the arrest of senior leaders. However, if the Naxals attacked, the commandos would exercise their right to defend themselves.

As the red dot of sunrise pierced the dark sky, the teams were prepared for action. The anger in their eyes was palpable – none showed signs of fatigue despite the hours of travel. Suddenly, gunshots rang out, accompanied by a cloud of smoke. A bullet narrowly missed a commando's ear, fired by a Naxal sentry who had spotted him hiding in the bushes. This was exactly the 'warm welcome' the commandos had been expecting. They retaliated from all directions – a single shot to the sentry's head proved fatal. Another commando discharged a grenade from an Under Barrel Grenade Launcher, enveloping the area in smoke.

The surprise attack threw the encampment into chaos. Some Naxals were woken from their slumber, while others who were bathing near the river or preparing breakfast were called to attention. All at once, the Naxals grabbed their guns and scattered in every direction. Those who had just woken up perished in the crossfire; those seeking refuge behind trees were soon taken down by bullets too.

Inside the camp, there were numerous women Naxals. Among them was Madhuri, who joined the movement in 2002 after she was kidnapped from her village, Gattepalli, in the fifth grade. She was indoctrinated into the dalam and received weapons training. In 2010, she married a fellow Naxal, Kartik Vike. However, after she developed epilepsy, Madhuri was assigned non-combatant responsibilities within the dalam. Madhuri was all set to participate in a motivational session held every morning in a corner of the camp when the encounter began. The sudden eruption of gunfire triggered an epileptic seizure, causing her to collapse on the ground.

The commandos relentlessly fired as they encircled the camp, causing several Naxals to plunge into the river in an attempt to escape the barrage of bullets. The air was filled with screams, cries and a volley of expletives exchanged between the warring parties. The deafening sounds of gunfire and explosions reverberated through villages located 3–4 kilometres away.

About an hour after his commander first informed him that the encounter had begun, Abhinav received a second call. He was told that twelve Naxals had been eliminated thus far. News of the encounter had already spread to senior officers and even local journalists. Abhinav, being fully engaged in supervising the operation, was unable to attend to calls from media personnel seeking more information. Without official confirmation, the news began to circulate in a distorted manner. A rumour soon spread that six C-60 commandos had perished in the operation. This eventually reached Chief Minister Devendra Fadnavis in Mumbai, causing him great concern. An anxious Fadnavis personally called Abhinav, seeking an update on the ground situation.

'Deshmukh Saheb, what is the current status? How many of our men have been killed?'

'There have been no casualties on our side, sir. In fact, our C-60 commandos have eliminated at least twelve Naxals. Our operation is progressing successfully,' Abhinav responded confidently.

Upon hearing Abhinav's report, Fadnavis let out a sigh of relief. He assured Abhinav that he would provide any necessary support and ended the call.[5]

The firing that began at daybreak lasted for five hours.

As the encounter raged on, the commandos received accurate information that helped them identify Sainath among the Naxals. Just one day earlier, he had sought refuge in a nearby hamlet called Boriya, along with two other accomplices. Throughout the day, the trio had stayed in a villager's home and only arrived at the camp after nightfall.

Sainath was washing his face when the combat started. He immediately rallied his comrades to take up arms and fight back. Allegedly, the man himself fired his AK-47 indiscriminately at anything that moved. The Naxals around him fell one by one, and he soon ran out of bullets. Undeterred, Sainath picked up a fallen comrade's weapon and continued firing. He ran out of ammunition again. The commandos stopped firing and urged Sainath to surrender, but he ignored them and rushed to grab a rifle from another fallen Naxalite a few metres away. Just then, a grenade detonated near him, enveloping him in a cloud of red smoke as he let out a piercing scream.

Amidst the chaos, the commandos heard someone shouting instructions in Telugu.

'Cover the right side, all of you!'

'Yes, Shinu Anna,' one of the Naxals responded.[6]

Some of the C-60 commandos understood Telugu and the name Shinu Anna sent a shiver down their spines. The dreaded Naxalite Srinivas, also known as Vijender, was called Shinu Anna by his comrades. The fifty-one-year-old hailed from the Warangal district of Telangana and was wanted for eighty-two cases of murder, robbery and extortion.[7] While Srinivas was giving instructions to his comrades, a bullet struck him, and he collapsed.

By 11 a.m., the intensity of the Naxals' firing had decreased and the commandos had made significant progress towards the camp. Before entering the grounds, they used a landmine detector to search the bloodstained soil. The lifeless bodies of the Naxalites were scattered throughout the area, along with their weapons, spent bullet casings, jerry cans, toothbrushes, soaps, medications, footwear, clothes and Maoist literature. The essentials that each Naxalite carried – a plastic mat, uniform, steel plate, medications and toiletries – were strewn about. Once the operation was over, the commandos gathered the dead bodies and placed them in a corner. The same thought was on everyone's mind: if they hadn't killed the Naxalites, they would be the ones lying dead.

In a preliminary search, the C-60 commandos and CRPF personnel recovered a cache of firearms, including AK-47s, INSAS rifles, self-loading rifles and twelve bore guns. The Naxalites had taken these weapons from the police officers who were killed during ambushes. Now, these same weapons were being used against the commandos. A gun has no loyalty; it belongs to whoever wields it. Meanwhile, Abhinav received information that some Naxalites had escaped to the Rajaram Khandla forest. He immediately dispatched a team to locate them. A few hours later, news came that six Naxalites had been killed in a confrontation at the second location.[8]

The bodies of the Naxalites who had plunged into

the Indravati in a bid to escape soon began floating to the surface. The river, which runs through Odisha, Chhattisgarh and Maharashtra, is infested with crocodiles. When the Naxalites panicked and jumped into the river, they were attacked by the reptiles. With the help of locals, the police began retrieving the half-eaten and mutilated corpses. In total, forty alleged Naxalites had been killed across both locations – seven women among them. It was remarkable that there were no police casualties during such large-scale encounters. It soon became clear that this was a historic anti-Maoist operation in India. The Naxals who had been killed had a combined bounty of ₹82 lakh on their heads.[9] Leaders such as Sainath and Shinu Anna had perished. Naxals from the Permili, Sironcha and Aheri dalams had convened in the camp, and all three dalams were completely wiped out in the aftermath. A dalam typically consists of fifteen to twenty members.

At the entrance of the Gadchiroli police headquarters, a display board showcases the names and photos of top Naxalites. It serves not only as a record of the C-60's accomplishments but also as a source of inspiration for its personnel. Once the operation concluded, the jubilant commandos used a sketch pen to mark an X on the faces of Sainath and Srinivas.

Abhinav was pleased with their success, but he knew that a significant challenge was close at hand. After the encounters became public knowledge, several human rights groups and individuals sympathetic to the Naxal cause began to question the actions of the police. They alleged that the Naxals had been brutally killed by the police while they were attending a wedding in the nearby Kasansur village. Some even claimed that the food given to the Naxals at the wedding had been poisoned. There were also doubts raised about whether the individuals who were killed were actually Naxals.[10] As usual, Abhinav diligently prepared the required reports for the state and national human rights commissions after the encounters. He knew that the Maoists would eventually attempt retribution, and he had to be on alert.

900 kilometres away, Fadnavis expressed his admiration for the C-60 commandos and the CRPF during a press conference in Mumbai. Retired IPS officer Krishipal Raghuvanshi keenly watched the news unfold from his home in Thane, coffee cup in hand. The anchor's shrill words – 'The biggest campaign against Maoists in Maharashtra's Gadchiroli! Forty Naxals killed!' – resonated with Krishipal. As the founder of the C-60 force, he still closely followed its activities. He called Abhinav Deshmukh to hear the story straight from the source. 'Congratulations, Abhinav. Has the team returned safely?'

Abhinav thanked him and gave a brief account of how the operation was carried out. As Krishipal listened, he swelled with pride. The C-60 force was the crowning achievement of his thirty-five years of police service; it had turned the tide in the bloody war against the Naxals. Nostalgia washed over him, reminding him of his long journey from a timid boy to a fearless cop.

2

TIMID BOY BECOMES A COP

Despite being a brilliant student with a knack for mathematics, Krishipal failed his fifth-grade district board exam in the subject. During the paper, a classmate sitting behind him kept pestering him for help by pulling on his shirt. Peeved, Krishipal turned to rebuke his classmate, only to be caught by the stern gaze of the examiner. Suspecting the boy was copying his work, the teacher demanded, 'What's going on? Do you need a thrashing?'

Panicked and embarrassed, Krishipal's hand accidentally knocked over his inkwell, spilling the dark liquid all over his carefully written answers. His mind went blank, unable to salvage the situation as time ticked away. When the bell rang, signalling the end of the exam, the unforgiving teacher swiftly snatched away Krishipal's answer sheet. He was awarded a disastrous zero marks.

Krishipal hailed from Kutbi-Kutba village, nestled about 115 kilometres from Delhi in the heart of western Uttar

Pradesh's Jatland, where life revolved around agriculture. As he trudged homeward from the village's zilla parishad-run school, tears welled in his eyes, dreading the disappointment of his parents. Krishipal's grandfather had opted against educating his father, training him to labour in the fields. However, Krishipal's father, embracing a more progressive mindset, offered his seven sons a choice: to toil on the family farm or pursue education. Initially inclined towards the former, Krishipal soon realized his passion for learning and was enrolled in school.

Though a dedicated and successful student, the humiliating events of the exam day left Krishipal questioning himself. What would his father think? Was he no longer committed to his studies? Had he become careless? These thoughts weighed heavily on Krishipal's mind as he walked towards his home on the thin pathway that bisected the farm.

Suddenly, he spotted a police jeep zipping into the village, leaving a little sandstorm behind. The arrival of cops in Kutbi-Kutba was a big deal. Krishipal noticed the absence of the usual hubbub in the streets, the desolate emptiness of the village. There were no elders gossiping in the verandas. Doors of houses had been shut from inside, which was unusual in the afternoon. Some people watched the police jeep's movements from half-opened windows, their eyes scared. Krishipal sped up his steps, an ominous feeling coming over him.

Upon reaching home, Krishipal was informed that there had been a murder in the village, and a team from the police station in Titavi had been sent to investigate. He still couldn't understand why the villagers were so terrified at seeing a police jeep. Only the actual culprit needed to be afraid – why was the entire village acting guilty? It was only after overhearing discussions among the elders that Krishipal realized everyone was afraid of the police. The khaki uniform had such a forceful grip on their psyche that no one dared to step out of their homes when faced with it. In school, he had been taught that cops were public servants and protectors of the people, but in reality he saw that the villagers considered themselves subservient to the cops. Krishipal was astounded by the power that the police wielded. He wanted to understand the magic of that khaki-coloured garb and resolved to wear it himself. To become someone who commands both fear and respect seemed a worthwhile goal.

Krishipal failed grade five and had to repeat a year. His academic performance was scrutinized by his father and his elder brother Omprakash, who was posted in Muradabad as an additional development officer. In time, Krishipal realized that if he wanted to become a senior officer, he had to fully devote himself to his studies. Krishipal enjoyed watching '*Saang*', musical theatre. In Saang, heroic stories of the historical figures like Prithviraj Chauhan and Rani of Jhansi were told through songs. Krishipal used to get overwhelmed with enthusiasm and patriotism after watching them. But gradually he stopped visiting Saang performances and focused on his studies. The village had no electricity supply and during nights he studied by making a lamp of a used glass bottle filled with kerosene. Krishipal topped in his school when the results of the board examinations of grade ten were out. The school added his name in the 'Roll of Honour', which was displayed outside the principal's office. That evening, the villagers gathered for a hookah session at Krishipal's home and showered him with praise.

In every Jat family, the hookah is a ubiquitous presence that has come to represent the community itself. Watching the elders gurgling hookah, Krishipal was often curious about the sensation but could never gather courage to even touch it. One of the servants of the house, Deenu, was a chain-smoker. Krishipal had often seen him puffing a beedi and thought it would offer the same sensation as a hookah, since both involved inhaling smoke. One day, when Deenu lit up a beedi while taking their buffalo to the village pond for bathing, Krishipal asked for a drag. He took the first puff and started coughing. Coincidentally, one of Krishipal's elder brothers was passing by and noticed him holding a beedi. When Krishipal reached home that day, his father thrashed him black and blue. Though he confessed to trying the beedi, Krishipal said in a rebellious tone, 'One day, I will smoke a beedi with my money.' Little did he know that he would one day become a police legend in a place known for producing beedis.

Krishipal moved to Sirsaganj to pursue his higher education. He lived with his elder brother, Rampal, who was a marketing inspector in the Food and Civil Supplies Department. Rampal was a simple yet stern man, which made Krishipal fearful and cautious around him. As soon as Rampal entered the house, he would pick up his books and start studying, for fear of being reprimanded if he was caught doing anything else.

One Saturday, a regional food controller who was an Indian Administrative Service (IAS) officer unexpectedly visited Rampal's office. Rampal immediately stood at attention and offered the officer his chair, nodding respectfully as he issued instructions. Rampal then asked Krishipal to fetch a glass of water for the officer, since the office peon was off duty. After the officer left, an impressed Krishipal asked his brother, 'Why did that man seem so arrogant and full of himself, as if he is the wisest person on this Earth?'

'He is an IAS officer. IAS officers rule the country. They are considered the most powerful people in India. Some of them become collectors, treated like kings of their districts.'

'Are they more powerful than the police?'

'Yes. The police are under them.'

In that moment, Krishipal resolved to become an IAS officer. 'I may fear my brother,' he told himself, 'but my brother fears that IAS officer. Why not strive to become someone like him?'

Krishipal enrolled in Meerut University for a post-graduate degree in science. The campus was only a few kilometres from Meerut city and on the weekends, Krishipal and his friends went there for outings. Before returning to their hostels, they often drank milk from a local shop, served in earthen cups called *kulhads*. They enjoyed flinging empty kulhads beside the road, delighting as they cracked with a loud sound. At the time, Emergency had been imposed in India and the police were constantly on alert to detain protestors. Police atrocities were rampant. Cops carried blank warrants with them, so they could write the names of the people they arrested.

One Sunday night, when Krishipal and his friends were smashing kulhads as usual, a police team mistook them for anti-Emergency protestors. They were detained, showered with expletives and taken to the police station. After being held for a couple of hours, their names were taken down in a diary and they were let off with a warning. Everybody was worried that their police records would be spoiled, harming their chances of getting a government job. Krishipal was deeply hurt by the behaviour of the police. He had always believed police officers must be kind and just people who use their powers for public interest. This interaction with the cops was a wake-up call that the men in uniform could make or break people's lives. After being impressed by Rampal's boss, Krishipal had aspired to become an IAS officer. This incident once again drew him to choose the IPS.

Krishipal's father advised him to keep appearing for competitive examinations but take up a job until he was recruited. Krishipal began working as a temporary lecturer of Botany at I. P. College, Bulandshahr. In 1977, he was selected as a permanent lecturer in Janta Vedic College, Baraut. However, the college principal refused to approve his appointment. Krishipal heard from some people that the principal wanted him to marry his daughter. The principal had subtly hinted his wishes during their interactions, but Krishipal had not been able to comprehend these indications. Ultimately, after the vice chancellor intervened, he was able take the charge after waiting for over four months.

Krishipal began preparing for the Union Public Service Commission (UPSC) examination while working as a lecturer. In 1979, he appeared for Indian Forest Service and the civil service examinations, both conducted in Delhi. Hari Singh Nalwa, one of Krishipal's college friends, invited him to stay in his hostel room along with another common friend and UPSC aspirant, Yogesh Malik.

There were several major changes to the examination system in their batch: common selection examinations were being conducted for various services like IAS and IPS, and preliminary exams had been introduced. Due to the unprecedented selection process, the examinees weren't sure what was going to be asked of them. Krishipal's job proved to be advantageous – whatever he studied, he revised while teaching the students. Though he was unsure whether he would be able to crack the exam on his first attempt, the results proved him wrong. He achieved a decent rank in the merit list and was selected as an IPS officer.

Krishipal enrolled in Sardar Vallabhbhai Patel National Police Academy (SVPNPA) in Hyderabad, which was spread across 277 acres of land. He was impressed by the academy's mission statement: 'The purpose of this academy is to prepare leadership for the Indian Police, who will lead the force with courage, uprightness, dedication and strong sense of service to the people.'[1]

During British rule, there were provincial police training schools and every province trained their cops differently. Policemen across the country were disparate and knew little about each other's ways of functioning. When India attained independence, the country's first home minister, Sardar Vallabhbhai Patel, found such an arrangement absurd. He believed that to keep the country united, there must be a single administrative and policing system. Since the concept of an all-India police service was Patel's brainchild, the academy was given his name.[2]

The curriculum at SVPNPA included maintenance of law and order, crowd control, forensic science, crime investigation, interrogation techniques, scene of crime survey, legal documentation and provisions of various laws. The trainees were taught rock climbing, swimming, martial arts and how to handle different types of weapons. They were also instructed in horse riding, to prepare those who might join the mounted police units introduced by the British and maintained by state police after Independence.[3] Krishipal enjoyed handling horses but lost interest after he narrowly avoided a grievous accident.

It was paradoxical that on one hand the IPS trainees were being taught a wide range of subjects and on the other hand, no training was being given to counter Maoism, though many areas like Srikakulam, Adilabad and Karimnagar in Andhra Pradesh – where the academy was located – had become hotbeds of Maoist violence. No training was given to counter the guerrilla warfare techniques adopted by the Maoists, nor were the trainees sensitized to the Maoist ideology.

An IPS officer's fate in terms of state cadre is uncertain – they could be posted anywhere in the country. Thus, trainees are taken on a countrywide tour, known as 'Bharat Darshan', to expose them to a plethora of cultures, lifestyles, cuisines and social structures. This tour is a chance for the young officers in their mid-twenties to forge lasting friendships, bond with their peers and let their hair down. Trainees are divided into different batches, each visiting a different set of states and Union Territories. Krishipal's batch went to Maharashtra, Rajasthan and Delhi.

While he enjoyed the entire tour, Krishipal found Maharashtra particularly fascinating. He was amazed to see the ancient architectural work in Ajanta and Ellora; to learn about the Mughal–Maratha conflict while visiting Aurangzeb's tomb near Aurangabad (now Chhatrapati Sambhaji Nagar). When he reached Bombay, he saw the sea for the first time in his life – the mighty waves of Arabian Sea clashing with the tetrapods of Marine Drive. In Film City, Krishipal got a chance to witness a movie shoot; in Igatpuri in the Nashik district he was mesmerized with the abundance of nature's beauty. At every turn, Krishipal was in awe of Maharashtra's rich cultural heritage and the warmth of its people.

While in Bombay, Krishipal's friend who worked in the

custom's department invited him for a night out. He took Krishipal to a cabaret bar in Colaba which, in reality, was a striptease joint. Young girls came onto the stage one by one in a hall with a mini theatre-like seating arrangement and stripped before the audience, who cheered with every garment the dancers removed. For a man like Krishipal, born and brought up in a conservative village family, witnessing such an event was a cultural shock. He found it difficult to sleep that night.

Shortly after the Bharat Darshan tour was completed, the cadre allocations were announced. In those days, cadres were allocated only near the end of their training. On the day of the announcement, Krishipal's heart was pounding like all his other batchmates, in anxious anticipation. His future was going to be shaped by the state he was assigned; the state where he would spend the rest of his policing career. That afternoon, Krishipal was allotted the Maharashtra cadre. He had hoped to be posted in his home cadre of Uttar Pradesh, but Maharashtra was not bad. Krishipal was ready to devote the rest of his life to Maharashtra.

After completing his training, Krishipal was sent to the Akola district of Maharashtra as a probationary officer in 1982. During the probation period, an officer is expected to familiarize himself with the functioning of the police on ground and gain practical experience. Krishipal's began his service at a time when low-ranking policemen across the state were rebelling for better working conditions and housing. During those days, each district had a union for the police which was supported by politicians. The incumbent politicians appeased police union leaders to use them in their power games.

In Bombay, the rebellion had turned violent. Members of the Bombay Police Union wreaked havoc on the city after their organization was banned. A bloody conflict ensued between the rebels and those loyal to the government. At the request of the state government, Prime Minister Indira Gandhi asked the army and paramilitary forces to quell the uprising. The government imposed a curfew in Bombay, but this did little to contain the violence. Shops were looted, trains pelted with stone, airport operations suspended and hundreds of buses, trucks and cars torched. Ultimately, the army had no choice but to open fire on rebels. Four people died and over thirty were injured.

Undercurrents of a similar conflict were being felt in Akola. The fire of police rebellion had spread to its neighbouring districts, like Nagpur and Amravati. One afternoon, the SP of Akola, Surendra Mohan Shanghari, received the dreadful news that a group of rebel constables had planned to loot the armoury that night. Shanghari asked Krishipal to lock the armoury and leave the district police headquarters with the key in his care on the pretext of going for an anti-dacoity operation. Krishipal followed his orders and the loot of the armoury was prevented.

Although the armoury was secured, weapons were also available at other locations like police stations and chowkies. The fear was that the rebels could snatch weapons from these less-protected sites. Even the loyal cops who were part of Krishipal's team were viewed with suspicion as there was a risk that they would switch sides in the prevailing atmosphere. Under these circumstances of fear and distrust, Krishipal continued his training, which included working as a police station in-charge and as a sub divisional police officer.

Even after Krishipal's training ended in April 1983 he remained in Akola, as his next posting had not been announced. Meanwhile, an officer one year junior to him came to Akola for his own training. This tall and fair-skinned young man from Bombay was Rakesh Maria, who became one of the most celebrated cops in the country at the peak of his career. Krishipal accommodated Maria at his residence and helped him get acquainted with the area. One month later, Krishipal got his orders to be posted in Pune. His life as a police officer was set to begin.

3

THE CHALLENGE OF COMMUNAL VIOLENCE

By the time Krishipal became an assistant superintendent of police (ASP) in Pune (Rural), he was already a married man and a father. In May 1982, his parents had arranged his marriage to Sarita, who was pursuing an MA in Nainital. She too belonged to a police family. Her grandfather had been a much-feared police officer under the British Raj, known as Darogaji (police inspector) even after his retirement. Not long after, Krishipal and Sarita became parents of a girl whom they named Garima. Filled with joy and excitement about the future, Krishipal relocated to Pune with his family to assume his new responsibilities.

Eager to immerse himself in his role, Krishipal diligently familiarized himself with the district, forging connections with the locals through regular meetings and social engagements. He met people from various backgrounds, including politicians, businessmen, social workers, lawyers and former criminals who now worked as police informers. These relationships proved invaluable as he handled cases of murder, attempt to murder and dacoity as ASP.

However, the unpredictable nature of the police force was a bitter truth that Krishipal was about to taste first-hand. In his line of work, stability was a luxury – senior officers and politicians wielded the power to transfer personnel at whim, without prior notice. Just six months into his tenure in Pune, Krishipal found himself abruptly uprooted from his newfound routine. He received an unexpected transfer as ASP, Solapur, forcing him to leave behind the networks he had painstakingly built and the comforting familiarity of Pune. Rumour had it that Krishipal's sudden transfer was a political decision taken by the powers to be, who wanted their own loyalists on the force.

At Solapur, he had a ringside view of the menace of the local gang lords who terrorized the entire city. They extorted money from shopkeepers and small businessmen, and were involved in bootlegging on a large scale. These criminals had no fear of the law and rampantly molested women. Despite the looming danger, the citizens of Solapur didn't trust the police to ensure their safety. Krishipal resolved to change the reputation of his force. He personally pursued every complaint received against the gang lords and made several public arrests. When he first took charge at Solapur, many cases of theft and dacoity had been left undetected. He directed the police stations to relaunch these investigations and many cold cases were solved. His efforts were celebrated by the local press and citizens' organizations.[1]

Solapur was a communally sensitive city and there had been a number of clashes between its Hindu and Muslim populations. After the 1981 mass conversion controversy in the Meenakshipuram village of Tamil Nadu, the Vishva Hindu Parishad (VHP) and other saffron organizations began organizing rallies across India to prevent a repeat of such an event.[2] In March 1984, riots broke out when such a march passed in front of a mosque in Solapur. Many shops were burnt down. Krishipal dealt stringently with rioters from both communities. As peace was slowly restored, another incident triggered tension – the murder of a Muslim youth.

That day, friends and relatives were visiting from Mumbai and Pune to celebrate Garima's first birthday. A party had been planned for the evening – all the preparations had been done – but Krishipal was unable to reach home that day. An agitated crowd surrounded the police station, demanding justice for the murdered teen. All efforts to pacify the mob failed. At last, some protestors relented and said that they would trust justice would be done if Krishipal personally investigated the case. The matter reached Vilasrao Deshmukh, then Maharashtra's home minister. With Deshmukh's approval, Krishipal stood on the bonnet of his police jeep and announced that he would be taking the investigation into his hands; that the culprits would not be spared irrespective of their religious identity. After Krishipal's announcement, the mob dispersed.

Although the tension was temporarily diffused, another challenge loomed the next day, when the funeral was set to take place. The police had received intelligence that an emotionally charged, possibly violent mob was likely to gather and called for preventive measures. Krishipal decided that he would pilot the funeral procession with his men. His idea worked and the young man was buried peacefully. Soon, Krishipal arrested the murderers as well.

The news that a novice officer had skilfully defused a communally charged situation reached the political leadership of the state. At the time, many areas of Maharashtra had been gripped by communal tension – Krishipal's deftness could be utilized there. So, in the same year, Krishipal was appointed a deputy commissioner of police (DCP) in Bombay's neighbouring city, Thane. The rank of a DCP in a commissionerate is equivalent to that of an SP in a district. However, a DCP has a little more authority, including the ability to exercise quasi-judicial powers such as sanctioning preventive arrests, the externment of criminals and the issuing of prohibitory orders.

The primary reason for Krishipal's transfer was to manage communally sensitive areas like Bhiwandi and Kalyan that fell under the Thane Commissionerate. Just before his transfer, Bhiwandi – a city known for its power looms – had endured a communal frenzy that shocked the whole nation. The Hindu–Muslim violence resulted in hundreds of deaths and several people were grievously injured. It was the Bhiwandi riot that established Shiv

Sena as a militant Hindu organization.[3] Having already proved his mettle in defusing tense communal situations without resorting to violence in Solapur, Krishipal was initially given charge of the Crime Branch of the Thane City Police but later made a zonal DCP in Kalyan.

Adjacent to Bhiwandi, Kalyan was just as communally volatile. Every police station in the town had a 'Good Morning Squad' – early morning patrols that alerted senior officers of troublesome incidents. On the morning of Ramadan Eid, a sub-inspector (SI) called Krishipal's home number in a panic.

'Sir, a white animal has been found at a mosque.'

'What?' Krishipal was unable to comprehend what the inspector meant by 'white animal'.

In a hesitant tone, the SI explained, 'Sir, the headless body of a piglet has been found outside the gate of Doodhnaka mosque.'

The words jolted Krishipal. He quickly realized that this was a conspiracy to ruin the festival and start a riot. People would soon pour into the mosque to attend the Eid namaaz. Krishipal rushed to the scene and asked his team to cover the dead piglet with flowers. He then met with the trustees of the mosque, who were still unaware of the incident, and pleaded, 'I request you to not discuss this incident with anyone, at least till afternoon.'

'You are trying to cover up this crime and shield the culprit!' an enraged trustee alleged.

'See, if this news spreads, it could lead to heavy bloodshed. After fasting for a month, do you want to spoil your festival like this? The people who have done this intend the same. I assure you that the perpetrators will not be spared.'

Convinced, the trustees agreed to Krishipal's request and kept mum. He immediately got the place cleaned up and disposed of the body. Eid was celebrated peacefully.

Having prevented riots in the city, Krishipal now had to make good on his promise and identify the conspirators. Since their attempt to incite violence had proved unsuccessful, he was sure the culprits would try again. Krishipal deployed his best officers to crack the case. A few days later, the cops came across an eyewitness who had seen three men carrying a squealing piglet in an auto-rickshaw. The witness remembered a distinctive painting of a man on the back of the vehicle. Shortly, the auto-rickshaw driver was traced and he confirmed that three men had travelled in his vehicle the previous night. He led the cops to the farmer from whom the culprits had bought the piglet under the guise of organizing a 'pork feast'. Based on the information provided by him, the cops traced the three men to Sangli and arrested them. They were members of a fundamentalist religious organization.

Unfortunately, luck did not always favour Krishipal. Not long after, Kalyan was once again on the brink of Hindu–Muslim riots. The last day of the Ganesh festival coincided with Muharram. The procession to immerse the Ganpati idols was set to pass through Ahilyabai Chowk. In an adjacent street, Muslims had installed Punjatans – symbols of five prominent figures in Islam, revered primarily by members of the Shia sect – from which the Holy Quran was to be recited. To prevent a confrontation between the two communities, Krishipal had asked the Muslims to finish their event by 3:30 p.m. On the other hand, the organizers of the Ganpati festival had been asked to delay their procession so they would reach the chowk by 5:30 p.m. If all went according to plan, the groups would not come face to face and the police would have ample time to deploy security arrangements along the immersion route.

However, the Muharram event continued after the scheduled time and the immersion procession also reached the spot an hour early. Krishipal immediately directed a police truck to block the entrance of the street where the Muharram event was ongoing. When the procession reached the chowk, a few Hindu participants became agitated on seeing the vehicle. 'In this country do Hindus need to celebrate their festivals in the shadow of police?' someone yelled.

Soon, others joined him and demanded the police truck be removed. They surrounded the vehicle and some threw stones and glass bottles towards the Muslim gathering. The youngsters who had gathered for Muharram also became aggressive and prepared to retaliate. The situation became explosive within minutes.

One of the inspectors shouted at the top of his lungs, 'Sir, the situation is getting out of hand! Give us the order for firing!' Faced with such an impossible situation, Krishipal's mind went numb. Unable to make a decision, all he could do was ensure that his distress did not reflect in his body language. Krishipal ignored the pleading officer and, to look nonchalant, lit up a cigarette from his pocket and inhaled deeply. The smoke blurred his vision momentarily and when it cleared, he recognized a familiar figure amongst the aggressive mob.

Bald and stout, the man had a thick moustache and wore several thick gold chains on his neck. He was a local strong man with whom Krishipal had cordial relations. Just a few days earlier, Krishipal had postponed the externment of a goon on his request. He immediately approached the man and pulled him aside by his collar. 'You motherfucker, was it for this that I did a favour to you?' he demanded. 'I want this fracas to end now.'

'Sir, please remove your police truck from the chowk,' the man pleaded. 'I will convince the crowd to leave the place then. I promise you that the situation will be defused.'

Krishipal had two options: either order his men to lathi-charge or worse, fire at the crowd, or risk following the man's advice. If he did the former, a few people would certainly be killed or injured. This could trigger violence elsewhere or ignite a political controversy, leading to him and his men getting suspended and facing an enquiry. The second option was also risky. If the police truck was removed, the Hindu mob could enter the street where the prayer meet was taking place and spark a violent confrontation. Krishipal was caught between the devil and the deep sea.

'Okay. But if situation worsens, you will be the first one

whose ass I will pump with bullets.' Krishipal delivered the warning with a smile and then directed the truck driver to pretend that he was shifting the vehicle by igniting its engine. The revellers were pacified and the procession started moving.

Krishipal then went to the Muslim camp, where the agitated young men were getting ready to confront the Hindu rioters. His efforts to placate them were in vain. Instead, he requested some of the women in the camp to pacify everybody. He warned them that if violence broke out, he would have to order a firing, putting them all at risk. The mob dispersed shortly.

After this incident, word spread in the police department about how tactfully Krishipal handled a very sensitive situation, without a single shot fired. The State Intelligence Department (SID) which briefed the CM regularly also lauded Krishipal in its report.

It was often said that no police commissioner of Thane could complete their tenure due to recurring communal violence in Kalyan and Bhiwandi. In just three and a half years, the Maharashtra government had cycled between five police commissioners. Despite the issues in the region, the then police commissioner, N. C. Venkatachalam, was happy with Krishipal's work. Even in the face of frequent precarious situations, Krishipal never allowed them to escalate to the level of bloodshed.

The city had another major problem, Kalyan bandhs. These were city-wide shutdowns perennially called by political parties. In the 1980s several local politicians had been murdered in quick succession. Over half a dozen such murders had happened within a year. Some of these politicians had a criminal background and were killed due to their past enmities and rivalries. Their parties would then call for a shutdown in the city to protest the killing. Shops, schools, colleges, public transportation – all had to be shut in fear of violence on the bandh day.

Once a group of shop owners led by a jeweller met Krishipal in his office. They complained that the frequent bandhs in the city had made their lives miserable and led to losses. Krishipal told them that while voluntarily closing one's shop was acceptable, nobody could be forced to do so. He advised the delegation to disregard any bandhs organized by political parties going forward. All shopkeepers could keep their establishments open like regular days with the assurance that the police would deal with the troublemakers. The shop owners trusted his words, but Krishipal knew he had taken a monumental risk by making such a promise. It would antagonize the incumbent politicians and potentially ruin his career.

A few days later, a local leader of a political party was killed in Kolshewadi. As usual, the party announced a Kalyan bandh through its notice boards across the city. Not a single shop owner downed their shutters. A senior leader of the party who later became a union minister, AUM (named changed), was riled to see the normalcy in the city. He announced that the funeral procession would proceed from the home of the deceased leader to the crematorium, passing through various parts of the city. Fearing violence during the procession, Krishipal denied them permission.

An enraged AUM barged into Krishipal's office with his minions and ranted, 'We have lost an important leader. First you don't allow the shutdown and now you are denying permission for the funeral procession. Isn't this atrocious?'

'Mr AUM, it is not the job of the police to shut down the city. If shopkeepers want their establishments to remain open, we will protect them. It is a crime to force them to shut down. As far as the funeral procession is concerned, will you take responsibility if there is violence?'

'Yes. I will take the responsibility,' AUM responded, thumping his chest.

'Okay. Give that to me in writing.'

'What?'

'Yes, you heard that right. If you give me a written assurance that no riot will happen during the funeral procession, I will allow it.'

AUM had no option but to do so. He couldn't backtrack on his words in front of his party workers. If he refused to give a written assurance, his subordinates would consider him a weakling.

After getting a letter from AUM, Krishipal gave him permission but asked him to take the procession through a shorter route. However, this route included passing through a market. Krishipal deployed uniformed policemen on both sides of the road. Thousands of political workers participated in the funeral procession, shouting slogans in praise of their deceased leader. When the procession reached the market, all the shops were open. Seeing this, some of the party workers lost their cool. A man broke the police cordon and rushed towards the footpath. He swiftly picked up a bundle of buckets displayed outside one of the shops and struck the glass door. It shattered into pieces, triggering a riot. As if they had forgotten about their bereavement, many of the mourners went on a rampage and damaged the shops while shouting expletives. Krishipal, who was present in the market, ordered a lathi-charge. As the cops began suppressing the rioters with their batons, Krishipal remembered AUM.

'Where is that AUM?' he asked a constable. The officer pointed in the distance, where AUM was trying to pacify the rioters, who were unwilling to listen to him. Krishipal ran angrily towards him, baton in hand, and forcefully hit him twice on his buttocks. His subordinates were amazed at Krishipal's audacity – AUM was an emerging name in politics, after all. Nevertheless, Krishipal held him by the wrist and shouted, 'This mayhem is all your handiwork. If you couldn't control the mob, why did you come up with such an idea?' AUM screamed in pain and ran away after freeing himself from Krishipal's grip.

Krishipal asked the family members of the deceased to finish the funeral quickly. He then summoned the shopkeepers and asked them to file a complaint against the rioters. Based on this complaint, the rioters were arrested and produced before a magistrate. The procedure continued until late at night. Krishipal had planned to go out with his family that evening, but his Sunday was ruined. Following this incident, however, Kalyan was free from relentless calls for bandhs by political parties.

4

'BHAIYA' DCP

Bhaiya may be the Hindi word for brother but in Mumbai, it has a different connotation. It is used to refer to a person from UP or Bihar, often in a derogatory and condescending way. Six years after joining the Maharashtra cadre, Krishipal realized that he too was viewed as a bhaiya when a complainant from UP approached him for help while he was posted as a DCP, Zone-1 in Thane in 1985.

One afternoon, when Krishipal returned to his office after eating lunch at home, a bearded old man wearing a skull cap suddenly entered his office, clung to his feet and started crying. 'Sir, please save us. You are our only hope. I have heard a lot about your work. People have told me that you are a Bhaiya DCP and will surely help people who hail from your state. I come from Jaunpur in Uttar Pradesh, sir. Please save us from Abdul.'

Bhaiya DCP! Krishipal wondered what that meant. He asked the man to sit on the chair before him and offered him a glass of water. 'Don't worry. Tell me what's the matter,' Krishipal encouraged in a comforting tone.

The aged man was Nuruddin Ansari (name changed), who ran a small sweet shop in the Rabodi area of Thane. His wife had died a decade ago and a few years later, his son and daughter-in-law had also passed away after suffering from tuberculosis. Ansari now lived in a chawl near his shop with his sixteen-year-old granddaughter Afshan (name changed). A local *gunda* (thug) named Abdul had become a menace in their locality and all the residents were terrified of him.

'Sir, Abdul came to my home two days ago and threw a bundle of notes at me – ₹2,000. He asked me to keep Afshan, my granddaughter, ready in two days, when he would come to pick her up. I have been coming to your office for the last two days, but I was told that you had gone out of Thane. Fortunately, you are here today. Sir, my granddaughter is not a prostitute. How can I allow that bastard to take her away? I am too old to fight that beast. Please help us, sir. Both of us will commit suicide if Abdul tries to do anything to her. Our lives are in your hands.'

Alarmed, Krishipal rang the in-charge of Thane Nagar Police Station, under whose jurisdiction Ansari lived. The officer confirmed that a gunda named Abdul was active in the area. Abdul was a migrant from Madras and lived in Rabodi with his mother. There were several cases of murder, attempt to murder, rape, molestation and extortion registered against him in police stations across

Thane. He possessed a country-made revolver and didn't hesitate to fire at cops when confronted. Krishipal asked the in-charge to immediately detain Abdul, but was told that he hadn't been seen in the area for the last few days.

Krishipal then requested Ansari to file a formal complaint at the police station. However, Ansari was afraid that Abdul would harm Afshan if he caught whiff of the complaint. Krishipal assured Ansari that he would ensure both his and Afshan's safety and asked the police officer in-charge to post uniformed constables outside their home.

While the elderly man's story left Krishipal enraged at Abdul's audacity and resolved to teach him a lesson, the words 'Bhaiya DCP' continued to revolve in his mind. After Ansari left his office, Krishipal called the peon and asked, 'What is this "Bhaiya DCP"? The old man who left just now called me that.'

The peon was taken aback, and visibly amused, by the question. Hesitantly, he explained, 'Sir, bhaiya in Mumbai means someone from UP or Bihar.'

'Hmm.' Krishipal could only assume that since he had given public speeches in his western UP-accented Hindi during meetings of the mohalla committees, which had been set up to prevent communal clashes, people might have become aware that he was from UP.

As Krishipal was about to leave his office that evening, Ansari came rushing in again. 'Sir, please remove the constables posted at my place. It is very dangerous. If Abdul gets to know that I have complained to the police, he will kill us sooner or later. For how long can you guarantee us protection?' Understanding Ansari's request, Krishipal ordered that the uniformed personnel be replaced with plainclothes officers from the Detection Branch (DB) squad.

Confusion prevailed over the whereabouts of Abdul. While Ansari maintained that the goon was hiding somewhere in Rabodi and could swoop in to grab Afshan at any time, the Thane Nagar in-charge suggested he might be in Madras. Suspecting the in-charge was in cahoots with Abdul, Krishipal decided to rope in another officer from a different police station. Nagesh Lohar, who was posted in a neighbouring police station, was a close confidant of his and an excellent detective. Krishipal asked him to track Abdul and within a day, Lohar reported that the criminal was very much in Thane.

As the days passed, Krishipal became increasingly frustrated that Abdul remained at large despite being identified. One evening, while Krishipal was discussing another case with his officers at the DCP office, the landline on his table rang. The caller was Sub-Inspector Lohar, and he had a major update. 'Sir, we have received intel that Abdul is going to visit Hotel Golden Gate, near Castle Mill, in some time. I am leaving with my staff to trap him.'

Krishipal agreed to meet the team there. When he reached the rendezvous spot, he witnessed a truly *filmi* scene. Lohar, with a revolver in his right hand, was running behind Abdul while signalling for his team members to surround him with the left. He shouted, '*Dhara madarchod la*!' (Catch the motherfucker!)

However, Abdul was too smart to be caught. He was familiar with the by-lanes surrounding the mill and ran from one narrow gully to another, shouting expletives at the cops pursuing him. After an hour-long chase, he escaped under the cover of the darkness that had descended by then. A combing operation of the area was immediately conducted, but in vain.

Although the attempt to capture Abdul had failed, it confirmed that he was certainly in Thane. Two days later, Krishipal called Nuruddin Ansari to check on him. With fear seeping into his voice, the old man told Krishipal that although Abdul hadn't contacted him, one of his henchmen had forced his way into their home. He said Abdul was furious about the police complaint and menacingly warned Ansari to be ready to face the consequences. After the threat, Ansari had started packing his bags to leave Thane forever. Krishipal convinced Ansari to remain in town with the guarantee that Abdul's story would end soon enough.

Meanwhile, S. K Padwal, an inspector who had worked for the Mumbai Crime Branch, was transferred to the Thane Police Commissionerate. Padwal was known for his brilliant policework and had been responsible for arresting notorious criminals. Krishipal sought his help in apprehending Abdul. Padwal had heard about the infamous Abdul and assured Krishipal that he would pursue the man with full concentration.

The case was far from closed. Abdul realized that Padwal was pursuing him and fled to Madras. All of Padwal's efforts to trace Abdul proved unsuccessful. He interrogated Abdul's mother, but she denied knowing his whereabouts. However, Padwal learned from his informers that Abdul often spoke to his mother on her neighbour's phone. Though he didn't have Abdul's address in Madras, he had his mother's address in Thane. These two key facts were enough to set a trap that would deliver Abdul to the police.

Padwal went to a post office and issued a money order for ₹5,000 in Abdul's name. When the postman reached his Thane residence, Abdul's mother informed him that her son was not home. The postman refused to hand over the money, since only Abdul could receive it. Three or four days later, the postman returned to Abdul's home with another money order for ₹5,000. Once again, he left without delivering the money as Abdul was absent. A week later, the postman visited Abdul's mother one more time with a fresh money order for ₹7,000. Predictably, Abdul wasn't home and the money could not be delivered.

During this period, Abdul's mother presumably informed him about the money orders and the postman's refusal to deliver the money. Abdul assumed that somebody wanted to give him a *supari* (contract to kill someone) and hence was sending him the money. ₹7,000 was a big amount in the mid-eighties, too tempting for Abdul to pass up. He needed to sustain himself while hiding in Madras, and the monetary temptation overruled his caution.

A week later, when Krishipal was about to retire for the day, his home landline rang. The caller was a control room officer, informing him that an exchange of fire had taken place. During a showdown with the cops, a civilian had sustained bullet injuries and was taken to Thane Civil Hospital. Immediately after the control room's call, Inspector Padwal phoned Krishipal and told him that the injured civilian was Abdul. Padwal recounted that he had received a tip-off that Abdul was back in Thane and hiding near the water pipelines in Wagle Estate. When Padwal and his force tracked down Abdul and asked him to surrender, he shot at them with his country-made gun. In the retaliatory fire, the fugitive collapsed.

When Krishipal reached the hospital, doctors informed him that Abdul had died of bullet injuries – including one shot that had disfigured his face. Although Krishipal had wanted to catch Abdul alive, he was content that his reign of terror in Thane had come to an end. He congratulated Padwal and his team and said that he would recommend their names for a reward.

As he was talking to Padwal, a constable from Naupada Police Station who was on hospital duty approached Krishipal with a request to speak to him in private. Krishipal agreed and followed him out of the mortuary.

'Sir, the man who was killed is not Abdul,' the constable whispered once they reached a silent corner of the hospital compound

'What? How can you say that?' Krishipal was flabbergasted, afraid that they were dealing with a case of mistaken identity.

'Sir, I arrested Abdul many years ago. I know him well.

This man doesn't look like Abdul. He is someone else.' There was no doubt in the constable's voice.

Krishipal immediately went to Padwal and confronted him with the constable's revelation. The inspector, though confused, maintained that the man he had killed was Abdul. Krishipal had been excited to share the news of the encounter with the police commissioner, but now fear had replaced the excitement. There would be major consequences for both him and Padwal if the dead civilian turned out to be an innocent.

Stepping out of the building, Krishipal lit a cigarette to keep him company as he organized his thoughts. How could they ascertain the identity of the deceased? How would they face the police commissioner if the body belonged to someone else? Suddenly, he remembered that Abdul's mother lived nearby and asked Padwal to bring her to the hospital.

When she reached the hospital, the cops took Abdul's mother to the mortuary. They showed her the dead body and asked whether she recognized the deceased. After a few seconds of looking at the corpse, the old woman started wailing and showering expletives at the cops. 'You people have killed my Abdul!' she cried.

Krishipal sighed, both in relief and commiseration. Padwal had killed the right man. The constable had been confused because Abdul's face had swollen due to the bullet injury, rendering it unrecognizable. Even Abdul's mother had identified him by looking at the rings on his fingers and the shirt he was wearing.

The newspapers carried reports of Abdul's death the next day and many lauded Krishipal for ending his hold over the city. He received congratulatory calls from the police chief as well as his other colleagues. A day after the encounter, while Krishipal was going through the newspaper clippings, Ansari visited his office along with Afshan. He asked Afshan to touch Ansari's feet.

'No, no ... in our culture, we don't allow girls to touch another's feet,' Krishipal protested, standing up from his chair and walking a few steps away.

Ansari had brought a box of sweets called choorma to express his gratitude towards Krishipal and offered him that instead. 'Sir, today we are safe just because of you. You have proved to be a *farishta* (angel) for us.'

Krishipal took a bite and smiled. 'I may be a Bhaiya DCP, but that doesn't mean that I will only help bhaiyas like you. I don't consider anybody's state or religion while discharging my duty. I would have done the same even if you were from Gujarat, Maharashtra, Tamil Nadu, West Bengal or any other part of India.'

'I will pray to Allah to give you abundant happiness in life.' With this blessing, Ansari left Krishipal's office for the last time.

5

BOMBAY BURNS OVER A BOOK

Krishipal and Sarita had their second child in 1986, during his posting in the Thane Commissionerate. A boy, whom the couple named Abhijeet. By this time, riots and communal incidents in Kalyan had decreased substantially, allowing Krishipal to spend more time with his children after work.

Although Kalyan had cooled down, severe communal riots had broken out in Aurangabad, a prominent city in the Marathwada region of Maharashtra. The city was named after the Mughal ruler Aurangzeb and had a history of communal violence. That year, the unrest began after the results of the Aurangabad Municipal Corporation election were announced. The Shiv Sena, despite emerging as the single largest party, failed to install its mayor due to a hurried post-poll alliance by the Congress and other parties. The Shiv Sena challenged the mayor's election in the Bombay High Court on technical grounds.[1] When the court didn't offer any immediate relief, postponing the matter to another date, around 2,000 Shiv Sainiks attacked Muslim neighbourhoods. This provoked a violent backlash.

The riots soon spread to surrounding areas of Aurangabad and over thirty people were killed in two days.[2] Such was the intensity of violence that Union Home Minister Buta Singh had to fly down to Aurangabad to take stock of the situation. He issued a warning that the political parties spreading hatred would be banned.[3] The state government was under tremendous pressure to contain the tumult, but it had escalated out of the control of the local police. Amid the furore, Krishipal received a call from Maharashtra Police Chief D. S. Soman.

'KP, you have been transferred as Senior SP, Aurangabad. Rush there immediately and take charge.'

'But sir …'

'No ifs and buts, please. This is an express order from CM Shankarrao Chavan. You are required to go. You were originally supposed to be transferred to Bombay – I'm not sure why CM sir has transferred you to Aurangabad.'

This sudden order was a shock to Krishipal's system. His father-in-law had recently been diagnosed with cancer and he was coordinating every aspect of the treatment. In his distress, he reached out to his immediate boss, Additional DG (Law and Order) S. P. Singh. When Singh expressed his inability to help in the matter, Krishipal sought an appointment with CM Chavan himself.

It was a Wednesday when Krishipal travelled from Kalyan to the Mantralaya in south Bombay. He had been told that he would only get five minutes with the CM and that too just before the weekly cabinet meeting. The CM's secretary warned him to be on time, as Chavan was a strict disciplinarian. Chavan's image was like that of a stringent school principal; several members of the Council of Ministers feared him.

There was already a queue of senior cabinet members outside Chavan's chamber when Krishipal arrived. After his name was called, he entered Chavan's chamber, saluted him and stood at attention. Chavan was sitting behind his desk, his posture upright, holding a cup of tea in one hand and signing files from the other. He paused for a moment to look at Krishipal then quickly became engrossed in signing the files again. '*Bola Raghuvanshi. Kay bolaychaaahe*?' (Yes Raghuvanshi, what did you want to say?)

Krishipal, who was not yet fluent in Marathi, replied in Hindi. 'Sir, I have been transferred to Aurangabad.'

'Yes, yes ... go to Aurangabad. It is a very important posting – the senior-most superintendent is posted in Aurangabad. After that, they are directly promoted to deputy inspector general (DIG). I have heard a lot about your efforts to contain communal tension in Solapur and Kalyan. I believe that you are the right choice for Aurangabad, where the riots are still ongoing.'

'Sir, I have a request. My father-in-law is suffering from cancer ...'

'Don't worry, there is a good medical college in Aurangabad,' Chavan interrupted. 'He will get excellent treatment there. You can keep your official Kalyan residence as long as you want.'

Krishipal felt stuck. Gathering some courage, he said, 'Sir, even if I move to Aurangabad, I will be working half-heartedly and will not be able to meet your expectations. Hence, I request you to transfer me anywhere in or around Mumbai. After my father-in-law's treatment is complete, I will go anywhere you say.'

Chavan paused signing the files and considered Krishipal's request for a few moments, a stern look on his face. 'Hmm. Okay. If you don't receive a revised order by Friday, leave for Aurangabad on Saturday and take charge.'

Krishipal returned to Kalyan with a heavy heart. He could tell from Chavan's body language that he was unlikely to be considerate and scrap his transfer to Aurangabad.

CM Chavan was very particular about his public image. In the 1970s, various areas of Maharashtra had been gripped by communal violence. A commission set up under Justice D. P. Madon to conduct an inquiry into the riots had passed many adverse comments against the Maharashtra government and police.[4] Chavan wanted to avoid any strictures on his government and hence deployed all the available means to contain the riots.

Apart from protecting his public image, certain undercurrents in his party – the Indian National Congress (INC) – were unsettling Chavan. A faction within the party had ganged up against him and were looking for an excuse to remove him from the post of CM. Chavan's detractors pressurized the party high command to disempower him, citing the dismal law and order situation in the state. Among them was Sharad Pawar, who had rebelled against INC to form his own party only to return two years ago. Sending Krishipal to Aurangabad was part of the CM's strategy to counter the charge of inefficiently handling the communal situation.

Krishipal reluctantly began packing up for Aurangabad, still awaiting the CM's order as the last ray of hope. That same evening, he received the order revoking his transfer to Aurangabad and appointing him DCP, Zone-1 in Bombay instead. In their power games, politicians seldom account for the sentiments and needs of police officers, focused only on saving their chairs. In this case, however, Chavan turned out to be different. He was kind to Krishipal, who was only a junior in the IPS hierarchy at the time. Within a month, Shankarrao Chavan lost his chair. On 24 June 1988, Pawar became the CM of Maharashtra again.[5]

In his new posting, Krishipal had to report to Bombay's police commissioner, Vasant Saraf. The police commissioner's office is located in south Bombay's Crawford Market, housed in a grand Anglo-Gothic style building that was constructed by the famous architect John Adams in 1896. While walking its corridors for the first time, Krishipal was mesmerized by the grandeur. The building befitted the stature of the police chief of the financial capital of the nation. Most IPS officers of the

Maharashtra cadre wished for an opportunity to occupy that fancy office.

After waiting for some time outside the commissioner's cabin on the first floor of the building, Krishipal was called in. He saluted Saraf and stood at attention. Unexpectedly, Saraf's face was red with anger. He furiously demanded, 'So you directly asked the CM to get posted as DCP, Zone-1? How dare you? At the most, you should have asked for a posting in Bombay Commissionerate, but you directly asked for Zone-1! And why did you avoid going to Aurangabad?'

Krishipal was shocked by the police commissioner's dressing-down. He tried to clear the air by telling Saraf about his father-in-law's cancer, his request that the CM keep him close to Bombay; that ultimately, it had been the CM's decision to send him to Zone-1.

Saraf heard him out, then said, 'I am posting you as the DCP of the Armed Police Headquarters in Naigaon. Tata Memorial Cancer Hospital is within walking distance. It will be easy to get your father-in-law treated there.'

Being posted as DCP, Armed Police was perceived as a downgrade. If an enquiry was pending against a cop for corruption or professional misconduct, they were transferred there. It took Krishipal a few days to comprehend Saraf's fury. DCP, Zone-1 was among the most high-profile posts. Many vital sites came under its jurisdiction: the Secretariat and Mantralaya, the Reserve Bank of India and Bombay Stock Exchange, star-graded hotels like Taj Mahal and Oberoi Towers, prominent railways stations like Victoria Terminus (now Chhatrapati Shivaji Maharaj Terminus [CMST]) and Churchgate, the headquarters of the Mumbai Municipal Corporation and Air India, and even tourist attractions like Gateway of India and Marine Drive. Generally, this zone was considered peaceful and the crime rate was minimal.

It was the prerogative of the commissioner to assign zones to the officers within the commissionerate, not that of the CM or home minister. Commissioners usually assigned Zone-1 to their favourite officers and Krishipal had encroached upon the Saraf's power by getting direct orders from the CM. He assumed that Krishipal had pulled some strings to get the plum posting, which hurt his ego. Krishipal wasn't unhappy about being thrown into the Armed Police Headquarters, but the misunderstanding with his boss bothered him. It was his first posting in Bombay, and it wasn't a good feeling to start his stint in the bad books of his boss.

However, on the bright side, Krishipal was relieved to know that Tata Memorial Cancer Hospital was close to his office. Though his father-in-law passed away a few months later, it made treatment accessible and convenient in his final days.

Around this time, the city's underworld, previously dominated by Karim Lala, Haji Mastan and Varadarajan Mudaliar, was giving way to organized mafia run by the likes of Dawood Ibrahim, Arun Gawli and Amar Naik. These gangsters not only fought among themselves but also extorted and killed businessmen, builders, film-makers and hoteliers to establish their regime.

Most police officers who were active in Bombay during that era have interesting anecdotes about its underworld, but Krishipal was the exception. As chief of the Armed Police, he was responsible for maintaining discipline in the armed reserved force and providing supplementary strength to the local police in case of riots. His men were deployed whenever any major event was arranged in Bombay or if a VIP visited the city. Krishipal had nothing to do with the investigation of crimes or combatting the underworld. Those responsibilities lay with the Crime Branch, whose chief was an officer close to the police commissioner.

In February 1989, a controversy erupted over author Salman Rushdie's book *The Satanic Verses.* The supreme ruler of Iran, Ayatollah Khomeini issued a fatwa to kill Rushdie and in India, Rajiv Gandhi's government had banned the book in consideration of religious sentiments. Even after the ban, Muslim organizations in Bombay called for a march from Nagpada to the British consulate in south Bombay.

Several hours before the march was scheduled to begin, the cops detained its organizers. However, people still gathered at the pre-decided spot in Nagpada and the leaderless mob marched towards the consulate. When the mob reached Mohammed Ali Road, it turned violent. Enraged protestors pelted stones at cops and fires broke out. At first, the police lathi-charged the crowd, but this proved ineffectual. The police then shot tear gas shells, but to everybody's surprise, they failed to explode. As a last resort, the police began firing on the rioters, killing twelve. Krishipal and his team, too, were present at the scene to help contain the riots.

In the aftermath, the question was raised: why hadn't the tear gas shells exploded? An investigation revealed that the shells were past their expiry date. It was the responsibility of Krishipal and the Armed Police to supply tear gas shells across the Bombay Police Commissionerate. The director general of police (DGP) of Maharashtra wrote a hard-hitting letter to Commissioner Saraf, blaming his force for the deaths, along with a circular from the manufacturers of the tear gas shells stating that they had expired after three years of unuse. The DGP's letter was a personal embarrassment for Saraf, one he blamed Krishipal for.

When Krishipal heard about the DGP's letter, he was worried. He was already in Saraf's bad books and now the letter added insult to injury. Krishipal, already wracked with guilt, feared that he might face disciplinary action. While he was pondering over what he could say to defend himself before Saraf, his colleague Inspector Khanolkar came excitedly to his cabin with a piece of paper in hand.

Krishipal read its contents and all his worries evaporated. He thanked Khanolkar and rushed to the police commissioner's office. When he arrived, Saraf's secretary informed Krishipal that an enraged Saraf had refused to meet him. Gathering courage, Krishipal forced himself inside the chamber.

'Sir, please listen to me once,' he pleaded. 'After that, I am ready to accept any punishment. I have the latest circular issued by the manufacturer in my hand. The DGP didn't mention this circular in his letter and jumped to conclusions after referring to the previous circular. As per this document, the shells were supplied well before their expiry date.'

Saraf thoroughly parsed the circular and immediately summoned his stenographer to dictate an equally harsh reply to the DGP's letter. Saraf minced no words while telling the DGP that the latter's office had misguided him by giving him the wrong circular, and that the lifespan of the tear gas shells was four years. In closing, he told the DGP that such communication from his office demoralized the field officers. Saraf's anger towards Krishipal had run its course and after this incident, the commissioner realized that he had misunderstood his new DCP.

That year, on Dussehra, tensions erupted in Bombay once again. The Shiv Sena was at loggerheads with various Dalit organizations like the Dalit Panthers and Republican Party over the name of Marathwada University in Aurangabad. The Dalit organizations were demanding that the university be renamed after Dr B. R. Ambedkar, while the Shiv Sena was against this.[6]

That evening, at their annual rally, Shiv Sena supremo Bal Thackeray delivered a fiery speech at Shivaji Park expressing his disapproval to the renaming. On their way back from the rally, Shiv Sainiks from Thane clashed with members of the Dalit organizations in Ramabai Nagar, Ghatkopar. The Eastern Express highway that connected south Bombay to the northern suburbs turned into a battleground between the two groups as they threw stones, glass bottles and tube lights at each other and damaged vehicles. That area fell under the DCP, Zone-6, who became so overwhelmed with the situation that he went incommunicado.

Krishipal was ordered to reach the spot with his armed policemen. Instead of ordering a lathi-charge, he approached leaders of the Shiv Sena like Anand Dighe and Eknath Shinde. They had known him since his stint in Kalyan and held him in high esteem. Krishipal managed to convince the Sainiks to leave the place. The frenzied violence ended within a few minutes. The Special Branch of the Bombay Police, which served as its intelligence wing, reported to Commissioner Saraf how Krishipal had swiftly defused the situation. Impressed, Saraf decided to transfer Krishipal from the Armed Police Headquarters to Zone-6 – a sensitive zone which had a high crime rate and a long history of riots.

6

PUNISHMENT POSTING

In 1990 Saraf was promoted to DGP of Maharashtra. Till then he had been responsible only for protecting Bombay; now the onus of the whole state's security was on him. From his time as commissioner of the SID, Saraf knew that the north-eastern district of Gadchiroli had become a canker for the Maharashtra police. Naxalites rampantly slaughtered policemen and ran a parallel government of their own. No officer was willing to go to Gadchiroli, and those who were assigned there were too scared to do anything. Dr Satyapal Singh, the incumbent SP of Gadchiroli, had been selected for a deputation to the central government. There was an urgent need to fill the post he had vacated.

The role had to go to an audacious officer who could think out of the box. As Saraf was pondering over potential names, a report in that day's newspaper caught his attention. Accompanied by a picture of Krishipal, it described how he had handled a recent conflict in his zone. Saraf's search had come to an end! Almost like Aladdin's genie, Krishipal appeared like a magical solution to Saraf's dilemma. He immediately summoned Krishipal to his office.

Saraf took the time to offer tea to Krishipal before uttering the shocking words, 'I want you to take charge as SP, Gadchiroli.'

Was it lightning that had struck Krishipal, or Saraf's words? Hesitantly, he replied, 'Sir, just a few months earlier, as police commissioner, you transferred me to Zone-6. Why are you sending me to Gadchiroli so soon?'

'You must go. I want you to deal with this Naxal problem. Don't you know how much trouble it has caused us?'

At that moment, Krishipal couldn't think of any substantial reason to avoid being sent to Gadchiroli. Impulsively, a pithy excuse slipped out of his mouth. 'Sir, my children's exams are coming up soon.'

'Hmm! Which grade are your children in?'

'Sir, my daughter is in grade two and my son is in Lower KG,' Krishipal replied sheepishly.

'Okay. Let them clear their exams. You go after that.'

Krishipal was relieved. His conversation with the DGP happened in January 1990 and his children's exams were scheduled for next March. He was sure that the government wouldn't be able to keep the SP, Gadchiroli post vacant for three long months. The Naxal problem was too pervasive to let it go unchecked for all that time. But Krishipal's assumption was wrong. In the last week of

March, Krishipal once again got a call from the DGP and was summoned to his office.

'I hope the exams of your children are over by now,' Saraf said.

'Yes, sir,' Krishipal replied in a dull voice.

'Good. Now pack your bags and leave for Gadchiroli.' The DGP delivered the order with a poker face.

As a last-ditch effort, Krishipal told Saraf, 'Sir, I am experienced in dealing with communal riots and detection of crimes but haven't ventured into the avenue of insurgency. I don't know whether I will be able to perform as per your expectations.'

At this, Saraf got up from his chair and went to the bookshelf in the corner of his cabin. He took out a book titled *Red Star Over China* and handed it over to Krishipal. 'Don't worry. This is for you. Start reading it. It will help you understand the Naxal problem.' Krishipal browsed through a few pages and then left Saraf's office after saluting him.

When he reached home that evening, Krishipal's wife Sarita sensed that he was not his usual self. Something was amiss. 'What happened? Is everything okay?' she asked in a worried tone.

'Yes, everything is okay. Get my bags packed. I have been transferred to Gadchiroli.' He tried to convey the news nonchalantly, as if he was unaffected by the transfer.

'What? Surely you are joking!'

'This is no joke. I was just at the DGP's office. He has asked me to take charge of Gadchiroli at the earliest.'

'Why does this happen to you every time? Despite the CM's order, you were not allowed to take the high-profile role of DCP, Zone-1. Instead, you were transferred to the Armed Police where nobody else wants to go. You were made DCP of Zone-6 just a few months ago. Now, without completing your tenure, you are being thrown into a death trap in Gadchiroli. You have proved yourself at every turn; this kind of treatment is nothing but gross injustice!'

'I am a government servant. The government has all the right to send me anywhere it wishes. This is not a big deal. Somebody has to go there, whether me or anyone else.' Krishipal tried to underplay the development, though he had been shocked too.

Sarita knew what it meant to be posted at Gadchiroli. She recollected conversations with Krishipal's friend who had been posted there, Satyapal Singh. He hailed from a village that neighboured Krishipal's childhood home and had been his batchmate in the police academy. During his tenure in Gadchiroli, he visited their residence whenever he was in Mumbai. Over tea and dinner, he had shared stories of the difficult and dangerous life in Gadchiroli. Sarita's apprehensions were evident on her face. She had mentally accepted the fact that, as a government worker, her husband would frequently be transferred from one place to another. But she could not accept that Krishipal was being transferred to a black hole, from where returning alive wasn't certain.

'The government will allow us to keep this home.

Till the time my tenure gets over, you can stay here with kids,' Krishipal told her in consolation.

'What do you mean "stay here with kids"? We all will go together. The children can't live without you. If you stay there alone, I will be always worried about your safety. Our life will become hell,' she shot back.

News of Krishipal's transfer to Gadchiroli had spread throughout the IPS circles. Those envious of him expressed happiness, others made taunting remarks: 'An officer who couldn't get his transfer stalled in three months is good for nothing.' Only the CM could revoke such a transfer order. Many officers used their closeness to the CM to get postings of their liking, but Krishipal had done no such thing. Not only did he lack the skill of gaining proximity with a politician – through flattery or becoming a 'Yes Man' – but also his conscience dissuaded him from doing so. He had never got close to any politician in his policing career so far.

A few days later, Krishipal received the formal order for his transfer. He departed for Gadchiroli from Victoria Terminus with Sarita and the children. Many cops came to see him off on Platform 8. There was a coupe reserved for his family in the first-class coach of the Bombay–Nagpur Express, its windows decorated with fresh flowers. The solemnity of the moment enveloped Krishipal; he felt the full weight of his departure. The sight of colleagues, friends and well-wishers bidding them farewell evoked a sense of readiness akin to preparing for battle. As the train gradually pulled away from the platform, Krishipal waved and offered a reassuring smile to those gathered outside. Yet, amidst the bittersweet farewells, a nagging question lingered in his mind: when would he have the chance to return and serve in the city again?

The train picked up speed a few minutes after leaving Victoria Terminus. Both children had claimed the window seats and were engrossed with the view outside. Sarita tried to keep herself busy with a magazine. Just as the train rattled on the tracks, several thoughts rattled in Krishipal's mind. The journey felt like a great paradox. He was leaving behind a glittering city that was full of life, modernity and luxury and heading for a far-flung, depressing land marred by backwardness and desolation, where death played hide-and-seek on a daily basis. He was staring into an uncertain future. *Will I be able to meet the expectations of the government? How will I manage the children's education? Will my family be safe there?* As night fell, Krishipal found his mind trapped by these questions. His eyes grew heavy under their weight and sleep soon embraced him.

7

FROM GERMANY TO GADCHIROLI

Chai garam! Chai garam! Chai garam!
Poori bhaji!
Vada pav!

The familiar hustle and bustle of the station, coupled with the distinct calls of hawkers, stirred Krishipal from his slumber. Glancing at the clock, he noted that it was 7 a.m. and the train had arrived at Ajni, the station preceding Nagpur. Sarita, already awake, had spent a restless night plagued by anxiety. With Nagpur only half an hour away, Krishipal roused the children. As he gathered their belongings and ushered his family towards the exit, his sense of anticipation grew, mingled with apprehension of the unknown.

Krishipal had informed the Range DIG T. K. Choudhary of their travel plans before leaving Bombay. As the train chugged into Nagpur Station, an SI and a few constables from the DIG office were already there to receive the family. They helped Krishipal unload the luggage from the train and into the jeep and car parked outside. The bags were unusually heavy since the family anticipated a long stay in Gadchiroli and Sarita had packed many household essentials.

After Krishipal reached the Nagpur circuit house where the family had been temporarily lodged, he took a bath, wore his uniform and went to meet DIG Choudhary. Although Choudhary was the DIG of a hazardous area like Gadchiroli, his office was in a safe zone in Nagpur, 170 kilometres away. Choudhary briefed Krishipal about his responsibilities in Gadchiroli.

'Raghuvanshi, you have been successful in urban policing, but this is a different ball game. You have to be very careful.'

'Yes, sir. I understand,' Krishipal said confidently.

'Always travel with strong police escort and don't rush immediately to the spot when you hear about a crime committed by Naxals. It could be a trap to ambush you.'

'Sure, sir. I will follow your advice.' Krishipal saluted Choudhary and left his office.

A few minutes after exiting Nagpur, the road to Gadchiroli took them through the Dandakaranya forest. Spread across an area of about 92,000 square kilometres, Dandakaranya encompasses parts of Madhya Pradesh, Orissa, Maharashtra and Andhra Pradesh. Krishipal's car was traversing through India's most paradoxical region. The forest is rich with iron ores and deposits of bauxite and manganese.[1] It has an abundance of Sagwan trees whose wood is highly valued internationally. The availability of tendu leaves and bamboo allows beedi production and paper mills to flourish. However, Dandakaranya is also home to one of India's most impoverished populations, who have had to endure malnutrition, lack of connectivity and healthcare facilities, as well as atrocities by corrupt government officials.

The forest finds a mention in the epic Ramayana, which says that when Rama was exiled for fourteen years by his father, he spent ten years there. On Dussehra, while Hindus across north India celebrate the victory over evil by burning effigies of Ravana, he is venerated in Dandakaranya by the Gond people. In a village named Paraswadi, a procession is carried out wherein an idol of Ravana is mounted on an artificial elephant amidst slogans like 'Ravan Raja *ki jai*', 'Jai Gondwana' and 'Raja Ravanna'. During the festival, some Gond homes keep idols of Ravana. The Adivasis of Paraswadi consider themselves to be Ravanvanshis and believe that Ravana was a Gond king who was killed by Aryan invaders. They believe that the kingdom of Ravana was not in Sri Lanka but in the central India.[2]

The name Dandakaranya has several meanings and one of them is 'forest of punishment'. In Sanskrit, *danda* means punishment and *aranya* means forest.[3] The Naxal movement had literally made the lush wilderness a forest of punishment for the police officers who were transferred here.

Naxalism travelled to Gadchiroli from a village 1,500 kilometres away in West Bengal named Naxalbari, though the movement had its roots in Germany, Russia and China. Naxalism is an extreme form of the ideology the world knows as communism. The fathers of this ideology were Karl Marx, a German philosopher, economist and revolutionary, and his friend and comrade Friedrich Engels. In the face of rising inequality after the industrial revolution, Marx and Engels were convinced that a social revolution by the working class was imminent.

In the 1960s, India was undergoing a food crisis and many died of starvation across the country. Land suitable for farming was owned only by the elite few and frequent droughts exacerbated the situation. It had become difficult for peasant families to survive, let alone thrive. Against this backdrop, Charu Mazumdar, Kanu Sanyal and Jangal Santhal – followers of the communist ideology in West Bengal – started a peasant's movement. Landless peasants began snatching food grains from the storehouses of landlords. They started occupying privately owned land and burning documents related to its ownership. The landlords also retaliated violently.[4]

Just a week after the agitation began, on 21 May 1967, a sharecropper named Bigul Kisan was attacked by his landlord's men. Bigul Kisan worked under the *adhiyari* system, which meant that half the agricultural produce he cultivated was owed to the landowners. After being evicted by his landlord, Bigul Kisan had approached the court for justice and won the case. Frustrated by the legal defeat, the landlord asked his henchmen to teach the farmer a lesson.[5]

The agitation intensified after Bigul Kisan was attacked. When a team from the Naxalbari Police Station led by Inspector Sonam Wangdi reached the spot, it had been surrounded by over 1,000 agitated tribals. In the melee, somebody began shooting arrows at the police team, three of which struck Inspector Wangdi. He died instantly.[6] Other policemen fled, leaving their weapons on the spot. This was the first time in the history of the movement that a cop had been killed.

Another police team reached the scene two days later to investigate Inspector Wangdi's murder. The cops were furious and when a crowd of villagers prevented them from entering the village, shots were fired. The police killed nine people, including women and infants.[7] After this incident, Charu Mazumdar mobilized landless labourers and tea garden workers and announced a war against landlords and the government. Armed with bows and arrows, axes, spears and sticks, they began attacking police stations. Many government officials, landlords and shopkeepers were lynched.[8]

The Chinese government was elated when it received the news of the uprising. Radio Beijing broadcasted that it was willing to lend support to Charu Mazumdar-led movement, whether through financing it or supplying arms.[9] Mazumdar too vocalized his support for China, stating that 'China's Chairman [Mao] is our Chairman', though he withdrew this slogan later in his life.[10]

After the Naxalbari campaign, similar incidents began happening in adjacent areas. Considering its roots, the rising wave was referred to as the Naxal movement or the Maoist movement interchangeably. Teams of peasants armed with weapons like bows and arrows, axes and knives began looting houses of landlords, burnt land ownership documents and captured farmlands. A series of murders were committed. After killing landlords, the Maoists wrote revolutionary slogans on the wall with the blood of their victims. The West Bengal administration collapsed totally; the government felt helpless. Many students from Kolkata also joined the agitation. Mazumdar named the campaign 'Khatam', which meant 'complete annihilation'. Their targets were 'class enemies' – not only landlords and moneylenders but also policemen and government officials.[11]

The Naxalbari movement inspired many such agitations in other parts of India. The key affected zones were Bihar, Madhya Pradesh, Orissa and Andhra Pradesh, though its presence was felt in a few other states as well. Gadchiroli fell in this red corridor and shared borders with both Madhya Pradesh and Andhra Pradesh. The Naxals noticed that the socio-economic conditions in Gadchiroli were conducive for an armed struggle. The residents, primarily tribals who survive on forest produce, had been oppressed by tendu leaf and bamboo contractors and government officials. The contractors used them as labourers for plucking tendu leaves and cutting bamboo but paid extremely low wages. The forest department didn't allow the Adivasis to use resources from the jungle, citing various laws. Under British rule, there had been a rule that tribal land could only be sold to a tribal. However, after India became independent, big tracts of land were bought by rich landlords and moneylenders. The government officials indulged in corruption, and tribal women were frequently sexually exploited.[12]

The creation of the People's War Group (PWG) in Andhra Pradesh set the ball rolling for the Naxal movement in Gadchiroli. A Hindi teacher from Warangal named Kondapalli Seetharamaiah was influenced by communist thought and joined Charu Mazumdar's Communist Party of India (Marxist–Leninist). After the death of Mazumdar weakened the party, Seetharamaiah broke away from CPI(ML) to establish PWG in April 1980. PWG rejected electoral politics and launched an armed struggle against the Indian state. Seetharamaiah formed dalams – small groups of five to ten youngsters who would work to achieve PWG's goals. Two months later, in June 1980, seven such dalams entered the forest areas of Maharashtra while others were dispatched in adjacent Madhya Pradesh.[13]

The dalam that entered Gadchiroli was led by twenty-three-year-old Peddi Shankar. Peddi Shankar hailed from the Bellampally district of Andhra Pradesh. His father worked in a coal mine. After passing grade ten, Peddi Shankar started working as a bus cleaner but continued his studies. Once he graduated from school, he became a member of the Radical Students Union and started participating in various social movements. He took up the issue of coal workers and led an eighteen-day long strike to demand permanent jobs for temporary workers. In 1977, he opened a library in his locality through crowdfunding. To counter increasing cases of theft in the workers' colony, he organized a vigilante group of youngsters to keep watch.

In 1978, a woman named Rajeshwari was raped and murdered by a coal mine official. Peddi Shankar organized an agitation by surrounding the local police station. To disperse the aggressive mob, the police fired a few rounds of bullets, killing two people. A case of dacoity, arson and snatching of police weapons was registered against Peddi Shankar. After this, he went underground.

During this period, Peddi Shankar began collaborating with Naxalites, and by twenty-three, he was made in-charge of the Naxal movement in Maharashtra. On 2 November 1980, he sought refuge in Moyabinpetha village along with four companions. Located close to the Maharashtra–Andhra Pradesh border, Moyabinpetha had a population of around 700 people who were mostly Gond and Mahar tribals who spoke Marathi and Telugu. Like other tribal areas, dwellers of this village were oppressed by the forest officials and contractors of tendu leaves and bamboo. By then, the Maharashtra government had received intelligence that the Naxal movement had taken root in the Chandrapur district, of which Gadchiroli was a part at the time. Hence, two companies of the State Reserve Police (SRP) had been deployed in the area. A moneylender's servant caught whiff of Peddi Shankar's presence in the village and immediately tipped off the SRP team patrolling nearby.

On receiving this information, the SRP team leapt into action. Within a few minutes, they had encircled Peddi Shankar and his teammates. As per the police, the group was asked to surrender but they hid in the jowar farms on the outskirts of the village and fired upon the police squad. Peddi Shankar was killed in the retaliatory fire, while his four accomplices escaped by rushing towards the Pranhita river that was flowing nearby. The police claimed to have recovered a 12 Bore gun, first-aid kit and ration kit, along with Naxal literature which depicted the police as the biggest nemesis of their struggle. A magazine named *People's War* was also found.

The encounter led to a tremendous uproar. A few human rights activists formed their own fact-finding committee to investigate the encounter. They concluded that Peddi Shankar wasn't killed in an exchange of fire but murdered. Peddi Shankar had been shot dead in an open ground where there was no scope to hide. No villager had seen Peddi Shankar firing at the cops and there were discrepancies in various police reports about the encounter. One report mentioned that Peddi Shankar shot two bullets, another mentioned that he shot four.[14]

Whether Peddi Shankar really died in an exchange of fire or was killed in cold blood, this incident is considered the first encounter between Naxalites and the cops in Maharashtra's history. Peddi Shankar's story may have come to an end but it marked the beginning of an era that would paint the green Dandakaranya forest red.

As the Raghuvanshis' car passed that troubled landscape, every passenger was thinking differently. The children were enjoying the view – it was no less than a vacation for them. For Sarita, the journey was like travelling into a black hole of uncertainty. Krishipal looked towards the jungle as a challenge. He was reaching Gadchiroli ten years after the Naxal movement had started in the district. In the time since, the Naxalites had strengthened their base and were ruling it with an iron fist. They had no fear of the state and its law enforcement machinery. In fact, it was the other way round. It was now Krishipal's responsibility to clean up the area and free it from the clutches of Naxalism.

In the same forest, away from Krishipal's eyes, there was a semicircle cluster of tents. A middle-aged man with grey hair and stubble, wearing a camouflage uniform, was addressing a small group of young men and women. A gun hung on his left shoulder. The youngsters sat on the ground; every person had a weapon kept next to them. Beside the group, a man had been tied to the trunk of a tree. Clad in a torn undershirt and lungi, the man had injuries all over his body and looked half dead.

'Comrades, Charu baba showed us how to take the struggle forward before he left. He wrote eight documents guiding us on how to attack and defeat the class enemies. As recruits, it is very important that you understand his thoughts before implementing them. In our struggle, we have to free ourselves from the fear of death. Before I speak further, I need to ask: are you free from the fear of death?' The man spoke in Hindi, with a distinct Telugu accent.

'Yes, Santosh Anna,' the group, which had members ranging from the ages of fifteen to thirty, replied in chorus.

That man, named Santosh Anna, was a dalam commander and one of the most wanted Naxalites. His real name was Yerakal Burgaiya and he hailed from Adilabad, a village near the Maharashtra–Andhra Pradesh border. He had dropped out of school after grade four and joined the Naxal movement as a teenager. Despite suffering from gangrene in his left foot, Santosh was notorious for abducting cops and forest officials and slaughtering them brutally. Policemen shivered on hearing his name and considered him a monster who mutilated the bodies of his victims. He had over forty murder cases registered against him.

Santosh Anna looked into the eyes of the recruits one by one and said, 'Charu baba had certain rules for guerrilla fighters. The identity of the members of a guerrilla squad must be a secret. The name of the class enemy to be killed must be a secret. Nobody outside the squad must know about the timing of the attack.'

He then removed the gun from his left arm and pointed the barrel towards a recruit as if he was going to shoot him. Unfazed, the youth looked straight into Santosh Anna's eyes. After a few seconds, Santosh Anna moved the gun away and raised it with his both hands.

'This is not our weapon to eliminate the class enemy. Instead of guns, we must attack our enemy with a knife, sickle or axe. When we have ascertained that the enemy is coming to a particular spot, we must first spread around. We must behave in a manner that ensures people don't get an idea of who we are. Then, when the enemy arrives, we must pounce on him and kill him. Keep in mind that we must not be impatient.'

Suddenly, a man in his late twenties rushed in. Raising his right fist, he greeted Santosh Anna. '*Laal salaam* (red salute), Santosh Anna. We have received information that the government has sent a new SP to Gadchiroli. His name is Krishipal Raghuvanshi. Earlier, he was posted in Bombay. He is known for being an honest and strict police officer who is close to the DGP. He is arriving in Gadchiroli today and will take the charge tomorrow.'

'If he is close to the DGP, why is he being sent here? For so many months, the government was not able to pin down a scapegoat. Now he has been found,' Santosh Anna sighed.

He then addressed the Naxalites sitting on the ground. 'The government has sent a new pawn to fight us. We will welcome him with blood. Charu baba once said, any revolutionary whose hands have not been dipped in blood is not a communist. Your actual test is going to happen now. Are you ready to dip your hands in blood?'

'Yes. We are ready, Santosh Anna.'[15]

8

A BLOODY WELCOME

'Please get some ice cream for the kids,' Krishipal requested the caretaker of the guest house. It was sweltering in the first week of June in Gadchiroli and he wanted to alleviate the discomfort of his children.

'Sir, you can get ice cream only tomorrow.'

Krishipal was taken by surprise. 'What? Why tomorrow? Why not now?'

'Sir, there is no ice cream shop in Gadchiroli. We will have to send someone to Chandrapur to fetch the ice cream. It will take a whole day to make a round trip.'

Although Gadchiroli and Chandrapur were just 90 kilometres apart – in fact, they were considered the same district until August 1982 – the terrible road conditions prolonged the travel time between the two places. Krishipal and his family found themselves thrust into an environment that felt utterly alien. The conveniences of urban living that they had taken for granted were conspicuously absent.

While Krishipal had previously served in both rural and urban settings, Gadchiroli was essentially a hamlet nestled amidst a dense jungle. Despite being granted independent district status by the government eight years earlier, the transformation on paper had failed to manifest in reality. As Krishipal surveyed his new surroundings, he couldn't help but feel a sense of unease.

Upon their arrival in Gadchiroli, Krishipal and his family found temporary lodging at the Maharashtra Industrial Development Corporation (MIDC) guest house. Unfortunately, the accommodation left much to be desired and maintenance was sorely lacking. Pests like rodents and lizards moved around freely. The paint on the walls was peeling; taps in the bathroom were leaking. Despite its dilapidated state, Krishipal had no choice but to endure the substandard conditions, as the official bungalow designated for the SP was uninhabitable. Months of vacancy had taken their toll, shrouding it in a thick layer of dust and turning it into a sanctuary for pigeons and rodents alike. Cobwebs draped over the corners of the rooms, adding to the overall sense of neglect and decay.

The enthusiasm of the children had gone, and Sarita's worry had turned to sadness. Krishipal was a movie buff and during his college days, sometimes even watched the same movie twice in one day. While in Bombay, he often took Sarita to watch the latest movies on the weekends. Their south Bombay residence near Azad Maidan was close to many famous cinema halls like Metro, New Empire and Regal. But in Gadchiroli, there wasn't even a decent restaurant where Krishipal could take his family to dine out, let alone a cinema hall.

Power cuts were frequent and nobody could predict when the supply would resume. A stormy day in Gadchiroli was bound to result in a breakdown of the electricity supply which, apart from shutting down tube lights and fans, also made the TV set dysfunctional – their only window into the outside world. Still, Krishipal was aware of his family's privilege. Only a few households of the 15,000 villagers even had a TV set. The district headquarters and a few sub-district headquarters, known as talukas, were fortunate to have at least an irregular electricity supply. A major area of the district had no electricity at all. Inventions like electric bulbs, fans and refrigerators may have changed the world, but not this part of India. In a situation like this, it felt odd to complain about the lack of theatres and restaurants.

In his very first week as SP, Krishipal visited a few police stations and outposts and met several policemen deployed at different locations across Gadchiroli. Most of the police stations were housed in dilapidated buildings that hadn't been repainted for a long time. The police outposts were little more than tin huts. Generators were used to keep the structures running, since one could not rely on the electric supply. The outposts were protected by SRP guards from all sides. Hiding behind the gunny sandbags, these guards were always on alert, with their fingers on the trigger of their rifles. Krishipal found it strange that more than half of the platoon was deployed just to protect those tin structures erected to control the Naxalites. The bitter reality of Gadchiroli was that a policeman felt safer in civil clothes than the khaki uniform.

One day, Krishipal noticed some off-duty policemen watching a cockfight near their station. Most of them had been transferred to Gadchiroli from distant areas like Mumbai, Konkan, Marathwada, western Maharashtra and Khandesh. With no other means of recreation available, their leisure time was spent betting on cockfights. Several empty bottles of liquor lay beside them on the road. Alcohol had become an evening companion for the homesick cops.

It was true that many of these dejected officers had been dumped there as a punishment for indiscipline, corruption, dereliction of duty and other charges. But not all cops posted at Gadchiroli were guilty; some simply hadn't been able to pull enough strings to escape the posting. In such a dire state, being able to take their next breath must have felt like an achievement for these cops. Everyone's faces were marked with depression. Apart from the lack of basic facilities like comfortable places to sleep and eat, clean toilets and bathrooms, the area was occupied by swarms of mosquitoes that took flight as dusk fell. Many policemen had succumbed to malaria and dengue.

Seeing the plight of the policemen, Krishipal wondered how he would be able to fight the Naxals with these living corpses. However, among the numerous cops he met, one man stood apart. His name was Tarachand Meshram. Of average height with a distinctive thick moustache, Tarachand appeared to be cheerful and unaffected by the strenuous life in Gadchiroli. He was talkative, but Krishipal noticed that his words had substance. Tarachand was quite knowledgeable about local affairs. While talking to him, Krishipal realized that Tarachand nurtured a deep animosity towards the Naxalites in his heart and was willing to risk his life for the fight against them.

One day while sipping tea at the guest house, Krishipal picked up a local Marathi newspaper. He was flabbergasted to see the headline: 'Naxals Welcome New SP with Blood!' Underneath it, equally sensational subheadings read 'Police Patil Killed!' and 'Body Cut into Pieces!'

The front page also carried a gory picture of a man whose head was hanging from a tree. In those days, publishing graphic and grisly photos of mangled dead bodies was not considered unethical by newspaper editors; no self-censorship was practised. Krishipal called up the control room to get details on the case.

Naxalites had kidnapped a Police Patil from his village and taken him into the jungle a few days prior. On paper, the police had launched a search, but in reality no efforts had been made to find him. The local cops believed that to rescue one Police Patil, the lives of several policemen would be jeopardized. Their experience was that once a policeman was abducted, there was a very low possibility of finding him alive. Since the Police Patil was not an official policeman, his life was seen as even more expendable.

The system of Police Patils is unique to the rural areas of Maharashtra. The government appoints representatives of the police in every village, selected from among those who have been educated till at least grade ten. The Patils act as a bridge between the administration and their fellow villagers. It is their responsibility to alert the cops about any suspicious activity in the village. The Police Patil also assists the investigation team if some crime is committed in the village and offers support during elections. The person selected as a Police Patil must not have a criminal record. They function like a policeman without a uniform. The post commands great honour among the villagers; however, a large number of Police Patil posts remained vacant in Gadchiroli as the ones occupying them were targeted by Naxalites.

On the day of his murder, Naxals brought the Police Patil back to his village and, in the presence of the villagers, chopped off his head. It was then hung from the tree in the centre of the village using the lungi he was wearing. His hands and legs were also severed and hung from the tree. The police had received the news of this murder through newspapers, as nobody from the village dared to inform them. Krishipal quickly hid the newspaper in a file lying close by. After staying in Maharashtra for a few years, Sarita could understand Marathi. Krishipal worried that if she read the newspaper, her fear would intensify. He immediately donned his uniform and left for the office.

Krishipal told his staff that he wanted to visit the scene of the crime. As he sat in his Gypsy, Tarachand joined him. As they traversed through the muddy and pothole-ridden roads, Krishipal took the time to get to know his new colleague. Tarachand was a head constable in the SID. He was a resident of the Etapalli village in Gadchiroli and married to a local tribal girl.

'Sir, this is most likely the work of Santosh Anna,' Tarachand said with confidence.

'Who is Santosh Anna?'

'Santosh Anna is a demon disguised as a human. He is the most active dalam commander in our area nowadays and has killed many of our men like this. He kidnaps people, tortures them for days and then slaughters them. Sometimes the bodies of his victims are never found. Santosh Anna has been part of many ambushes, too, in which there have been heavy casualties.'

'Why haven't we caught him till now?'

Tarachand chuckled for a few seconds. 'Forgive me for this, sir. Every senior officer who is posted to Gadchiroli asks such a question in his initial days. In fact, it is the other way round. The police here feel fortunate that Santosh Anna hasn't caught them till now. Santosh Anna is the king of this jungle, and he rules it through fear.'

'Have some shame, Tarachand. Being a policeman, how can you glorify such a criminal?' Krishipal was on the brink of losing his cool.

'I am not glorifying anybody, sir. I am just telling you the reality. In some time, you will realize why I am saying what I am saying.'

'Tell me, why is our situation like this in Gadchiroli?

Across the world, criminals fear the police but here, the police fear these criminals. Why are they able to beat us?' Anger seeped into Krishipal's words.

'Sir, your questions are straight and simple, but the answers are very complex. Our government is as responsible as the Naxalites for the bloodshed in this area.'

'Okay, I will speak to you about this later.' Krishipal thought it prudent to change the topic since the wireless operator and driver present in the Gypsy were within earshot. 'Tell me, how many Naxalites are operating in Gadchiroli?'

'Around 125 Naxalites, sir.'

'And how many policemen are deployed here?'

'Around 1,600, including the local police and SRP forces.'

Upon reaching the village, Krishipal inspected the crime scene. The newspapers had reported that the Police Patil was killed in full view of the villagers, but the village was now deserted. Tarachand informed him that such a scene was common whenever a police team reached the spot after a Naxalite incident. Only the women, old and ailing people were left in the village; everybody else disappeared. Nobody wanted to invite death by meeting the police. When nobody came forward to register a complaint, the policemen themselves became the complainants. The fearful avoidance of the police reminded Krishipal of his own village.

The head and other limbs of the dead man were still hanging on the tree. Nobody in the village had dared to take them down. The cops collected them and sent them for a post-mortem exam. There were dry bloodstains on the tree as well as the victim's clothes. Krishipal then met the family of the deceased. They were speechless, though the tears rolling out from their eyes reflected their agony. Krishipal assured them that the police would try to arrest the murderers as soon as possible; that he would ensure that the family received some financial relief from the government. Their faces clearly conveyed that they thought Krishipal's words were hollow promises.

This was Krishipal's first time visiting a tribal village. He walked through it with Tarachand and a few other policemen with the intention of acquainting himself with tribal life. Krishipal noticed a few huts which were far larger than the rest. Tarachand told him that these structures were called ghotuls. Ghotuls are unique to Gond and Muria tribes living across Chhattisgarh, Madhya Pradesh, Maharashtra and Andhra Pradesh. They serve as community centres and are an inseparable part of tribal life, allowing the community to transfer its culture from one generation to the next. The youngsters are taught traditional arts, like singing and dancing, as well as skills required for livelihood like fishing, weaving, farming and hunting.

'Sir, boys and girls are introduced to each other for marriage here,' Tarachand explained. 'Premarital sex is not considered taboo in this tribe's culture. On full moon nights, groups of boys and girls dance together. If one expresses their liking for another then the couple may spend the night together. If the wedding is fixed then the bridegroom pays hunda money to the bride's father, unlike the dowry offered to the bridegroom among Hindus. The bridegroom has to stay at his father-in-law's home till the hunda is paid. Otherwise, he cannot claim any rights as a husband.'

'Interesting! It seems that women have the upper hand here,' Krishipal remarked.

On the outskirts of the village, there were some huts that served as granaries. They were erected at a height above the ground and were built with mud and bamboo. Their roofs were made of dry leaves and grass.

'Sir, these huts are used to store food grains by the Adivasis. But they have also been used for some other purposes which have contributed to the growth of Naxalism.'

'What else used to happen here?'

'Tribal women have been sexually exploited and raped in these structures. Some forest department officials and government workers have been involved in such crimes.'

It was dusk by the time Krishipal returned to Gadchiroli. By killing the Police Patil, the Naxalites had openly challenged him. Although he had promised that the killers would be brought to justice, Krishipal wondered how he would do so with the ragged force he was heading.

He now found himself faced with an inner conflict. He had three options. First, seek a deputation in the central government and escape Gadchiroli. Second, be passive and wait for his tenure in Gadchiroli to end. Third, take the challenge head-on and do something unprecedented that would cause lasting damage to the Naxal movement.

Krishipal's conscience didn't allow him to accept the first option – he would be seen as a coward and escapist. The second option was better, but there would be no difference between him and the constables who were killing time by betting on cockfights. The third option – though most outlandish – would make him immortal, one way or another.

9

A DEEP-ROOTED PROBLEM

In his early days in Gadchiroli, Krishipal often went to the banks of the river close to his office after work. He spent time contemplating his next course of action over bottles of warm beer. The fridge never seemed to cool them, even when there was electricity.

Ultimately, he chose the third option. Though it might prove fatal, he would do something that the Naxalites would never forget. To do this, he had to make a sacrifice even before his actual plan began – to stay away from his family. To fight this war, he needed to concentrate completely on his work. If his family stayed with him, he would be distracted while taking care of their security and comfort.

That night, over dinner, Krishipal informed Sarita of his decision. She lost her cool, demanding how he could take such a decision unilaterally. After a prolonged argument, Krishipal proposed that Sarita go to his native village along with the children for a few weeks. Once he oriented himself to the area and the Naxal problem, Sarita could return. Though unwilling, she accepted his suggestion.

Though he would miss them, Krishipal felt relieved after seeing off his wife and children. With their safety guaranteed, his complete focus was on the target: eliminating the Naxal problem from Gadchiroli. He started travelling across the district to get an in-depth understanding of its issues, meeting teachers, journalists, social workers and politicians alike. He also reached out to those retired cops who had been posted at Gadchiroli for a long time. From them, Krishipal got valuable insights into the causes for the advent of Naxalism in Gadchiroli and the helplessness of the police in containing the violence.

Considering the backwardness of the area and the prevalence of Naxal violence, the Maharashtra government had offered an economic package of ₹100 crore to the local administration as part of a special action plan. The fund was to be utilized under a two-pronged strategy. First, to improve health and education facilities, transportation and generate employment opportunities. Second, to strengthen the security apparatus in the region.

From 1988–9, the fund was used in a variety of ways. Eight companies of the SRP were given special training in Pune and deployed at Gadchiroli. Twenty-four police outposts were constructed across the district. Two additional SPs, five deputy SPs, fourteen inspectors and seventy sub inspectors were posted at Gadchiroli. However, these measures failed to have a significant impact on Naxal activity.

Beyond the lack of resources and infrastructure, Krishipal observed that the Gadchiroli police were negatively affected by the subpar information system. Without quality intelligence in advance, the cops failed to arrest Naxals and were killed by them instead. The local people's support was crucial to defeat the Naxals, but the sentiments of tribals were with the rebels and against the police.

Understanding why the tribals supported the Naxals was a key piece of the puzzle. The reason for the proliferation of Naxalism in Gadchiroli was different from other regions of India. In West Bengal, the atrocities committed by zamindars against landless labourers had fuelled the unrest, while in Andhra Pradesh moneylenders oppressed the tribals. In other places, miners had joined the Naxal movement to resist their exploitative bosses. In Gadchiroli, it was government officials – especially from the Forest Department – who were the villains. They not only siphoned off the money sent by the government for the welfare of the tribals but also treated them brutally. If a local wanted to get official work done, such officers used to tell them '*Bai aana, Batli aana*' (Get me women, get me liquor). The sexual exploitation of Adivasi women had become common – there were several cases where corrupt officials had raped minor tribal girls.[1]

The survival of the Adivasis was largely dependent on forest produce, but the forest officers restricted access, citing legalese. If an Adivasi had to clear a piece of land for shifting cultivation, they were restrained from doing so. The Forest (Conservation) Act, 1980 had been implemented in a manner that snatched away the rights of the Adivasis and threatened their livelihood. They were not allowed to collect dry wood for cooking food. Though bamboo shoots were part of their diet, the Adivasis weren't permitted to cut bamboo since it was used for manufacturing paper. They had to bribe the forest officials to use the natural wealth their communities had treasured for generations.

Just before harvest season, government officials would summon Adivasis and threaten to burn down their agricultural produce. Already impoverished, they had to pay bribes to save their yield. On the other hand, the governmental agencies allowed companies selling Sagwan wood to operate after receiving kickbacks. The Adivasis were also exploited by the contractors of tendu leaves and bamboo and paper mill owners. They were paid a pittance for back-breaking labour. The bitter sentiment stirred up by these many injustices was capitalized on by the Maoists.

In various villages, the Naxals had set up units called 'sangams', meaning confluence. Sangams acted as a bridge between the cadres and Adivasis. Their members didn't participate in the armed conflict but supported the Naxal movement on the ground. The sangams functioned as a de facto administrative order, parallel to the gram panchayat system. Members resolved petty disputes amongst themselves and set up jan adalats (public courts) to punish those accused of crimes. They also influenced local youths into joining the Naxal movement.

The sangams were the eyes and ears of the Naxals. If anybody was suspected of working as an informer for the police, the local sangam passed on their details to the dalams. Sangams helped the Naxalites punish or eliminate those government officials who were accused of oppressing tribals. A brief trial would be arranged in the open ground of a village after which jan adalats delivered punishment, which could range from thrashing to beheading the culprit.[2] By way of sangams, the Naxalites had established their supremacy in tribal villages. They also compelled the tendu leaf and bamboo contractors to pay higher wages to the Adivasis by threatening to harm them or burn down the stocks they procured.

Apart from dealing with the atrocious government personnel, the Naxals attempted to redress problems of agriculture and accessing forest resources. Only a fraction of Gadchiroli's land was irrigated, so the Naxals helped the tribals build tanks in their villages. A co-operative system was introduced wherein two to four families ploughed fields and collected firewood together. This not only encouraged a sense of unity among the villagers but also respect for the Naxalites.[3] Dalam members were addressed as anna (elder brother) by the Adivasis. The ultimate aim of the Naxal movement was to establish a janata sarkar (people's government) in the region which would run as per the Communist ideology.

The Naxalites also made extensive use of poetry, folk music and drama to win over the hearts of the Adivasis. Programmes were organized in villages where Naxal supporters sang upbeat songs of rebellion and reminded locals of the atrocities committed by the government. The tribals were told that they had full right over forest land; that non-tribals, with the help of the government, were plundering them away. The underlying message was that to end the oppression, violence was the only option. The Naxals used tribal languages like Madiya and Gond to convey their points.

Later, in 1997, such performing arts units were formalized under the name Chetna Natya Manch (CNM). Many youngsters were influenced by the CNM and joined the dalams, viewing it as an opportunity to fight against the oppressive powers to be. Wearing the Naxal uniform gave them a sense of strength; they took pride in being part of a large and organized community. Since the tribals considered Naxals to be their well-wishers and the police their nemeses, they would pass on information about police movements to the dalams.

During his regular meetings with Gadchiroli police personnel posted across different units, Krishipal noticed that many cops on the desk jobs wore civilian clothes. One head constable posted in the headquarters was particularly conspicuous – he was nicknamed 'Red Shirt' by his colleagues, since he wore one nearly every day. His Bengali-accented Hindi made Krishipal even more curious to know more about him.

The constable's real name was Ashok Biswas. He hailed from a Bengali family that had settled in Gadchiroli in the 1970s, after which Biswas got a job on the police force. While talking to Biswas, Krishipal observed that he had a deep knowledge of the history and politics of the Naxal movement in India – not only the Gadchiroli dalams but also those in other states. Krishipal frequently called the constable to his office and chatted with him for hours.

Biswas told him that a year after Peddi Shankar was killed, an incident in the Adilabad district of Andhra Pradesh had played a major role in the proliferation of Naxalism. On 20 April 1981, the tribals of Adilabad had planned a big rally in Indravelli village to demand better wages for tendu leaf collectors and labourers working for government contractors. Another one of their demands was to free forest land that had been possessed by non-tribals. Although the police initially allowed the gathering, permission was withdrawn after they received intel that Maoists would also be participating.

A day before the rally, the police enforced prohibitory orders at the venue and deployed numerous cops. However, swarms of Gond tribals began reaching Indravelli from different parts of the state, most of whom were unaware of the prohibitory orders. The police tried to disperse the crowd by lathi-charging them and then began shooting the agitators. Several people were reportedly crushed by a police jeep. According to non-government sources, sixty-five people were killed, although the police maintained that there were only thirteen deaths. Many of the dead were allegedly cremated secretly without following the tribal rituals. The incident was widely compared with the Jallianwala Bagh incident during British rule.[4,5]

In 1983, three years after the Adilabad incident, a group of communists had organized a convention in Kamalapur village, part of the Aheri subdivision of Gadchiroli. One of the organizers of the convention was Eknath Salve, a lawyer and former legislator. Followers of the Communist ideology from across India were expected to participate. After getting permission from the Gadchiroli police, a 15-foot-tall stage was erected. The gathering was to be held in a ground that spread over 10 acres, one corner of which was converted into a kitchen to cater food for the participants. As preparations were in full swing, an intelligence report from the Andhra Pradesh Police rattled their counterparts in Gadchiroli. According to the report, Naxals from various parts of the country were also planning to participate, and the convention's hidden agenda was to intensify their war against the Indian state. The Gadchiroli police withdrew their permission.

Even so, the organizers insisted upon conducting the event. A crowd marched from Chavela towards Kamalapur, pelting stones when the police obstructed them. The officers then resorted to a lathi-charge. Despite firm action by the police, some protestors managed to reach the stage. After the clash, the police detained around 500 people. The Kamalapur convention may have failed, but it became a landmark event in the history of the Naxal movement in Maharashtra. In the aftermath, many young men and women began joining the dalams.[6]

With the help of Tarachand and Biswas, Krishipal tried to understand the tactics and modus operandi of the Naxals. To get insight into the weapons used by the Naxals, he visited the storeroom where seized firearms were kept with his two companions in tow.

'Sir, although we usually get beaten up by Naxals, sometimes luck favours us and we teach them a lesson,' Tarachand said. 'These weapons have been seized from them on such rare occasions.'

'They have all the same weapons as us!' Krishipal was shocked.

'Sir, these are our weapons.'

'What do you mean?'

'Sir, in Gadchiroli, policemen are being killed with their own weapons. When the Naxals ambush us, they steal arms from our dead and injured men. These are used during encounters and ambushes. On the other hand, when they kill civilians like informers or government contractors, then they use an axe or a knife,' Biswas explained.

'Essentially, those who can retaliate are dealt with using firearms, while unarmed people are butchered like goats,' Tarachand added. 'During the initial days, they used bows and arrows. Then they started using *kattas* (country-made pistols) and *bharmars* (muzzle-loaded short-range guns).'

'Sir, apart from this, they also liaise with insurgents from Assam, Manipur and Nagaland to obtain weapons,' Biswas supplied. 'Bangladesh and Burma, too. They also run arms manufacturing factories at some of their bases, like Abujhmad. They've even started making improvised explosive devices (IEDs), with a near-perfect success rate. We've heard rumours that the Sri Lankan group [Liberation Tigers of Tamil Eelam] LTTE have trained them in explosives and guerrilla warfare.'

'Where do they get the funds for all of this?'

'Sir, they don't have any dearth of money. They extort not only tendu leaf and bamboo contractors but also those who have been assigned to development projects like building bridges, roads or schools. When a contractor refuses to pay up, they are thrashed and their equipment is burnt down. If they approach the police to complain, they are killed. Apart from this, some amount of money is extorted from shopkeepers and moneylenders as well. While they are moving from one place to another, the Naxals take breaks at villages and expect the residents to take care of their food and accommodation.'

Krishipal noticed some firecrackers lying in a corner and looked at Tarachand for an explanation.

'During encounters, the Naxalites use such crackers to fool us. They throw lit firecrackers in different directions. Mistaking them for gunshots, our men misdirect their fire. Our bullets are wasted while theirs are saved. This is one of their tactics to mislead us.'

'Hmm. We, too, need to be as shrewd as them,' Krishipal sighed.

'Naxals have been using various unusual tactics to abduct or kill policemen,' Biswas expanded. 'For instance, they dig pitfalls and cover them with grass to trap unsuspecting cops. Traditionally, such pits have been used to hunt wild animals, but in the Naxal-infested areas, those conducting search operations or routine patrols in the forest have fallen victim to them.'[7]

That evening, after Krishipal got home from the storeroom, DGP Saraf gave him a call. 'How are you, Raghuvanshi? Hope you have settled by now.'

'Yes, sir. I am fine. The rains have started, so there is some relief from the heat. I am continuously trying to understand the problems affecting the area. I visit different police stations daily.'

'Then you'll know full well that our people are getting killed every day. I trust that you will stop this. You have everything you need: weapons, manpower, funds. Now I need to see results,' Saraf said in a solemn tone.

'Yes, sir. I will try my best.'

Krishipal had been frequently receiving phone calls of this kind from Saraf – reminding him of the stakes, of the pressure he and his team were under. In theory, he did have the resources necessary to wage this war at his disposal. But his short stint in Gadchiroli had already made one thing clear: this wasn't a battle that could be won through force alone.

10

THINKING LIKE A NAXALITE

Krishipal found a sense of purpose in overseeing the construction of the new SP bungalow, a project that offered respite during moments of overwhelming stress. His discussions with the Public Works Department engineer heading the construction were almost therapeutic – conclusive, easy, everything his work was not. For instance, he was able to request a mini pool on the bungalow grounds to cater to his love for swimming. Despite these moments of ease, one question remained in the back of his mind. How could he win the hearts of the tribals who consider the police their adversary?

The key to solving the Naxal challenge was hidden in the hearts of Adivasis, he realized. Intelligence was vital and the only way to get it was to earn the trust and support of the tribals. The police were still seen as cogs in a system that had oppressed them and rightfully so, given their treatment of the tribals so far. However, Krishipal was hopeful that someday he could better this image.

In the meantime, he turned his attention to more immediate steps. Though the government had sent a large number of police personnel to Gadchiroli under the Special Action Plan, there was no strategy on how to utilize them. Everyone was just dawdling. Nobody had the willingness or courage to fight the Naxals. Krishipal was dumbfounded to hear that, in some cases, the SRP platoons and dalams crossed each other while patrolling in the forest and the SRP men deliberately looked the other way. News of some forest guard or local land official being murdered often followed. Krishipal vowed to change this situation.

During those days, the district police was divided into three units: Sironcha, Aheri and Gadchiroli. Krishipal broke them down further into five, creating independent divisions for Kurkheda and Etapalli. He assigned an officer of the deputy SP rank to each division. The police stations under these divisions were headed by inspectors. Every police station had a few outposts. Earlier, these were manned only by the SRP, but Krishipal assigned an SI at each outpost. Additionally, he ensured that there were at least two constables who spoke the local languages at every outpost.

Before Krishipal took over the charge, officers were regularly sent on anti-Naxal operations along with SRP squads. Most of these operations were just an eyewash and concrete results were rare, especially since no teams ventured out after dusk. When the police received information about the presence of Naxals in a particular village, they would rush to apprehend them. However, as soon as the Naxals detected police movement, they vanished into the jungle. The cops usually returned empty-handed or, at most, with some leftover materials like backpacks, utensils or food.

One day, Krishipal called a meeting of his subordinates and announced something that surprised everyone. 'Henceforth, nobody will go for the anti-Naxal operations.'

The officers present at the meeting looked at each other in confusion. Some thought that Krishipal was a coward who wanted to avoid getting entangled with the Naxalites. Others believed that this was a sarcastic remark about their inefficiency. After letting the officers stew in their bewilderment for a few moments, Krishipal said, 'You might think that my decision is strange. I have been assigned to wipe out Naxalism from Gadchiroli but here I am, telling you not to fight Naxals. If the government gets to know about this, I could lose my job and embarrass the DGP. But I have taken this decision after much contemplation.'

'Sir, if we don't catch the Naxals, they will become more fearless and the problem will aggravate in the days to come.'

'Wow! You are saying this as if you are catching three or four Naxals every day. Instead, I have been hearing that Naxals are catching policemen. I know that most of us have been transferred here unwillingly. It's time we stop talking about catching Naxalites,' Krishipal said with a wry smile.

After listening to his words many officers lowered their eyes in shame.

'I haven't called you here to reprimand you. I have a plan which I believe will help mitigate this crisis, but it will take time. It is possible that by the time this plan starts delivering results, we will be transferred out of Gadchiroli or even out of this world by Naxal bullets.'

'Sir, we are excited to listen to your plan!' a young officer piped up.

'Nobody puts their life in danger for fun. We must understand why these boys and girls have chosen to leave their homes behind to live a difficult life in forest, constantly on the move. An extreme sense of victimhood has been pushed into their minds, systematically and forcefully, by the Naxalites. They feel that their way of living and their very survival is under threat. They are convinced that the state is their enemy; that we, who wear the khaki uniform, represent that enemy. Hence, they kill us without any mercy or guilt.

'These are not gangsters who kill for money or zealots who pick up guns due to religious radicalization. Our fight is not only against the symptoms but also the roots of the malady. As police officers, I know there is a very limited scope for us to work in this regard. Still, I feel we can put in our best effort. We are in the battlefield – we know the reality.'

'But is it possible to change their attitude towards us, sir?' another officer asked.

'Let's see. So far, we have been going to villages only when we receive intelligence inputs that Naxals were seen there. By the time we reach there, the rebels vanish and our men rough up and interrogate the villagers. From now onwards, every police officer will regularly visit the villages in their jurisdiction. We will not ask villagers about the Naxalites; instead, we'll ask about the locals' well-being and the problems they are facing. Keep a diary and make a note of these. Nobody is to misbehave with the villagers. Instead ... consider yourself a Naxalite.'

There was a burst of laughter in the meeting on hearing this.

'Yes. Those visiting the villages must consider themselves Naxalites. Try to figure out where you would hold a meeting in the village, if you were part of a dalam. In case of police raids, what would be the possible escape routes? Discreetly, make a rough map of such locations in the diary. Deposit one copy of the map with the local police station and another one with the Naxal Cell at the police headquarters.'

Before calling this meeting, Krishipal had set up a Naxal Cell in the District Special Branch (DSB) and appointed Ashok Biswas as its in-charge. The task of this cell was to track Naxal activities: names of the dalam commanders, cases registered against them, the number of members in a particular dalam, their area of operations and so on.

'Start executing this plan right away. If the villagers can't view you as their friends, they shouldn't consider you their enemies either.' With that, Krishipal concluded the meeting.

Afterwards, he overheard some officers ridiculing him in the corridor. 'He is a newbie here and hence has such odd ideas. His bubble will burst when he faces reality in a few days,' one person said. However, there were others who believed that there was substance in Krishipal's plan. 'All other ideas to finish Naxalism have failed. KP sir is thinking out of the box, and we must give it a shot.'

Soon, the on-ground implementation of Krishipal's strategy began. Most police officers visited some or the other village every day and met those who lived in their jurisdiction. They behaved courteously and in a friendly manner. Like well-wishers, they asked after the residents' health and if anybody was ailing, the details were noted down. The cops carried medicine for them during their next visit. In some villages, where many people were suffering from dengue or malaria, teams of doctors were sent on Krishipal's request.

Many shopkeepers charged the tribals exorbitant prices for salt. Krishipal arranged for cheaper salt packets for them. Earlier, shopkeepers registered with the Public Distribution System (PDS) were known to steal rations meant for the tribals. Under Krishipal, that changed and the tribals received their supplies in full.

If a local had been harassed by a government official, the report was sent to the official's higher-ups. As instructed by Krishipal, no questions were asked about Naxalites, but the visiting cops made rough maps of the villages. They also recorded details about the village residents: names of respected individuals, how many were employed and unemployed, whether the children were going to a government-run *ashram shala* for their studies and so on.

Krishipal formally named this endeavour the Gram Bheti Yojana (Village Visit Plan). He had set up a cell, headed by an inspector, to receive reports from the visiting police officers and compile the complaints of the villagers. The cell forwarded the complaints to the concerned departments of the Zilla Parishad. After a few days, the police revisited the villages to check whether the grievances of the villagers had been addressed.

Initially, the tribals were sceptical about the changed behaviour of the cops. However, in a span of six to seven months, they realized that their life was changing for the better and their problems were actually being addressed. They began opening up to the cops, offering them water to drink or a place to rest when they visited a village. The gorge between the two groups was reducing. However, Krishipal's strategy – that friendly relations with the tribals would fetch him good intelligence – had yet to show results. It was rare for a person to become a police informer purely out of patriotism or a social cause – in most cases, vested interest or monetary gain were involved. Krishipal's idea was to establish a network of informers who were as vested in combatting the Naxal movement as his team.

While interacting with the Adivasis, Krishipal realized that there was another reality beyond their apparent camaraderie with the Naxals. There was a section of the population that was tortured by Naxals and hated them but were powerless to resist their dominance. Once, while visiting a village, Krishipal noticed a middle-aged man overhearing his conversation. Both the man's hands were missing. When Krishipal enquired about him, he was told that the man used to be a teacher who educated students about democratic values and the rule of law. He disparaged the Naxalites and their ideology. One day, some Naxals came to his school and chopped off both the man's hands with an axe in front of his students.

Across Gadchiroli, there were many teachers like him, who had been killed or mutilated for speaking against the Maoists. On occasions like Republic Day and Independence Day, they raided schools and replaced the Indian tricolour with black flags. They forced teachers and students to raise anti-India slogans. If any teacher resisted, they were roughed up in front of the children. In the eyes of the Naxals, these teachers were class enemies who represented the oppressors. Fearing Naxal violence, many students avoided going to distant schools. Krishipal had also heard claims that Naxals sometimes robbed the food or supplies provided by the government for the children's midday meals.

Beyond encouraging the villagers to trust the police, Krishipal also had to get the police to trust him and each other. Camaraderie was important in a unit, and crucial when executing life-threatening missions. Krishipal refurbished a volleyball ground and badminton court on the campus of the Gadchiroli Police headquarters. Every evening, he spent some time with the constables playing these games. Generally, cops were required to keep their hair short, but there was no such compulsion in Gadchiroli. Some had shoulder length hair or long beards, since they might need to hide their identity while travelling. Instead of their police ID cards, they carried ones belonging to non-police departments like Agricultural or Health to mislead the Naxalites in case they were caught.

Krishipal maintained friendly relations with his subordinates, and they eventually opened up to him about their personal lives. Some of his men hailed from the Gadchiroli district itself. Once, a constable named Damu Kolha (name changed) became teary-eyed as he told Krishipal that he would never be able to return to his village. Two years earlier, he had left his home to participate in the police recruitment drive at Gadchiroli. When this news reached the Naxals, they tortured his parents and brothers. They tried to summon Damu back to the village, but he knew that returning meant death. The Naxals would chop off his head.

There were many like Damu, who were forced to abandon their homes forever after being recruited. In some cases, recruits went to meet their parents discreetly, but if Naxalites got a whiff, they raided the village and killed the recruit.[1] Sometimes Naxals would send a message to the recruited youth through some relative that his parents were very sick and wanted to see him for the last time. When the youngster gave into his emotions and went to the village, the Naxalites beheaded him. Generally, it was the parents of recruits who went to the Gadchiroli police headquarters and met them clandestinely. Even those who returned to their villages after being unsuccessful in the recruitment drive were often killed. Thus, leaving one's village for police recruitment meant you could never return – whether you were selected or not. Unsuccessful candidates hung around the police stations in Gadchiroli for a few nights, on the hunt for petty jobs.

By talking to constables belonging to Adivasi families, Krishipal realized that the Naxals didn't value their lives. Since 1982, they had started killing Adivasis as well. If they had the slightest suspicion that a villager was working for the police, they were beheaded. While passing through the village, if a policeman drank water from a tribal family or stayed with them for a few hours to escape the afternoon heat, the family had to face the wrath of Naxals. In some cases, the head of the house was killed.

For tribals, it was like being trapped between a rock and a hard place. If they helped the Naxals, the police tortured them; by cooperating with the cops, they invited the wrath of the Naxals. There had been several instances when Naxalites, intending to slay cops, had killed innocent villagers while blowing up buses or Jeeps carrying wedding parties. Whenever their recklessness was exposed, the Maoists simply washed their hands of their actions by issuing an apology. By some accounts, the Naxals had killed more than 700 Adivasis between 1982–2012, accusing them of being 'class enemies' or due to mistaken identities.[2]

The Naxals also used the tribals for their anti-police propaganda. Whenever there was some major police action, they pressured the tribals to protest, claiming that their human rights were being violated. They frequently called for bandhs to exhibit their strength. Meanwhile, they created impediments in the development of the tribal areas. They didn't allow contractors assigned by the government to construct roads, bridges and tunnels in remote regions. 'At first, the government didn't undertake any developmental work in this region,' one constable told Krishipal. 'Now, finally, when they thought of doing so, the Naxals are not allowing it to happen. Hence, Gadchiroli remains backward.'

To bypass issues like these, the government established the Border Roads Organization (BRO) in 1960. Operating under the Ministry of Defence, BRO has been tasked with constructing roads in India's border areas using teams of engineers who are enrolled in the army. It has constructed roads in the difficult terrain of north-east India and friendly neighbouring countries. To stall developmental work, several BRO engineers have been killed by the Naxalites.[3] Sarpanches (village heads) who supported the development projects have also been targeted.

Apart from extorting money from contractors and moneylenders, Naxalites have not always spared the tribals who collect tendu leaves. They force the workers to share a part of their earnings, claiming that their wages have increased because of the fear generated by the Maoists. The extorted amount is called a 'contribution' to the movement. If a worker refuses to part away with their hard-earned money, they are at risk of punishment and even beheading.

Krishipal felt shaken after learning about the atrocities committed against the tribals by Naxals. These stories had never been exposed. If some tribals had started working for the Naxals after being aggrieved by the government's actions, wasn't it possible that those tribals who had been victimized by the Naxals could work for the police? Couldn't the police seek their help in the fight against Naxalism? Why hadn't the police reached out to such people before? Suddenly, the problem that had been plaguing Krishipal had a very obvious solution: he had to think like a Naxal to defeat them.

11

THE C-60 COMES TO LIFE

One evening, Krishipal called all those policemen who hailed from the local tribes to his office for tea. After chatting with them for a few moments, he said, 'At the end of the day, this is your problem. I will be transferred out of Gadchiroli in two or three years, but you people belong to this place. Your families are here. Hence, it is you who will have to find a permanent solution to the Naxal situation. How long will your people be oppressed by these bastards? Consider this seriously. We will meet again in three days. Until then, think of ways to effectively deal with this problem.'

Krishipal's words touched the hearts of the gathered policemen. So far, those assigned to Gadchiroli had counted the days until their tenure was over. For the first time, it seemed that an officer wanted to free Gadchiroli from the clutches of Naxalism – to seek their opinion rather than simply ask them to implement strategies created by ministers and senior officers sitting in their plush air-conditioned offices. Even that implementation was only done on paper; there was no real action on the ground. If a policeman was murdered, the top brass and incumbent politicians just issued a statement condemning the incident and offered compensation to the family of the martyred. Krishipal, on the other, genuinely appeared concerned about Gadchiroli.

Three days later, the group met again as planned. When asked about their suggestions, the men echoed the same realization that Krishipal had recently come to.

'Sir, we must operate in the same manner as the Naxals.'

'As in?'

'Sir, Naxals work in dalams. Perhaps we could form dalams too and enter the jungle. All we need are weapons. We already know the topography of the area, and have knowledge of the best routes through the jungle. We know where the river is, the hills, the swamps ... We will hunt the Naxals down and finish them,' one constable said enthusiastically.

'If the Gadchiroli Police continues to work the way it has been, nothing will change,' another constable added. 'Meanwhile, the Naxalites grow stronger day by day. They know our vulnerabilities and our style of work.'

A third constable chimed in. 'And to top it all off, the Naxalites know that the police fear them. This can only change when they get a taste of their own medicine. You are right, sir. This is our issue to solve and we have to take accountability.'

'Sir, with full sincerity, we are ready to lay down our

lives in this war,' the first constable spoke again, his eyes reflecting his anger. 'If we don't come forward today, this crisis will go on and on. Some of us will lose our lives, but the Naxals will also get the message, that there are people who can respond in their language.'

Krishipal was elated after listening to the constables. 'You guys have offered a brilliant idea. This strategy will help us teach the Maoists a lesson, but I'll need permission from the government to form such "dalams". I'll speak to the DGP – it will be possible only with his approval.'

He went to the Maharashtra Police headquarters in Bombay two days later to meet DGP Saraf and propose the experiment in Gadchiroli. Krishipal narrated the conversation he had with the constables to Saraf, who remained unconvinced. 'Your proposal is brilliant, but I don't think that we can take such a risk. If we arm these men with automatic weapons, the Naxals could snatch them. It is also possible that some of these men might double-cross us and join the Naxalites. The world will laugh at us then.'

A disappointed Krishipal returned to Gadchiroli, the words of the constables still resonating his mind. The very next day, he gathered them and gave a fiery speech. To close it, he declared, 'Now, we have to launch our big fight against Naxals. We might lose our lives as well. Are you all ready?'

'Yes, sir.' All the constables replied in chorus.

Krishipal hand-picked sixty personnel who were tall and well-built – though even those who were physically frail were willing to join the war. He visualized this new team as a unique, superior and reliable force. He decided that the uniform of these commandos should differ from the regular police uniform. At first, Krishipal considered a dark green uniform, since the commandos would be working in forest, but it was too similar to the typical Naxalite garb. He settled on grey, to match the soil in the area. Krishipal bought the uniforms with the help of a friend in Bombay, using the Secret Service Fund given to SPs for cultivating informers to pay for them. No audit is done of the spending from this fund.[1]

The commandos were relieved of regular police functions. Krishipal began their training with a lesson in road opening – an exercise undertaken whenever a police or VIP convoy was passing by a road to ensure the Naxalites hadn't planted landmines there. Like most of the security-related practices adopted by the Gadchiroli Police, this technique was developed through their past mistakes.

During these early training days, DGP Saraf visited Gadchiroli. The Naxals learnt about his visit and killed a police informer within a 100-metre radius of the police outpost in the remote village of Damrancha. Through this killing, they intended to convey their supremacy in the district. When Saraf heard about the murder, he informed Krishipal that he wanted to visit the site. Krishipal accompanied Saraf in his Gypsy – it was perilous for the police chief to visit a Naxal-infested region. Any untoward incident would be a major embarrassment for the government and bolster the confidence of the Naxalites.

The route to Damrancha was fraught with muddy roads. Along the way, the Jeep piloting the DGP's convoy got stuck in mud, and it took a lot of effort to pull its wheels out. This often happened to police vehicles in Gadchiroli, as the Jeeps sanctioned by the DGP's office were not suitable for the terrain. Krishipal took this opportunity to convince Saraf that four-wheel-drive vehicles like Gypsies – of which he had only a few at his disposal – were required. Saraf accepted Krishipal's argument and said that the Gadchiroli Police would receive Gypsies instead of Jeeps.

As they continued their journey, Saraf spotted the road opening team that Krishipal had deployed. Astonished by their distinctive uniforms, he said, 'Raghuvanshi, these don't look like personnel of the Gadchiroli Police. Who are these people?'

'Sir, these are the Adivasi personnel that I spoke to you about during our meeting in Bombay. In my capacity, I have raised a special unit of a few well-built men. For the time being I am using them for road clearance.' Krishipal replied with a smile, but he was afraid of being reprimanded by Saraf for raising the unit without his approval.

'Hmm! So, is this your crack team?'

'Yes, sir. You can consider it that.'

'How many boys have you deployed in this way?'

'Sir, there are a total of sixty. I have placed thirty in Gadchiroli and the rest in Aheri.'

'Very good. So, this is your Crack-60 team. Go ahead.' After thinking for a few moments, Saraf continued, 'You should involve more people so that a strength of sixty men is always ready for deployment.'

Krishipal was relieved to see Saraf's change of heart. Not only had the DGP liked the idea, but he had also named the force.

Saraf then asked, 'You have removed these guys from normal police duties – what they will do when they aren't on some assignment?'

'Sir, they will train hard to become stronger and more skilful.'

'Excellent!' Saraf exclaimed. His remaining time in Gadchiroli went smoothly; the DGP's visit was a triumph for Krishipal and his newly christened force.

After Saraf returned to Bombay, Krishipal followed his advice and enrolled forty more men into the specialized force. His team was now 100 men strong. Thirty were deployed at Gadchiroli, thirty at Aheri and thirty were kept in reserve. The remaining ten commandos would step in when their fellows were absent due to leave or illness.

Krishipal then experimented with the command and control of the newly raised commando force. An inspector was made in-charge of the force for administrative purposes and the men were divided into sections comprised of ten commandos, each headed by a constable. Krishipal chose the party commanders by observing their skill and courage, not seniority. Hence, in many units, senior constables were led by their juniors. This made C-60 a unique commando force. Generally, in the armed forces, a section of soldiers is identified with names like Alpha, Beta and so on. However, Krishipal entitled the units based on the names of their commanders. If a section was headed by a constable named Devgi Madavi, for instance, it would be known as the 'Devgi Madavi Party'.

He now had a team of spirited young men and the tacit support of his superiors to fight Naxalism as he saw fit. However, one thing made him feel uneasy – these commandos only had basic police training. As tribals, they knew the forest well, but that only put them on equal footing with Naxals, not at an advantage. In case of a confrontation, his boys would need additional preparation to gain an upper hand.

While contemplating who could provide such advanced commando training, the Greyhounds Force of the Andhra Pradesh Police came to Krishipal's mind. Raised just a year earlier, in 1989, the Greyhounds had become a formidable force against Naxalism in a brief span of time. Sturdy policemen under the age of thirty-five years were recruited for the force and trained in jungle warfare. True to their name, the Greyhounds had started inflicting severe damage on the Naxalites as soon as the force was commissioned.

Krishipal wanted to see the performance of the Greyhounds in Andhra Pradesh replicated by his C-60 commandos in Maharashtra. After taking his superiors into confidence, Krishipal rang up the inspector general (IG) of the Greyhounds and sought his assistance. The IG readily agreed to the proposal but said that he could only arrange for the accommodation of the trainees. Krishipal would have to account for their food and travel. Once again, money from his Secret Service Fund footed the bill.

The Greyhounds began training the C-60 commandos

in batches. Their tasks ranged from climbing hills and walking through the jungle carrying heavy weights to jumping from heights and crossing rivers. The trainees also received lessons in handling different types of weapons and surviving in the forest. The two groups discussed their experiences with the Naxals and the Greyhounds offered insight into their modus operandi.

Six months later, the training was complete and the force, ready for action. Seeing them march for the first time, Krishipal was confident that C-60 would create history.

12

THE SAGA OF KAMALA ALAAM

'Try this chutney, sir. It tastes good with bhakri,' one C-60 commando proudly offered Krishipal on his first operation deep in the jungle. They had received information about the presence of a dalam commander and were on the lookout for him.

He had gotten fairly used to life in the forest, but some things took more time than others. Food was once such thing. Krishipal eyed the red powder with suspicion. 'What is this?'

'Sir, this is red ant chutney. We Adivasis regularly eat it. It's fresh – I just got it from there.' He pointed towards a tree which was crawling with ants.

Every commando carried bhakris, biscuits and chickpeas from the headquarters during missions – food that wasn't quick to go stale. Often, they had to spend days in the forest and such dry rations came to their rescue. Cooking during operations was forbidden, as the smoke could alert the Naxalites. However, as an accompaniment, the commandoes often prepared chutneys made of wild insects. By participating in the operations, Krishipal was getting exposed to tribal culture and food.

Despite his growing familiarity with local life, seven months was not enough to understand Gadchiroli and the complex problem of Naxalism that marred it. The bad roads, dense forest cover and uneven terrain – coupled with the constant shadow of death – meant that officers posted in Gadchiroli had little time to focus on anything else. Those who were accustomed to urban life found it tough to sustain in this perilous land. However, Krishipal was happy with the progress he had made. Despite adversities, he had come up with a solution that had the potential to get rid of the Naxal problem in the long run. He took charge as SP, Gadchiroli, on 11 May 1990; on 1 December 1990, the C-60 commando force, his brainchild, formally came into existence.

Soon after, the action started. With the help of the Naxal Cell, a list of dreaded cadres was made and the hunt for them began. The C-60 commandos often received intelligence from the contacts in their villages, which led them to their targets. Krishipal made it clear to his men that they should avoid being trigger-happy; killing Naxals was not their priority. They were advised to shoot only if their life was in jeopardy. Apprehending a Naxal alive was more advantageous as they could provide information about their accomplices. Killing a Naxal, on the other hand, would invite scrutiny from the government, human rights groups and media.

The operations conducted by the C-60 were largely successful and numerous infamous Naxalites were apprehended. Krishipal was rattled to see a number of tribal women among the dalams. The women's wing of PWG was led by Narmada Akka, who had joined the Naxal movement in 1980 as an eighteen-year-old. Apart from participating in ambushes, she also actively recruited Adivasi women. Interrogating the women arrested in connection with Naxalism was a challenge. The few women in the Gadchiroli Police at the time weren't from the area and did not speak the local languages. Krishipal realized it was crucial to recruit some Adivasi women to the force, but the problem was that there weren't many women in Gadchiroli who could meet the minimum educational qualifications.

One evening when Krishipal was staying at the forest department's guest house in Allapalli, a C-60 commando informed him that an Adivasi girl named Kamala Alaam wanted to meet him. She had been associated with the Maoists and had deep knowledge of the Naxal networks in south Gadchiroli. Krishipal agreed to the meeting and asked the commando to bring her to the guest house after dusk.

At the agreed time, a wheatish-skinned girl, frail but tall, appeared before Krishipal. 'Yes, Kamala. What brings you here?'

'Sir, I have heard of the new commando force of Adivasis raised by you. I want to join it.'

'Why do you want to join it?'

To answer this question, Kamala narrated her story.

Kamala hailed from Kamalapur village, where she had lived with her parents and siblings. She had worked in a paper mill close to the village. The Naxals held considerable clout in the village – many people Kamala knew had joined them. She, too, had participated in the meetings organized by sangams and developed an affinity towards Naxals. She had believed that they were well-wishers of the tribals and was taught to hate the governmental machinery – the source of exploitation, as per the Naxals.

During the Kamalapur convention organized by the Maoists, as mentioned in Chapter 9, twelve to thirteen motor pumps were installed in a well close to her house to supply water to the cadres' camps. As the police cracked down on the convention and began tracking down Maoist sympathizers, her village came under scrutiny. A police team recovered the motor pumps and singled out her grandfather, thrashing him brutally for allowing the Naxals to install the pumps. The cops then arrested him along with sixty-nine other villagers on charges of supporting the Maoists.[1]

Distressed with the arrest of her grandfather, Kamala approached the Naxals for help. Since they had some lawyers supporting them, she thought they would help her grandfather get bail. 'It is because of you people that my grandfather has been arrested. Now you should help us get him released,' she pleaded.

She was to be disappointed – the dalam washed their hands of the incident. Kamala returned to the village and informed the kin of the accused that they would have to fend for themselves. After some discussion, the families decided to hire a lawyer by pooling in their savings. The arrested villagers were released on bail, but some families went bankrupt between the lawyer's fees and bail money. Although Kamala was enraged to see the treatment meted out to her grandfather by the police, she was also appalled by the behaviour of the Naxalites. They had not only raised their cadres from the village but also often demanded food and shelter. Yet, in their time of need, the Naxals had abandoned the villagers. Henceforth, Kamala began questioning their ideology.

Meanwhile, another incident happened that furthered her disillusionment. In addition to the paper mill, Kamala worked as a temporary labourer on a paddy farm during the sowing season. One day, a Naxal commander named Bhupati Anna summoned her and asked her to demand twice her daily wage from the farm owner – ₹350 instead of ₹170. Kamala found the amount excessive and unfair, and refused to follow the diktat. Bhupati Anna then beat her with a bamboo stick as a punishment.

'My father is a small peasant and he too employs labourers for paddy sowing. If you fix such an excessive rate, then he won't be able to afford to pay. Hence, I will take just ₹170,' she tried to reason with her attacker while crying in pain.

The Naxals were infuriated by her disobedience and announced that her family was to be ostracized. They would no longer be invited to any celebrations, nor would anyone participate in functions organized by her family. They were also disallowed from using the village well. Kamala decided to return the favour. She told her family not to attend meetings called by the Naxalites or supply them with food. This was the beginning of her friction with the dalam members.

Just a few days later, Kamala had another confrontation with the Naxals. On 20 January 1986, her younger sister, Radhabai, took their cattle out for grazing. Kamala had gone to the paper mill and her father and brother were at the paddy field. The task usually took two hours but that day, Radhabai didn't return on time. The worried family began to search for her. Kamala's cousin, Nilabai, told her that she had seen Radhabai being taken away by Naxals. They were headed in the direction of the nearby Kolamarka forest.

A distressed Kamala sought help from Jagar Singh, her employer at the paper mill. The kind-hearted Sikh man brought out his Jeep to search for Radhabai. Singh was familiar with the Naxals, as they often extorted money from him. Through his contacts, Singh confirmed that a dalam had set up camp around 25 kilometres away in Kolamarka. It was possible that Radhabai was being held hostage there. He dropped off Kamala and her mother,

Ratnabai, 2 kilometres away from the camp. Singh thought it was not prudent for him to be seen by the Naxalites.

In the camp, a programme of folk songs and dancing was happening around a bonfire. The songs were about the atrocities committed by the state and how the tribals had united to fight back. Kamala recognized one of the campers, a man named Shankar Penta Atram. She approached him and pleaded for the release of her sister with teary eyes. Shankar confirmed that Radhabai was with them but refused to free her. Instead, he threatened to kill Kamala if she didn't leave the camp immediately. She obeyed but resolved to get her sister back at any cost.

The next morning, Kamala met with Baba Atram, a sitting Member of Legislative Assembly (MLA), and sought his help. When Atram suggested that she approach the cops, Kamala wasn't sure if they would help her. Her family was already in their bad books, ever since her grandfather's arrest. Out of options, she took a chance and went to Aheri Police Station. To her surprise, the cops registered her complaint and immediately swung into action. Two Jeeps and over a dozen armed personnel were dispatched. Kamala sat in one of the Jeeps to lead them to the Naxal camp.

When the convoy arrived at its destination, the Naxal cadres were having a meeting. Jagar Singh had also been summoned there to finalize the extortion amount. As soon as the cops exited their vehicles, they fired a few warning shots in the air. Chaos ensued as the Naxals started running helter-skelter. Kamala desperately searched the melee for her sister, shouting out her name. Suddenly, Radhabai appeared before her. The sisters hugged and started crying. Radhabai had been persuaded to join the dalam while in captivity, but she was rescued before the group moved on. The police took her to the government hospital in Chandrapur for a medical examination.

Apart from the rescue of Radhabai, the police raid also led to arrest of wanted Naxals like Pochya Torram, Shankar Atram and Shamrao Arigela, among others. As they were being taken into the custody, the notorious cadres stared at Kamala in an intimidating manner; one of them shouted that she would have to pay for what she had done.

Kamala knew that she had put herself and her family in danger by getting even with Naxals, yet she had refused to bow down. They never spared anyone who challenged their power and Kamala had already done so multiple times. Around a year and a half later, the arrested Naxals secured bail and were released from prison. They decided to avenge their incarceration. On 15 May 1987, half a dozen Naxalites barged into Kamala's house at 2 a.m., disguised as cops. A few began hitting Kamala with the butt of their guns, while others punched and kicked her. Bleeding from the injuries all over her body, Kamala thought that the Naxals were going to kill her. After she fainted due to the unbearable pain, the Naxalites left her for dead.

Apart from the physical trauma, the attack had injured Kamala's soul. It intensified her hatred towards the Naxals and she decided to dedicate her life to bringing them down. Kamala left her village for Aheri and offered her services to the police officers who had aided her sister's rescue. They readily accepted. She started working as an informer for the Gadchiroli Police and helped in the arrest of several cadres. One of the major victories was the arrest of a dalam commander named Bhuyanna Sayam. The police picked him up from his home, where he was recuperating from an illness, after being alerted by Kamala. A large cache of arms was also recovered based on her intel.

Soon, the Naxals realized that they had made a mistake in leaving Kamala alive. It was decided that she should be put to death for the damage she had caused to their cause. Special squads were formed to hunt Kamala down but she managed to outsmart them by moving to a different house in Aheri. There were a few instances when she came close to getting caught. Once, she clandestinely visited her village to see her ailing mother. After spending a night and day there, she left for Aheri. However, somebody had tipped off the Naxals about her trip. A squad comprising Gopanna, Bhupati and a few other cadres apprehended her beside a road in Repanpalli. As the sky darkened at dusk, they prepared to behead her. Luckily, just as one of her assailants lifted the axe to chop her head, a police Jeep was spotted approaching Aheri. The Naxalites panicked, assuming the cops were coming for them, and escaped. Kamala lived to tell the tale.

On another occasion, she was spending a few days

at her aunt's place in a village close to Kamalapur. One night, while the family was sleeping, her aunt's daughter-in-law woke up when the neighbourhood dogs suddenly started barking. She stepped out of the house to check what was happening, only to find that a group of men had surrounded the house. One man introduced himself as a cop and asked if Kamala was inside. Sensing danger, she told them that Kamala had visited their house but left in the evening. The men didn't bother checking inside the house and left, believing her words.

The next day, Kamala was shocked to learn that the men were actually Naxals. The group had been given a list of targets to eliminate, and her name was on it. That same night, they had killed the sarpanch of the neighbouring Rajaram village on suspicion of being a police informer. Before murdering Sarpanch Gangaram Atram, they had entered his home and shared a meal with his family. After, they had asked the other family members to leave the house and closed the door behind them. Two men held Gangaram's legs, two caught his hands and a fifth person beheaded him with a chopper. After they left, Gangaram's family found his body lying in a pool of blood with his head placed on top of his chest.

Krishipal was amazed by Kamala's story but remained sceptical. Though she could be a valuable asset to the police, it would be problematic if she went rogue. It was possible that her entire tale was an elaborate plot by the Naxals to infiltrate their ranks. Krishipal asked Kamala for a few days' time, during which he pondered the risks and advantages of inducting her and discussed the case with his superiors. After a lot of thought, Krishipal decided to take a chance on her. On 1 January 1992, Kamala was recruited as a police constable.

Krishipal attached Kamala with C-60, making her the first woman member of the elite unit. Assigned to question the arrested women, she initially proved to be a very harsh interrogator. However, with time, she developed an interrogation technique that was based on compassion rather than threats. Krishipal mentored her closely during this time. She learnt to treat each case differently and use appropriate tactics on each detainee. Her talent for getting the detainees to confess sensitive information resulted in more arrests and the recovery of arms and ammunition.

Her recruitment encouraged more women to join the police and soon, two dozen tribal women had donned the uniform. Kamala's impressive performance led her to be promoted to commander of a party that comprised of both men and women. As per the naming convention in C-60, this was called 'Kamala's Party'.

She proved to be a very effective leader. In one instance, Kamala received information that several dalams were coming together to celebrate 'Naxal Week' in the forest of Khanda. Maoists celebrate Naxal Week in memory of Charu Mazumdar every year, from 28 July to 3 August. As her party moved towards the Naxal camp, they were faced with a wide nullah (stream) that was overflowing due to heavy rains. While Kamala and her colleagues were thinking of ways to cross the raging nullah, the Naxalites noticed their presence and started firing. Kamala's Party also returned fire. By the time the commandos entered the camp, most of the Naxals had escaped. However, Kamala's Party managed to arrest six of them and recovered a huge number of arms. Through such operations, Kamala was able to arrest most of the Naxals who had harassed her and her family.

Like many other police personnel from the tribal community, Kamala had to make immense sacrifices. She could never return to her village, even when the Naxalites repeatedly beat up her parents and brother to force them to call her back. Her dedication to her mission has left a lasting legacy. Her son also joined the Gadchiroli Police as a constable in June 2006.

13

THE ABDUCTION OF BABA ATRAM

'Raghuvanshi, I want you to find him alive at any cost. And if you can't find him alive, I should see the dead bodies of some Naxals alongside his.'

Receiving such an extraordinary call from Maharashtra CM Sharad Pawar raised Krishipal's heart rate. He was facing what was perhaps his biggest challenge since he had been posted to Gadchiroli: the abduction of Dharamrao Baba Atram, also known as Baba Atram, a sitting MLA from the ruling Congress (I) party. Baba Atram was not just any politician; he hailed from the esteemed Atram family, whose influence and authority encompassed Gadchiroli and its surrounding regions.

Representing the Aheri Vidhan Sabha seat, Baba Atram's legacy extended beyond politics. He was also an educationist and had played a pivotal role in establishing Gadchiroli as an independent district. The news of his abduction had sent shockwaves across the nation, triggering a sense of urgency and concern among the top echelons of the Congress party at the centre. The formidable reputation and widespread influence wielded by Atram underscored the gravity of the situation. Krishipal and his team were under immense pressure to ensure that the MLA was found safely.

It was 1991 and preparations for the parliamentary elections were on in full swing. Former prime minister Rajiv Gandhi was confident of returning to power after a gap of two years. Two prime ministers, V. P. Singh and Chandra Shekhar, had failed to sustain the government and mid-term elections had been announced. Gandhi was spearheading his party's campaign and touring across the country. Maharashtra was very important for any party or coalition that aspired to form a government at the centre. The state sent forty-eight members to the Lok Sabha, the third highest after UP and undivided Bihar.

When Gandhi heard about the abduction, he called CM Pawar – who was a member of Congress – and asked him to ensure Atram's safe return. Gandhi feared that Congress's electoral performance would be adversely affected if Atram was not available for the campaign. Under pressure from the president of his party; Pawar bypassed hierarchy and protocol to speak directly with Krishipal and had been keenly monitoring the rescue efforts.

This episode started on the afternoon of 27 April 1991. The political temperature in the Vidarbha region was as hot as the weather. Atram had gone to Medpalli village to address a campaign meeting for his party's candidate, Shantaram Potdukhe. Atram also had to attend the wedding of a party worker on the same day. With two major events scheduled for the day, there were over 1,000 people crowding the village. Atram and his maternal uncle, Ramachandra Talate, stopped by a school to chat with the villagers. Suddenly, five men wielding automatic firearms emerged from the crowd and demanded Atram and Talate go with them. The villagers protested and surrounded the armed men, refusing to allow Atram to be taken away. The furious crowd was on the verge of lynching the Naxalites when the men pointed their rifles towards the civilians and threatened to fire.

Fearing a bloodbath, Atram pacified the villagers and said that he was ready to go with the armed men. The crowd obeyed and the Naxals took the duo to the outskirts of the village, where another twenty armed men in green uniforms were waiting. Some villagers had followed them but retraced their steps when the Naxals threatened them. By this time, Atram had realized that he was being abducted by PWG.

One of the Naxalites asked Atram and Talate to sit on the ground. 'We have kidnapped you. Now we will send our demands to the government. Until they are met, you will remain with us. Please cooperate.'

Atram was shocked by this turn of events. He had never been targeted by the Naxals, having never acted against them or said anything to provoke them. Considering how popular he was among the tribal population, it was believed that the Naxalites would never harm him. So far, Naxals had never touched anybody from the Atram family to avoid inviting the ire of the Adivasis. Now, they had broken their self-made rule. Though Atram's uncle was let go after a few hours, he remained under lock and key.

Soon after, the kidnappers revealed their demands through a pamphlet. Their primary demand was the release of a Naxal named Shivanna, along with sixteen other prisoners. Additionally, they wanted police camps removed from certain areas of the forest and for a Maoist memorial that was damaged in a police action to be rebuilt. The Naxals gave the government one day to meet their demands. If they failed to do so, the abductors threatened to kill Atram.

A member of the Permili dalam, Shivanna had been arrested three years earlier under the stringent Terrorist and Disruptive Activities (Prevention) Act (TADA). Apart from being involved in the killing of several government officials and policemen, he had managed the finances of his group. Shivanna heavily extorted the bamboo contractors, demanding up to ₹10 per tonne of bamboo. He was known for speaking roughly with the bamboo contractors and their workers. Once, after he misbehaved with some workers, they informed the police of his whereabouts. A trap was laid. When Shivanna came to collect money in Chandrapur, he was taken into custody. The arrest of such an important leader was an enormous blow to the local Naxal movement.

The Naxals in Maharashtra had repeatedly used this tactic of abducting important persons to press their demands. Days earlier, members of PWG had kidnapped a junior government engineer along with another officer. In another incident, PWG cadres held a constable from the neighbouring Bhandara district hostage. They released him after their demands were met. However, this was the first time that a politician of such a stature had been abducted by them.[1]

At the time of Atram's abduction, Krishipal was in Nagpur to meet with his superiors. After receiving a wireless message about the incident, he rushed back to Gadchiroli. Krishipal was surprised that the Naxals had abducted Atram. According to the grapevine, the MLA had won his last election with their support.

The Naxals had a paradoxical relationship to the election process. They opposed elections, engaging in violence during the voting and counting days. In their eyes, the elections were nothing more than a pseudo-democratic way to strengthen class enemies. On the other hand, they were willing to accept money from candidates who wanted their approval. In fact, candidates could only campaign in Gadchiroli if they paid up. Krishipal assumed that Atram might have failed to keep some of the promises he had made to the Naxalites, leading to his abduction. However, Atram had consistently denied that he got any support from the Naxals, maintaining that this was a false narrative spread by his detractors.

Krishipal summoned the C-60 commandos to his office

as soon as he reached Gadchiroli. Some of them were sceptical about the abduction.

'Sir, I can't believe that Naxals would ever kidnap Baba Atram. The whole incident seems scripted. Do you think this could be a case of friendly kidnapping?' a commando asked. So-called 'friendly kidnappings' are cases where the abductors and abductee are hand in glove, working together for some ulterior motive.

'You may be right. The primary information we've received may seem suspicious but we can't sit on it, assuming it's a fake case,' Krishipal replied curtly. 'On paper, an MLA has been taken away by Naxals at gunpoint and we don't know his whereabouts. It's our responsibility to search for him. His life might genuinely be in danger. If something happens to him, our reputation will be tarnished.'

With that settled, the team began pondering the best course of action. One commander said, 'Sir, we still have two or three hours of daylight left. Allow us to use the sniffer dog. We'll take a sample of Atram's clothes and instruct the dog to follow his trail from the place where he was abducted in Medpalli.'

Krishipal liked the idea. Since the Naxalites didn't use motorized vehicles – preferring to walk on foot – they could not have gone far. A sniffer dog would be able to trace them swiftly. But what if the commandos and Naxals came face to face? If there was an exchange of bullets, Atram would be caught in the crossfire. This operation needed to be planned thoroughly – any impulsive action could jeopardize Atram's life.

He sought advice from his superiors on whether to use the dog. DIG P. K. B. Chakraborty seemed equally confused and advised him to seek permission from DGP Saraf. Krishipal rang Saraf's residence in Bombay, only to be told that he had gone to Bangalore to participate in a conference and was inaccessible.

It wasn't until the next day, after receiving news of the abduction, that Saraf called Krishipal. Sending the dog squad after such a delay was useless, he said; Krishipal should have taken a call about it on the day of the abduction itself. Time was running out. It was Sunday, the deadline for the ransom, and they had no leads. Ultimately, going against Saraf's advice, Krishipal decided to deploy a sniffer dog to trace Atram. A black Doberman, part of the dog squad of the Maharashtra Police, was called to action.

Atram's kurta and pants were brought from his home and offered to the police dog to sniff. The handler then took the dog to the school and the outskirts of Medpalli village, where Atram was last seen. As the handler shouted his command – 'Smell follow!' – the dog ran towards the jungle. An armed party of C-60 commandos trailed behind, with their rifles loaded and ready to shoot. They waited with bated breath for the dog to signal Atram's presence with a bark.

The dog kept moving for several kilometres once they were inside the forest. The already arduous journey was made worse by a bout of unseasonal rainfall that left the ground slippery. The C-60 commandos were unaffected due to their stringent training, but the dog handlers were tired after hours of walking. Ultimately, the dog stopped at the bank of the Bande river. Crossing the river and chasing the smell – already diluted by the rain – was beyond the dog's skill. Perhaps the Naxals had anticipated that sniffer dogs would be used and crossed the river to throw them off the scent. Everybody was disappointed. However, Krishipal noted a positive outcome: he now had an idea of the direction the abductors had gone in. The trail indicated that they had taken Atram north of Medpalli, towards Allapalli, a quiet village in Aheri.

By this time, some of Krishipal's superiors had landed in Allapalli to discuss further course of action. They decided to mobilize all available police personnel to locate Atram. Apart from the C-60 team, Krishipal had seven companies of the SRP at his disposal. He was allotted additional men and a company of the Border Security Force (BSF). A total of twenty-four companies from various law enforcement agencies were deployed under him. Since it was likely that Atram was near Allapalli, the base camp for the operation was set up at the forest department's guest house there. The DGP asked two of Krishipal's superiors, the IG and DIG, to be present at the camp.

Usually, a topographic map was consulted ahead of such operations, providing a bird's-eye view of the region. But no topo-sheet was available at such short notice, so Krishipal had to rely completely on human intelligence to plan the rescue. Some officers were made to fetch intel while others conducted searches inside the jungle. Krishipal's team received conflicting information regarding

Atram's location. One informer claimed to have seen Atram with the abductors towards the north of Allapalli, while another maintained they were in the south. Krishipal realized that the operation might stretch for many days and divided his men into day and night shifts. Although the Naxals had only given the government a day's time to accept their demands, the police were making operational decisions independent of the negotiations. It was two days before they could even procure topo-sheets from the Nagpur office of the Geological Survey of India.

While the police relentlessly searched the forests, Atram and his abductors moved only after dusk. They hid out during the day, taking turns keeping a watch out for police movement. The Naxals had their own intelligence network that alerted them when search parties were nearby. There were a few occasions when the police came close enough for Atram to see them, but he couldn't ask for help since his mouth was stuffed with a piece of cloth whenever a police team was around. However, the kidnappers didn't torture Atram and behaved politely with him, offering him the same food they ate. The only discomfort was the sheer amount of walking. The Naxals constantly changed locations and crossed 30–40 kilometres of forest every day. Once they reached the border of Madhya Pradesh, they changed course again to some other location.

Although the Naxals didn't threaten or misbehave with him, Atram feared that he would be killed if their demands were not met. The dalam commander was kept abreast of the developments through the informers who came to their hideouts. He muttered expletives when they told him that the government was taking time to consider their demands. On such occasions, Atram was petrified as he observed the enraged face of the commander. He also feared that he would be killed in the crossfire between Naxals and the cops.

With the Sunday deadline long passed, the government had still not taken a call on the demands. In return, there was no news from the Naxals about the fate of Atram. When the search parties came up empty, the police broadcasted an appeal to the Naxals asking for some more time. Daily newspapers criticized the government's inaction and the Opposition parties capitalized on this friction. Former MP and Janata Dal leader Vishweshwar Rao demanded the resignation of CM Pawar, stating that 'Congress has no business to make claims of providing a stable government when it has not been able to provide security to its own MLA.' BJP leader Sudhir Mungantiwar publicly claimed, 'Atram's kidnapping is the result of the paralysis of state administrative machinery.'[2]

On 2 May, a Nagpur Bandh was called by various organizations to protest Atram's abduction. Markets, schools, colleges, eateries and bus services were shut for the day. Prakash Javadekar, a BJP politician, demanded that security personnel from the central government be deployed during the elections, as one couldn't rely on the Maharashtra Police for security. He feared that people wouldn't come out to vote because of the Naxal threat.[3]

The situation was growing more precarious. The chief

minister called Krishipal twice every day for an update on the progress of the search operation. Pawar was scheduled to visit Aheri to address a public meeting. Ahead of his visit, he called Krishipal and asked solemnly, 'Tell me without any hesitation, is it possible to rescue Atram within forty-eight hours? If yes, I will announce it to the gathering.'

Krishipal knew he couldn't make such promises. 'Sir, we are trying our best, but I can't give you any assurance on how long the rescue will take.'

It was then that Pawar told him that if Atram was not found alive, the dead bodies of a few Naxals must be recovered with his.

On 3 May, a week after the abduction, there was shocking news. The government had announced its willingness to talk to the captors. Krishipal felt dejected, wondering whether the CM had lost faith in his efforts. In reality, Pawar adopted a two-pronged strategy. The government would appoint a negotiator who could talk to the abductors. Meanwhile, the search operation would be intensified. His government even approved an aerial search of the forest. DGP Saraf landed at Gadchiroli to personally supervise the operation.

One afternoon, while sleeping at a Naxal hideout, Atram was awakened by the loud sound of a helicopter. He looked up but couldn't see through the dense foliage.

The Naxals panicked, assuming that the police had located them and were dropping combatants to the ground. One of the Naxals pointed his rifle at Atram while others aimed for the sky. The aircraft was carrying an additional superintendent along with a few commandos. Though they were equipped with hi-tech binoculars to scan the forest, they were flying hazardously low and could only see the green cover. The forest was so dense that even sunlight couldn't penetrate. A few minutes later, the chopper's sounds faded away, much to the Naxals' relief. However, Atram was disappointed – those sounds had evoked a hope of freedom in him, only to be snatched away.

As the police were planning more aerial sorties, news from Andhra Pradesh rattled everyone. On the morning of 7 May, a fifty-four-year-old MLA of Anantpur named S. Channa Reddy was reading a newspaper at his home while sipping a cup of tea when three men in police uniforms barged in. They saluted Reddy and before he could speak, shot him over sixty times. The investigation revealed that the assailants were Naxalites who had disguised themselves as cops.[4] The assassination of Reddy was worrying. Like Reddy, Atram was a legislator. By killing Reddy, the Naxalites had proved that they were not averse to murdering politicians and their threats were not hollow. Congress leaders feared that Atram would meet the same fate. While the Andhra Pradesh Police launched a manhunt to find Reddy's assassins, pressure also intensified on their Maharashtrian counterparts to locate Atram soon.

More bad news from Andhra soon followed. On 12 May, Rajiv Gandhi was scheduled to address a public meeting at Nizam College, Hyderabad. A few hours before Gandhi landed, MLA P. Sudhir Kumar – son of former union minister P. Shiv Shankar – was abducted from his home in the city by Naxals. During the confrontation, they shot his aide, a former cop named Narayanswami. Shortly after, a PWG spokesman telephoned the office of the United News of India and claimed responsibility. He demanded that four of the top Naxal cadres arrested by the Andhra Pradesh Police be released and threatened to kill Sudhir Kumar if this wasn't done within twenty-four hours. The Andhra Pradesh government immediately reverted that it was willing to negotiate.

It had become a regular strategy of the Naxalites in Andhra to abduct senior government officials or politicians. The Greyhounds were regularly undercutting their movement by killing and arresting some of their top men. In response, the Naxals resorted to abductions to get their arrested colleagues out of prison. It appeared that their comrades in Maharashtra were adopting the same tactics, feeling the heat of the aggressive pursuits of C-60.

One day, an informer came panting to the Allapalli guest house and told Krishipal that the Naxals had been spotted on a hillock around 10 kilometres away. Krishipal immediately picked up a carbine and headed into the jungle along with fifteen commandos. After a four-hour trek, the team reached a riverbank. Since the commandos had been trained by the Greyhounds to cross rivers, the task was accomplished swiftly. The next challenge was to stealthily reach the hillock and surround the Naxalites. They were on higher ground – in warfare parlance, a 'dominant height'. It would be easy for them to spot the movement of the commandos and shoot.

Krishipal continued to strategize how to rescue Atram safely, since it was imminent that the Naxals would fire at them. After another two hours, Krishipal and his team reached the plateau of the hillock. They hadn't encountered any resistance while climbing – Krishipal believed that success was close at hand. This hope fuelled the team's enthusiasm and they didn't feel tired despite the physical strain.

On reaching the hilltop, Krishipal instructed the commandos to move forward in a semicircle, maintaining some distance from one another. But he was taken aback when, after scouring the area, no Naxals were found. There weren't even any traces of human presence, like footprints or leftover food, on the desolate hillock. Krishipal concluded that the tip had been a red herring, or the Naxalites had caught a whiff of their presence and escaped, ensuring that no evidence was left behind.

Krishipal ordered his team to return to Allapalli, aiming to reach before sunset. Everyone was dejected and demoralized. In such a mental state, tiredness got the better of them. After climbing down the hillock,

Krishipal decided to rest for ten minutes. He sat down on the ground and rested his back on the trunk of a tree. However, just as his back touched the trunk, the carbine hanging from his right shoulder fell off and ...

BOOM!

The sound of a gunshot led to a panic among the relaxing commandos; they rushed to find cover, fearing an ambush by Naxals. One SI was shivering due to shock – he thought that a bullet had hit him. Fortunately, the bullet had only brushed his hair. The man had felt a sudden flash of heat over his right ear and assumed that the bullet had hit his head. Even so, it had missed by a millimetre.

Krishipal was equally terrified. The accidental gunshot from his carbine could have killed one of his colleagues. Had the man died due to a bullet injury, the consequences would have been serious. Krishipal could have been suspended for negligence or even arrested on the charge of culpable homicide. As the shaken group walked back to their camp, Krishipal pondered the strange nature of luck; the creative ways in which it could delight or screw you up. Krishipal profusely apologized to the inspector and both of them thanked God that they had avoided a worse fate.

Sharad Pawar didn't want to prolong the situation any long. The police hadn't made a breakthrough and the pressure from both his party and the Opposition was mounting.

Taking a cue from his Andhra Pradesh counterpart, Pawar concluded that they had no choice but to accept the Naxals' demands.

For the negotiator, he chose Eknath Salve, who was a social activist, politician, lawyer and novelist from Chandrapur. The septuagenarian was a former Congressman and had served as the MLA of Chandrapur from 1967–8. Salve commanded huge respect among Adivasis due to his social work in the backward areas of Vidarbha. As a lawyer, Salve had fought cases of youths who were booked under the stringent TADA law without taking any fees. His novel *Encounter* was based on Naxalism and considered a masterpiece in Marathi literature. The CM contacted Salve and requested his help in securing the release of Atram. Salve readily agreed to intervene but told Pawar that he couldn't guarantee that his intervention would fetch the desired result.

Unaware of their political master's move, Krishipal and his men continued their pursuit of Atram. The two suites in the Allapalli guest house were occupied by Krishipal's seniors, DIG Chakraborty and IG A. V. Krishnan. Hence, he had no choice but to stay in the storeroom of the guest house, which also functioned as a temporary control room. His men were accommodated in the houses of the forest guards.

While leaving Gadchiroli, he had brought along only a few extra clothes, not expecting that he would be away for around two weeks. They got soaked in sweat and dust during the long walks in the forest and it was unbearable to repeat them. Sarita had briefly returned to Gadchiroli with the children, so he wrote to her asking for more clothes. Every one or two days, police parties would travel from Aheri to Gadchiroli for official work. Since their home telephone was often out of order, Krishipal dispatched letters to Sarita through them. Theirs was a traditional arranged marriage and Krishipal had never written love letters to his wife. Under these adverse circumstances, however, his words were full of love; he wrote how much he missed his family and reassured her that he was safe.

Sarita too sent replies with the returning parties. In one letter, Sarita mentioned that she had received a threatening call on a day when the telephone was functional for some time. The anonymous caller had snarled, 'Tell your husband not to act smart. We will release the MLA, but he should be careful.' Some unknown people had also pelted stones at the bungalow in the night. This made Krishipal worried about his family's safety – he knew the Naxals could use this tactic to intimidate him.

One day, a reliable informer tipped the police off that the Naxalites were camping with Atram at a place which was just a two-hour walk from the base camp. The informer also provided details about Atram's captors. Initially, it was believed that the abduction was the handiwork of Santosh Anna of the Chamorshi dalam but a different name emerged now: Devji. He was the commander of two dalams, Aheri and Permili, at the time. There were around twenty-five cadres with him, playing hide-and-seek with the cops.

Thrilled, Krishipal ordered his commandos to get ready. He told his men to aim for getting Atram alive but if the MLA was killed, the Naxals must not be spared from the wrath of C-60. As the charged men were about to move towards the given location, Krishipal got a call from DGP Saraf.

'Raghuvanshi, immediately stop all operations to trace the MLA. Tell your men to relax.' Saraf sounded furious.

'What? Why, sir?'

'The government has decided to release Shivanna.'

'But sir, we have traced …' Saraf disconnected the phone before Krishipal could finish his sentence.

Krishipal clenched his fist in frustration. For around two weeks, he and his team had wandered the jungle searching for Atram and now, when rescue was possible, Krishipal had been asked to call off the operation. Although he was disappointed that their efforts had been wasted, what pinched Krishipal more was the decision to release Shivanna.

Seeing the changed expression on Krishipal's face, Tarachand asked, 'Is everything all right, sir?'

He remained silent for a few moments and then said in a sombre voice, 'We will return to Gadchiroli tomorrow. The operation has been called off. Shivanna is being released to get Atram back alive. The decision has been taken by the government.'

'Sir, this is wrong. Shivanna has killed many of our men and it took a lot of effort to arrest him. It was a blow to the Naxals when we caught him. It will be dangerous to free him. He will target us again. The time spent in prison doesn't deter these bastards.' Tarachand was enraged.

'I understand all this, but there's nothing we can do. I can't question the DGP and CM. We just have to follow their orders,' Krishipal tried to reason.

'I have understood one thing, sir. The life of a policeman is of no value. Only politicians' lives are valuable in this country. "Jai Jawan, Jai Kisaan" is just a slogan to be shouted on 26 January and 15 August.'

Since evening had set in, Krishipal decided to leave for Gadchiroli the next morning. In pursuit of Atram, the cops had been inspecting every vehicle that passed along the road where the Naxalites were suspected to be hiding. A superior sent Krishipal a message, instructing him not to check or follow any Jeep that was heading towards Bhamragarh. Krishipal understood the reason behind this instruction.

Eknath Salve got in touch with his Naxal contacts and met Devji in the forest. Salve conveyed the government's willingness to release Shivanna in exchange of Baba Atram. Devji agreed but said that Atram would only be returned when Shivanna reached them after being released from jail. At Salve's instruction, the public prosecutor filed a plea in a TADA Special Court and all the cases against Shivanna in Chandrapur and Gadchiroli were withdrawn expeditiously. However, the jail authorities refused to release him. In their records, Shivanna was also incarcerated for a case registered in the Wardha district. The prisoner couldn't be released until he made bail for all cases against him, or they were withdrawn. A team of government lawyers immediately worked to withdraw the Wardha case, clearing the way for Shivanna's release.

On 13 May, Shivanna was discharged from the District Jail in Chandrapur. A team of mediators from a human rights organization waited for him at the gate. Shivanna emerged and hurriedly boarded their vehicle, which then headed towards the forest area of Allapalli. After ascertaining the release of Shivanna, the Naxals blindfolded Atram and dropped him off on the Bhamragarh–Chandrapur road, where he was picked up by Eknath Salve in a police Jeep. Atram was taken to a government guest house where he met Sharad Pawar. The abduction crisis, which had stretched for seventeen days, came to an end.

An exhausted Krishipal was finally able to rest for the first time in two weeks. DIG Chakraborty and IG Krishnan had left, so he could sleep comfortably in one of the suites vacated by them. He relaxed by sipping two pegs of whiskey and then dozed off. At 4:30 a.m., somebody knocked on his door. It was Krishipal's orderly, informing him that Atram had reached his home.

With the release of Shivanna from jail and Atram from captivity, everybody was happy. The CM, Rajiv Gandhi, the Congress party – even the Naxalites. The only wretched ones were Krishipal and his commandos. He believed that releasing Shivanna had set the wrong precedent. The

Naxals would adopt similar tactics in the future to free their people from jail.

Krishipal wanted to speak to Atram and glean some insights about his time with Naxals. However, Atram didn't cooperate and Krishipal's superiors asked him not to disturb the MLA for a few days. A month later, the CM inducted Atram into his Council of Ministers. He was given charge of the tribal and forest development department. The entire episode proved to be demoralizing for Krishipal and the C-60.

14

THE ENEMY INSIDE AND OUTSIDE

'Jai Hind, sir. I have fantastic news. Six more Naxals have surrendered before the C-60 with their weapons. They have been involved in several cases; I am going to interrogate them now.'

Krishipal was full of excitement as he briefed Saraf over the telephone. Every week, the list of C-60's accomplishments was growing. Saraf, initially sceptical about the force, had a growing sense of admiration for Krishipal and his commandos. After his conversation with Saraf ended, he stood up to head for the interrogation room. Suddenly, Arnab Chandel (name changed) barged in. A senior administrative official in Gadchiroli, Chandel was fuming with anger. Krishipal returned to his chair and asked his unexpected visitor to sit.

'Raghuvanshi, I am not going to tolerate this. You need to arrest that man immediately and subject him to such severe torture that he never dares to do this again.'

Krishipal offered him a glass of water. 'What happened, Arnab? Let me understand the whole matter.'

'Call the police guard deployed at my bungalow right away and arrest him.'

'Why, what happened? Is he not punctual?'

The matter was much more serious. Chandel complained that the guard had misbehaved with his female relative and made some lewd comments. Krishipal pacified him and assured him that strict action would be taken.

Once Chandel left, Krishipal summoned the guard to his office. The man, who was in his early twenties, was a police constable from a local tribal village. Krishipal confronted him with the complaint. Punitive action would have to be taken, he warned, but he was willing to hear the constable's side of the story. Such distasteful behaviour by a constable was preposterous. On hearing Krishipal's stern words, the guard started weeping.

'Sir, there is no fault of mine. It is the other way round. The complainant is the one who has made objectionable gestures.'

After grilling him thoroughly, Krishipal realized that the guard was most likely not at fault. After spending years in the IPS and listening to thousands of people plead their case during interrogations, Krishipal had a knack of knowing when someone was lying. His hunch was that the guard was not guilty, and it went against his conscience to punish an innocent man. However, he suspended the guard until an inquiry was completed.

Chandel was not happy with Krishipal's decision and he did not hesitate to let him know. Krishipal stood his ground – he could not take Chandel's words as undeniable proof just because he was a high-ranking official. The altercation left Krishipal upset and in no mood to work, but questioning the surrendered Naxals was a top priority. He lit a cigarette and headed towards the interrogation room.

Krishipal had established a Naxal Cell under the Gadchiroli Police that maintained the records of Naxalites who had voluntarily surrendered. Details about their village, family, education and the criminal cases they had been charged with were stored in a database managed by the cell. It also monitored the activities of the surrendered Naxalites, helped them secure employment and access various government relief programmes. The surrendered individuals, in turn, offered valuable information about Naxal activities and helped conduct anti-Maoist operations. Some were inducted into the force as informants and got regular payments from the police fund.

When Krishipal entered the dimly lit room, the surrendered men were squatting on the floor, all in one row. They looked no different from any other Adivasis of the region – except for the fact that each one had several cases of murder, abduction and attempt to murder registered against them. At the time of surrender, they were also in possession of deadly firearms. Fear and worry showed clearly on their faces. Krishipal asked if they had been provided with water and something to eat. After they said yes, he started interrogating them one by one.

Krishipal used a soft hand with Naxalites who voluntarily surrendered. He tried to make them comfortable and spoke empathetically. He assured them that they would be protected by the police, since they feared being targeted by the dalams they had betrayed. This method worked well; the former Naxals often spilled more information than expected.

On that day, the interrogation session continued for over four hours. Krishipal finished several cups of coffee and smoked more than his daily quota of cigarettes. Nearly every man he spoke to had a similar story. They were school dropouts who had been picked up by the dalams at fourteen or fifteen years of age. In some cases, the Naxals had identified the recruits during cultural programmes organized by sangams. The Naxalites then indoctrinated them using recorded speeches of senior Maoist ideologues. They were told that the government was snatching away *jal* (water), jungle and *zameen* (land) from their rightful owners. The teenagers were made to believe that the state could be crushed with the power of a gun.

After being inducted into various dalams, the teenagers were first assigned non-combatant responsibilities like cooking, cleaning the camps, collecting firewood and sticking posters with slogans in villages. After a few weeks, they were trained to shoot. Using air guns, they practised shooting both moving and stationary targets. At the next level, recruits were taught to handle various firearms and camouflage the camp using leaves and branches. During the last stage, they were made to walk in the jungle and execute an ambush. Recruits from Maharashtra were also taken to the camps of Madhya Pradesh and Orissa as part of their training.

One of the boys being interrogated was Sunil (name changed), who was the only child of his parents. They had supported the Naxals by providing food and shelter but never thought that their son would join them. When the infamous dalam commander Santosh Anna came to pick up Sunil, his father pleaded for him to be spared with tearful eyes. However, Santosh told him to let the boy decide whether he wanted to go along with them.

Santosh then called the family outside the house, where a crowd of villagers had gathered on hearing the commotion. With the butt of his gun, he drew a line in the soil, similar to the one that is drawn during kabaddi matches. He asked Sunil to stand at one end of the line and said, '*Beta, tu faisla kar. Baap ke saath rahega ya hamare saath. Tu jo bhi faisla karega wo hamko manjoor hai. Hum kisi ko kucch nahi karenge.*' (Son, you decide whether you want to stay with your father or with us. We will accept your decision and not harm anybody.)

Sunil looked at his weeping father for a moment and then towards the ground. Everyone he knew was scared of the police, but he was aware that the police feared the Naxals. Believing that joining the dalam would empower him, Sunil defied his father and chose to become a Naxal. As he stepped towards the Naxals, all the dalam members clapped and Santosh hugged him. His enraged father turned away, pulled his mother inside the house and shut the door.

The Naxals took him to their camp and after completing his training, Sunil began participating in ambushes – some of which led to cops being killed. However, he soon became disillusioned with the movement and realized that life as a Naxal was very different from what he had imagined. The Naxals talked about equality and a classless society but didn't practice what they preached. Discrimination was rampant in the dalams. The top commanders ate better food than the recruits; they drank tea with milk, while the recruits were given black tea. The recruits were allowed to marry, but a vasectomy was compulsory before the wedding.

Sunil had also become terrified of getting killed in an encounter – the continuous anti-Naxal campaign of the C-60 had demoralized the cadres. As he told Krishipal, '*Apne mool maksad se bhatak gaye Naksali.*' (The Naxals have deviated from their core objective.) The other surrendered Naxals had similar stories and chose to give themselves up after being let down by the movement. They did not wish to die for a cause they no longer believed in. One of them said that he decided to quit as the Naxalites weren't allowing any kind of development in his area.

After the interrogation, Krishipal felt nothing but pity for the boys. He saw them as victims, not criminals. They had believed the misinformation spread by the Naxals, who capitalized on the maladministration and atrocities perpetrated by police and forest department officials. Krishipal sympathized with them and was left pondering how he could help them lead a normal life.

The next evening, Krishipal had to leave for his village to attend a family wedding. Before his departure he called a meeting to address officers who were ranked inspectors or higher.

'We must think of a long-term solution to the Naxal problem. Killing or arresting some cadres here and there is like giving paracetamol to a cancer patient. We need to go beyond such palliative measures. The Adivasis need to be encouraged to participate in the political process. They should speak up about the cruelty of the Naxalites. It is our responsibility to create an environment where they can do so without inhibition. Even if they are criticizing the government or police, let them speak. *Baccha jab tak royega nahi, maa ko pata kaise chalega ki wo bhukha hai?* (How will a mother know that her child is hungry until he cries?) These Adivasis are our own people. If they are speaking against us, we should not suppress their voices. We must redress their grievances.'

After the meeting, Krishipal headed to Nagpur to catch a train to Delhi. His speech had evoked mixed reactions among the police officials and a few of them gathered to confer over tea at a stall near the SP office. Some liked the idea, whereas others wondered how Krishipal could allow the tribals to speak against the government.

'The Naxals are already doing the needful,' one inspector commented satirically. A clerk working in Arnab Chandel's office overheard the conversation and joined the group to elicit more information about the meeting. As Chandel's sycophant, the clerk knew his boss nurtured a grudge against Krishipal, though he was not aware why. He immediately rushed to Chandel's office afterwards and narrated whatever the inspector had told him. Chandel hatched a plan to get back at Krishipal.

He hid a small tape recorder amidst the files on his desk and summoned the inspector to his office. When the inspector entered the room, Chandel offered him tea and asked him what Krishipal had told the officers during the meeting. The inspector was confused why an administrative officer was interested in the internal meetings of the police department but did not dare to question such a high-ranking person. He narrated Krishipal's words verbatim. The inspector left the office at Chandel's request with the sinking feeling that he had been dragged into a conspiracy.

As soon as the inspector left his cabin, Chandel checked the recording on the tape. The policeman's voice was clearly audible. He immediately rushed to Bombay and met with the chief secretary of Maharashtra to complain that Krishipal was planning to encourage disaffection towards the government by inciting the tribals to speak against it. Chandel insisted that Krishipal's action amounted to sedition and urged that strict action be taken.

This complaint rattled the chief secretary and he thought it pertinent to apprise the CM immediately.

Sudhakarrao Naik had replaced Sharad Pawar just a few months earlier. Naik was trying to build a clean image of the government and was known as a hot-headed politician. During the tenure of his predecessor, many people with criminal histories like Hitendra Thakur and Pappu Kalani had been given electoral tickets by the Congress.[1] The Opposition parties alleged that Congress was facilitating the entry of criminals into politics and helping them become legislators. Although these individuals had become his party colleagues, Naik dealt with Thakur and Kalani harshly and got them arrested under the stringent TADA. He was trying to send a message that anybody who maligned his party or the government wouldn't be spared.

Naik was enraged when he heard Chandel's complaint. He contemplated suspending Krishipal and summoned the additional chief secretary of the home department and the DGP to his office. They convinced Naik that Krishipal was an upright officer with a clean track record – it was unbelievable that he would do such a thing. However, Naik argued that a complaint from a high-ranking officer like Chandel couldn't be ignored, especially on such serious charges. Hence, he ordered an inquiry. A two-member committee was set up with the divisional commissioner of Nagpur and the commissioner of the SID as its members.

Krishipal's world was overturned when he heard about the allegations. He quickly realized that this was Chandel's handiwork, though he had never considered that the man could go to such sinister lengths. If the committee indicted him, Krishipal could be dismissed from the IPS under Article 311 of the Indian Constitution. As per the article, he would not even get a chance to defend himself if the government was satisfied that providing such an opportunity would go against the interest of state security.[2] There was also the fear of him being booked for sedition. However, Krishipal decided he wouldn't back down. He was innocent and had proof on his side. No matter how hard Chandel tried, he could not change the truth.

The investigators were diligent and spoke to the inspector whose voice was clandestinely recorded, as well as other officers who had attended Krishipal's meeting. It soon became clear to them that the allegations were hollow. Krishipal's intention was to make Adivasi voices heard and have them participate in local governance. His words had been deliberately misinterpreted. The investigators also found that the inspector's voice had been doctored to create a false narrative.[3] The committee exonerated Krishipal.

Ultimately, Arnab Chandel was transferred. Krishipal was relieved after being absolved but also learnt a valuable lesson from this experience. In Gadchiroli, the Naxals weren't the only enemy – his colleagues could be his foes too.

With the inquiry being closed, Krishipal's troubles were far from over. Santosh Anna was under pressure from top Naxal leadership to hit back at the police, who had done enormous damage to their movement since the C-60 was formed. He soon got his chance when an informer told him that an SRP platoon was moving towards Bhamragarh to relieve the personnel deployed there. Santosh immediately called a cadre meeting to plan an ambush.

On the following Sunday, Krishipal was teaching his kids to swim in the bungalow's much-loved mini pool. The idyllic morning was interrupted when he received a message on his wireless set. Naxalites had killed thirteen SRP personnel in an ambush at Hemalkasa, 175 kilometres from the town of Gadchiroli. They had blasted the vehicle carrying those men by triggering a landmine near a nullah. The Naxals had also looted their rifles, light machine guns, mortars and ammunition. The men in the SRP platoon had worked in the Gadchiroli district earlier and were aware of the hostile conditions there. However, no one is ever truly prepared for an ambush.

Krishipal immediately left home. He and his team would have to pick up the dead bodies and provide medical aid to the survivors. The scene of the crime was scattered with the mangled remains of the SRP men. Some of the injured men hugged Krishipal and cried. He had brought along ambulances that carried the victims to the nearest hospital. Meanwhile, he ordered that the bodies of the killed cops be sent to their native villages.

As the site was still being cleared, DGP Saraf summoned

Krishipal for an urgent meeting at the forest department's guest house in Aheri. The atmosphere in the meeting was tense. Krishipal and his fellow senior police officers sat before Saraf, who was fuming with anger. To defuse the situation, Krishipal asked a peon to serve a glass of water to the DGP.

'I don't want to drink your water. Tell me, what is the role of an SP?' a livid Saraf demanded.

'To look after the police administration of the district, sir.'

'Then why has this happened? Who is responsible for these deaths? Why was the platoon going directly to the site?'

Much before the ambush, Krishipal had created a system to prevent such ambushes. Any platoon coming to relieve an on-duty team would first be stationed at the Gadchiroli Police headquarters. They would leave for their destination only after two to three days of thorough briefing and conditioning. This ensured that the force was accustomed to the topography of the area and aware of the ground realities and threats. However, the SRP had a separate command and didn't adhere to this system. When a platoon was already stationed at a particular location, keeping another platoon at the police headquarters was seen as a waste of human resources. In line with this, the ambushed platoon had defied Krishipal's guidelines and headed directly to the location.

Faced with Saraf's temper, Krishipal feared that Saraf would recommend his suspension to the government.

However, gathering courage, he said, 'I take responsibility for this incident. I am guilty of these thirteen deaths. But I also want to submit that, when I was transferred to Gadchiroli, I was told that I would be getting SRP companies which were trained in jungle warfare. I am sorry to say that the unfortunate SRP platoon didn't follow the required steps after entering Gadchiroli.'

Krishipal then explained the findings of the initial investigation. 'The platoon had kept all its rifles chained up, while its other weapons were inside a locked box. When the Naxalites attacked, the police could not fire a single bullet. After blasting the vehicle, the Naxals broke the lock with a gunshot and looted the weapons. Why didn't the SRP personnel keep the weapons in a ready-to-shoot position while entering Gadchiroli, as is standard protocol?'

After listening to Krishipal, Saraf realized that the situation was not his fault. The SRP leadership had been negligent in this case. The very next day, he sent for all the senior officers of the SRP in Nagpur and admonished them. Krishipal's strategy – that any platoon going to Gadchiroli would first stay at the police headquarters for a few days to be properly briefed – was formalized into a rule.

15

LOSING A COMRADE

The wheel of time spins a tapestry of unique experiences in every man's life, blending moments of joy with those of anguish. While Krishipal found solace in the success of his brainchild, the C-60 force, the events of the last few months had cast a shadow over his spirits. The abduction of Baba Atram, the release of the notorious Shivanna, the inquiry against him, the unsettling Bhamragarh ambush – all of it weighed heavily on Krishipal's mind.

He often found himself lost in contemplation in those days. One morning, he was interrupted by Tarachand and another constable. Tarachand had a smile on his face, as was his habit. Even during tense situations, he cracked jokes that made everybody laugh. Since he had grown close to Krishipal, Tarachand didn't hesitate to speak his mind.

'Sir, you look sad. Don't show the C-60 commandos such a sad face, otherwise half of them will go back home.

Your words and the shine on your face are what charges them up.'

'I will suspend you, rascal. You speak too much,' Krishipal responded, cracking a smile.

'I will be happy to get suspended for the sake of a smile on your face. Anyway, getting suspended just means I will receive half of my salary for doing nothing.'

'Okay, tell me. Why have you come?'

'Sir, his son is getting married on Friday,' Tarachand pointed at the constable who had accompanied him. 'He wants to invite you but was hesitant to approach you. So, I brought him along.' The constable belonged to the local Madiya tribe and hailed from Aheri. After joining the police force, he had shifted to a village in north Gadchiroli where the Naxal influence was relatively less.

'Congratulations! I will definitely come.' Krishipal saw this as an opportunity to acquaint himself with local customs and traditions. Since he had taken the charge in Gadchiroli, he had not done anything social.

Once he had accepted the invitation, doubt started to creep in. Would it be safe for him and Sarita to visit a Naxal-infested area in the late evening? Would the villagers be harmed for inviting a senior police officer to the wedding? Krishipal discussed his concerns with the Police Patil of the village, who advised him to attend the wedding without any inhibitions. 'For how long will we keep fearing these Naxalites?' he questioned.

On Friday, Krishipal and Sarita reached the wedding venue, which was in an open area outside a ghotul. A group of boys and girls were dancing in a circle to the beating of drums. Their forward–backward movements were similar to Garba. The performers had drawn artistic tattoos on their faces and limbs and stuck peacock feathers on the back of their heads.

'Sir, often during such dances, boys and girls choose their partner for marriage. One wedding thus leads to many more,' Tarachand whispered in Krishipal's ears.

An artistic wooden pillar installed outside the ghotul caught Krishipal's attention, and he asked Tarachand about it.

'Sir, this is called a *mundha*. As per tradition, the bridegroom has to carve out this decorative object after his engagement. It is then displayed outside the ghotul during the marriage rituals,' Tarachand explained. 'We Indians often think that Western countries are more modern than us. But in some ways the tribes here are more or less like them.'

'What makes you say that?'

'Sir, most Indians see a live-in relationship as a Western concept. A man and woman living together without marrying is forbidden, but here it is a part of the culture. Unmarried boys and girls meet and mingle with each other in ghotuls. In some tribes, couples stay together for many days, even years, and only get married once the woman becomes pregnant. In other cases, couples may marry after a child is born or a man may have more than one wife.'

Noticing Krishipal's keen interest, Tarachand continued. 'During old times, if a Madiya man wanted to get married, he had to participate in a dangerous tradition. When a man proposed to a girl, she would ask him to kill a bison to prove his strength. The villagers, singing and dancing to drumbeats, would take him to the forest and leave him at a spot where a herd of bison had been spotted.

'The man was only allowed to carry a spear to fight and kill the animal. Very often these men would get injured after being struck by a bison's horns. However, the villagers were supposed to be mute spectators and couldn't help the man who was risking his life. If he killed the animal, the villagers would carry the body in a procession to the village. The man would present the horns of the bison as evidence of his valour. The girl would then do some artwork on the horn and on their wedding day, place it on the bridegroom as headgear.'

As Tarachand was explaining these unfamiliar rituals to Krishipal and his wife, a man came to invite them for dinner. The food was arranged in a corner of the open ground. The makeshift kitchen was just behind the eating area and delicious aromas filled the air.

'Sir, among the tribals, a wedding is not just an event for one household. The entire village has to participate. Villagers contribute to the wedding essentials as per their capacity: grains, chickens, goats, sheep, monkeys, frogs, fish, vegetables. Some bring firewood and help in cooking and making other wedding arrangements.'

A Madiya wedding is rarely deemed complete without partaking in the traditional Mahua wine. As the ceremonial rites drew to a close, revelry commenced and the guests began indulging in the prized beverage. Tarachand approached Krishipal with a cup of the aromatic brew. Though tempted, Krishipal hesitated, mindful that he had a meeting with a senior officer the following morning. Uncertain of the potential repercussions of consuming the tribal liquor, he courteously declined the offer. However, the host persisted, citing custom. Reluctantly, Krishipal acquiesced and took a cautious sip. After sipping on the bittersweet elixir, Krishipal bid farewell to the wedding party and headed home.

The next morning, after the senior officer's visit, Tarachand came rushing into Krishipal's cabin. 'Sir, I have got in touch with a man who has rebelled against Santosh Anna and wants to share his dalam's secrets. He said he will confess everything only after meeting you in person.'

'Can we trust him?'

'Yes, sir. I have cross-checked the information. He has truly rebelled against Santosh and is hiding in the forest area of south Gadchiroli.'

'Okay, let's meet him.'

Accompanied by his bodyguard, Ashok Waghmare, and Tarachand, Krishipal ventured into the forest the following morning. Although they waited for half an hour at the agreed upon spot, the man didn't turn up. Krishipal suspected that they were being fooled or worse, entrapped.

Just as the trio was planning to return, a man in green uniform appeared with a bharmar in hand. He had covered his face with a handkerchief. Waghmare immediately pointed his rifle towards the man, prompting him to drop his weapon and raise his hands. Only then did Krishipal speak to him. It turned out that Santosh had humiliated the man and, in retaliation, he had decided to spill the beans.

The man offered valuable intel about Santosh Anna's dalam and their hideout, including the location of their weapons. Krishipal couldn't believe his ears – the man was a gold mine of information. Krishipal suggested that the man surrender and told him that his rehabilitation would be taken care of. However, the man declined the offer and said that he planned to leave the state. On their way back to the headquarters, Krishipal was full of praise for Tarachand for connecting him with such a man.

The next challenge was to act on the information that he had received from the anonymous Naxalite. Soon, the C-60 began raiding multiple hideouts of Santosh Anna's dalam. Many dreaded Naxalites were arrested and a huge cache of arms was recovered. Krishipal and his men had severely undercut Santosh and his comrades. However, the man himself was too cunning and slipped away every time a police team was about to catch him.

Still, the crackdown on Santosh Anna's dalam had an enormous impact on the regional Naxal movement. Naxal incidents had seen a steep decline and Krishipal's superiors were happy. He felt that he was on the brink of winning what many had thought was an impossible war.

August 1991. Krishipal felt satisfied that within a year of becoming Gadchiroli's SP, his efforts were showing results. One rainy day, Krishipal was sipping hot ginger tea in his office while perusing the dossiers of wanted Naxals that remained at large. He asked someone to fetch Tarachand, as he wanted more information about a particular dalam commander.

Over an hour later, Tarachand still hadn't turned up. This was very unusual. Whenever Krishipal called for him, Tarachand came rushing within minutes, leaving all his other work aside. At Krishipal's request, it was confirmed that Tarachand had not reported to his office at the SID either. Worried, he sent one of his constables to Tarachand's residential quarters to check if he was unwell.

He drinks uncontrollably. Maybe he's still sobering up after boozing last night, Krishipal thought. However, Tarachand's wife told the constable that he hadn't been home for two days. She hadn't alerted anyone, assuming that he had gone on some secret operation on short notice.

Krishipal feared that Naxals might have kidnapped Tarachand. They knew that the man was his confidant and acted as his local guide in Gadchiroli. By the following afternoon, posters addressed to the police were put up in some villages that confirmed Krishipal's fear. They contained a simple message: it was futile to search for Tarachand; he would never come back.

Though he was dejected, Krishipal still hoped he might be able to rescue Tarachand from the clutches of the Naxalites. Some villagers claimed to have seen him alive on the bank of the Bande river around when the posters appeared. A search for Tarachand was launched based on the input of the villagers. Soon, the cops were able to locate a familiar tractor. The tractor belonged to Tarachand's friend and he often borrowed it to meet his sources. According to the eyewitnesses, he was last seen reaching the bank of the river on that very tractor.

Krishipal guessed that the Naxals had taken Tarachand to the other side of the river and decided to cross it to pursue the search. However, due to the heavy rains, the river was raging. He would need a motorboat to cross the river with a team of commandos. In those days, the Gadchiroli Police had no motorboats and had to request them from the neighbouring Chandrapur district. Krishipal asked the Chandrapur administration to send a motorboat urgently. However, it took over forty-eight hours for the boat to reach their location. Krishipal and his men were forced to camp at Etapalli, near the riverbank.

Even after two days, the river hadn't calmed down. The motorboat operator was terrified by the flow of the raging river. He refused to join the operation, saying that it was risky and he didn't have prior experience crossing flooded rivers. However, Krishipal insisted that they cross the river. Apart from his personal bond with Tarachand, it was his duty to rescue an abducted colleague.

He recalled how, just two and a half months ago, the whole governmental machinery was put to task to rescue MLA Baba Atram. From the prime minister to the chief minister, everyone had been concerned and monitored the rescue efforts. Apart from deploying numerous forces, they'd even sent helicopters to conduct the search. Now, nobody was bothered about a head constable whose life was in trouble due to his duty.

Krishipal remembered Tarachand's words when Shivanna was released, clear as day. '*The life of a policeman is of no value. Only politicians' lives are valuable in this country.*' In Krishipal's eyes, Tarachand's life had no less value than Atram's.

He announced that even if the boat operator refused to come along, he would cross the river. As a teenager, Krishipal used to sometimes cross the Hindon river near his village by swimming across it. This gave Krishipal the confidence that he'd survive even if the boat capsized. He sat on the motorboat and tied it to a tree on the bank with a 40-metre-long rope. He then asked the commandos whether they were skilled swimmers. Nine of them said yes and joined him on the boat.

'If something goes wrong while crossing the river, don't worry about your weapons. Throw them into the river and swim back to the bank. Your priority is to make sure you don't drown,' he instructed the commandos.

The ten men crossed the river after braving the heavy current and turbulence. The boat nearly capsized twice, but Krishipal maneuvered it safely to the other side of the river. Although they had overcome one challenge, there were three obstacles remaining. First, to locate Tarachand. Second, to rescue him from the abductors. And third, to return to the other side of the bank safely, with Tarachand in tow.

The task seemed insurmountable. It was unclear which direction the Naxalites might have taken Tarachand in after crossing the river. The dog squad couldn't be used to trace Tarachand as the rains had destroyed the trail. There was the additional risk of getting ambushed or stepping on a landmine. The intensity of the rain was increasing, and they did not have enough provisions to sustain them if they got stuck on the other side of the river for days. Krishipal's conscience now asked him a hard question: could he put the life of ten cops in jeopardy to find one? It would be unfair to Tarachand if his force stopped looking for him. However, keeping the safety of his other men in mind, Krishipal decided to abandon the operation for the moment.

The next day, an informer came to Krishipal with dreadful news. The Naxals had killed Tarachand the day before. He had been subjected to unimaginable torture before being murdered. His body parts were cut, one by one, before he was beheaded. The pieces of his body were then thrown into the same river which Krishipal had crossed. The informer also said that the Naxalites were camping close to the riverbank and warned Krishipal that he could be their next target.

Krishipal's mind seized with disbelief at the tragic fate that had befallen his closest confidant in Gadchiroli. Waves of guilt washed over him; each crest carrying the weight of his failure to rescue Tarachand. The realization that even his trusted allies were not immune to peril left him grappling with a profound sense of vulnerability and insecurity. Tarachand's radiant smile, etched vividly in his memory, now seemed hauntingly ephemeral – a poignant reminder of the fragility of life amidst the harsh realities of their environment.

He suspected that Santosh Anna was responsible. Although the place where Tarachand was killed fell under the Etapalli dalam, there were reports that Santosh had been spotted there. Full of rage, Krishipal decided that he must seek vengeance.

16

ESCAPING DEATH BY A WHISKER

Tarachand's murder shattered Krishipal – he missed his friendly presence and guiding hand. He took a few days off to recover from the gloom. Some part of Krishipal didn't feel like continuing in Gadchiroli, but he still had a few months of his tenure remaining. During this period, he resolved to continue his dual policy of aggressively combatting Naxalism while building bridges with the tribal population.

Once he returned to regular work, Krishipal was invited to inaugurate a two-day-long volleyball championship in the interiors of Etapalli. The Gadchiroli Police had organized it for the tribal youth, to strengthen their relationship with the community.

On the morning of the tournament, a convoy of three white Maruti Gypsies left the Allapalli camp. Krishipal sat in the front vehicle. It took them about four hours to complete the 70-kilometre journey to the venue due to adverse road conditions. Once they arrived, Krishipal was happy to see that a good number of youngsters were playing in the match. As a sports enthusiast, he couldn't resist participating in the game, which went on till sunset. Soaked in sweat from the exertion, he was in no mood to undertake the long and uncomfortable return journey across muddy and uneven roads. Though he had planned to return the same evening, Krishipal decided to remain at the SRP camp, where the event had been organized, for an additional day. Staying overnight also gave him an opportunity to chat with the youngsters around the campfire.

On day two of the tournament, Krishipal once again joined the players for an enjoyable game. The youngsters were pleasantly surprised that a senior police officer was playing with them. During the breaks, Krishipal ate with them and offered tips to those who were planning to appear for competitive exams. He displayed genuine concern for their well-being and assured them of his support. These gestures helped Krishipal forge strong bonds with the villagers. However, not everybody who came to watch or participate in the tournament wished well for the cop in their midst.

Krishipal left Etapalli in the early hours of the third day. As per standard procedure, Gadchiroli's SP was never supposed to return by the same route which he had taken to reach a particular place. This was done to pre-empt any attempt at a Naxal ambush. However, Krishipal was hesitant to use the alternate roads, which were in even worse shape. He assumed that the Naxalites would not sit in wait for three days and asked the convoy to retrace the original route. This time, Krishipal sat in the third Gypsy. The vehicles maintained a distance of about 20–30 metres from each other. Since Krishipal had gone to sleep very late on the previous night, after chatting with the local youths, he dozed off soon after he sat in the car.

Suddenly, the sound of an explosion jolted him awake. As the smoke cleared, he saw that the second Gypsy in the convoy had overturned. It appeared that the vehicle had passed over a landmine. Usually, Naxals orchestrated such blasts and hid behind the surrounding trees, ready to fire on the cops. The commandos in Krishipal's vehicle and the first Gypsy deboarded in a ready-to-shoot position, anticipating an ambush. However, there was no firing.

Although the intensity of the blast had upended their vehicle, the personnel sitting in the second Gypsy miraculously escaped without serious injuries. Krishipal and his men fanned out to inspect the area. He soon discovered that they hadn't triggered a landmine at all. Explosives had been hidden on the road, connected to a detonator 70 metres away through a wire that passed from a narrow nullah. The Gadchiroli Police had a list of spots where ambushes were likely to take place but this one, surprisingly, didn't figure on it. Krishipal had escaped certain death by a whisker. He felt guilty for choosing to return by the same route thus endangering everybody's life.

Another lesson learnt was that the Naxals had the patience to wait for their targets and a robust information network. It was because of this network that they knew when and by which route Krishipal was travelling. However, their incorrect assumption that Krishipal would be travelling in the second Gypsy had saved him. He felt fortunate that his mistake hadn't proved deadly and launched a manhunt to trace the perpetrators. Soon, three men were caught. When interrogated, they revealed that Santosh Anna had conspired to kill Krishipal.

Not long after this episode, an informer named Shikari requested a meeting with him. Shikari was a tribal man in his fifties who, until a decade ago, had worked as a guide for senior police officers and bureaucrats who were hunting game in the jungle. Observing Krishipal's solemn mood, he said, 'I understand you are very disturbed these days, sir. I know you sincerely want to free Gadchiroli from the menace of Naxals. I can offer you some help.'

'Yes, speak up. What can you do for me, Shikari?'

'I can arrange a meeting with Santosh Anna.'

Krishipal was enraged at Shikari's proposal. 'Why should I speak with Santosh Anna? The bullets of my revolver will meet that beast first.'

'Forgive me, sir. I know that he has inflicted a lot of damage, but we must keep the door open for dialogue. Think over it, sir. If Santosh Anna gives up arms and is ready to reform, it will be a big victory against the Naxal movement. Over the last two years, I have noticed that you prefer words over bullets. I am sure a brief chat with him will do the magic. I have a mediator who can arrange the meeting but we have to give an assurance that Santosh will not be arrested.'

Once his initial outrage had subsided, Krishipal seriously considered the idea for a while before asking Shikari to arrange the meeting. With his approval, Shikari informed the mediator that the SP was willing to meet Santosh Anna. The same was conveyed to Santosh. The commander had certain conditions. First and foremost, Krishipal would meet him at a location of his choice in the forest. He would also have to come alone, unarmed and without a bodyguard. Santosh threatened to change the meeting location at the last moment or cancel the meeting altogether if he sensed danger.

When these conditions were conveyed to Krishipal, he was torn. Meeting a dreaded Naxal alone in the forest sans a bodyguard and his weapons was perilous. At the same time, there was a likelihood of Santosh Anna's surrender, which would be an immense blow to the Naxal movement in Gadchiroli. When Krishipal sought advice from his superiors, they were aghast.

'Can you trust that bastard?' a riled senior shouted. 'Are you aware of the repercussions if he kidnaps or kills you? We will have to launch another operation to retrieve your body. Remember, Tarachand's corpse still hasn't been found.'

The proposal to meet Santosh on the conditions laid down by him was rejected outright. Through Shikari, Krishipal sent another message to the Naxal commander. Though he wasn't willing to meet Santosh alone in the jungle, they could meet outside

Gadchiroli, in Nagpur or Wardha. Santosh remained adamant.

In response, Krishipal sent a final message to Santosh Anna. 'Whenever I will meet you, either I will kill you or you will kill me. We're done talking now.'

17

FIGHTING RAKTABEEJ

1st July 1992

My dear Raghuvanshi,

I am sure, you are busy preparing to hand over your onerous charge to your successor and should also be looking forward to joining your new posting. I thought I must take advantage of this time and write to you to express my admiration for the hard work you relentlessly put in the district to curb the menace of Naxalites. If today there is some peace and feeling among the police that they are on the top, capable of handling any charges posed by the Naxalites, a large measure of credit goes to you.

I am sure, your successor will carry forward the task so doggedly shouldered by you and earn a good name for Maharashtra police and himself, as you have done.

Thank you for all that you have done for the Force and good-bye.

Yours Sincerely,
V. K. Saraf
Director General of Police, Maharashtra.[1]

Reading this letter from the DGP had made Krishipal tearful. Very few officers in the police force were fortunate to receive such kind words from their bosses. Though he had his fair share of misadventures and mistakes, Krishipal's two-year tenure in Gadchiroli had seen the police consolidate their position in this labyrinth of death. The acknowledgement of his efforts by DGP Saraf was the biggest reward. He was happy to leave Gadchiroli a satisfied man. However, he was worried about one thing – the future of C-60.

Many police organizations are plagued by what is known as the Predecessor–Successor Syndrome. This syndrome, usually fuelled by a desire to make one's mark, compels the successor to discontinue the initiatives of their predecessor. Krishipal wasn't sure whether the next SP, Subodh Jaiswal, would continue the C-60. Subodh was an upright officer but had a reputation for being an obstinate maverick. DGP Saraf was also due to retire shortly and there was no guarantee that the next DGP would allow the C-60 to live on.

Subodh arrived in Gadchiroli thirty days before the charge was to be handed over. He started living with Krishipal to orient himself to the area. Krishipal introduced him to the primary challenges in Gadchiroli, and the officers and informers who could help him fight the Naxalites. During their conversations, Krishipal subtly praised C-60 and explained how he had raised the force. Once, over tea, he told Subodh, 'I have just one regret while leaving Gadchiroli, that I couldn't lay my hands on that bastard Santosh Anna. He has been a big menace and brutally killed many of our men.'

Subodh nodded and then seemed to get lost in thought, gazing at the wall that listed the most wanted Naxals unblinkingly.

Before he knew it, Krishipal's farewell day had arrived. On 31 July 1992, the entire town of Gadchiroli poured into the SP's office: policemen, government officials and the common folk alike. Prominent social workers, local businessmen, teachers and journalists were also among the attendees. The Jeep in which Krishipal was to leave was decorated with beautiful flowers.

As soon as he emerged out of the office after completing the formal handover, the people showered him with petals and shouted in chorus, 'KP Raghuvanshi *zindabad*!' No outgoing SP in Gadchiroli had ever received such affection and respect from the personnel and local people before. Apart from his performance as SP, the people had been touched by his emphatic nature and approachability. Some of the C-60 commandos couldn't hold back their tears. To them, Krishipal wasn't just a boss but also a mentor – almost like a family elder. Among them was Kamala Alaam, who had received a new lease of life after Krishipal inducted her into C-60. She was inconsolable.

Before Krishipal left, Additional SP Ravindra Kedari

said in his farewell speech, 'Many IPS officers with high ego emit arrogance in their behaviour and behave with citizens like they are some monarch, but Krishipal sir was different. He behaved respectfully with everyone and showed genuine concern to resolve their problems.' As the Jeep carried him away from Gadchiroli, Krishipal was caught in a deluge of emotions. His time in Gadchiroli had forever changed him – as a cop, and as a person.

Krishipal's new assignment was to work as the SP of Ahmednagar district. It was not a troubled area and relatively close to Bombay. Shirdi's Saibaba temple and Shani Shingnapur – where devotees from across India and abroad throng – were under his jurisdiction. Over the previous two years, Krishipal had become conditioned to the stressful environment in Gadchiroli. In fact, he had started to enjoy that life and was missing the action. He found himself yearning to go back to Gadchiroli and hold the charge for some more time … at least until Santosh Anna was killed!

The commandos who had been recruited and trained by Krishipal kept in touch with him and often called to check that he was well. Subodh also spoke to him occasionally to get his perspective on certain cases. One day, just as Krishipal returned home after visiting Shirdi's Saibaba temple with his family, his phone rang. The call was from a constable of the Gadchiroli Police.

'Sir, we have finished your incomplete project. You must come to Gadchiroli to celebrate with us.' The constable's words were full of excitement.

'Why? What happened?'

'Sir, that mad dog Santosh Anna is dead! Now he will rot in hell for his sins.'

For Krishipal, this was bittersweet news. On one hand, he was happy that the most dreaded Naxalite of Gadchiroli had met his fate. On the other hand, he felt some regret that he wasn't the one who had brought Santosh to justice. Ashok Biswas of the Naxal Cell called with more details, sounding just as exultant. He had a personal stake in the case too, since Santosh's accomplices had once conspired to kill him.

Santosh Anna's death was a big achievement for the Gadchiroli Police in its war against insurgency. However, the Naxal movement itself seemed impossible to defeat. It was like a Raktabeej, a demon that multiplied with every drop of blood it spilled. Every time a major Naxal leader was arrested or killed, another took their place. The relief after Santosh Anna was killed soon evaporated as another challenger emerged: Shivanna.

Shivanna, also known as Vikasanna, was the same Naxal who was released from jail in exchange for Baba Atram. Harsh interrogations and time spent behind bars didn't deter him from joining the Naxal movement again. Krishipal, who kept tab on the happenings in Gadchiroli, had anticipated that releasing Shivanna would prove costly for the force. Then again, it seemed that nothing was more valuable than the life of a politician whose party was in power.

Shivanna started ambushing police parties within a few months of his release. His first hit was barely five months later. On 21 November 1992, he engineered a landmine blast at Tadgaon in which ten policemen perished.[2] Their vehicle was flung many kilometres away due to the impact of the blast, reduced to a mangled mass of metal.

In 2003, Shivanna's reign of terror caused considerable damage, culminating in a landmine explosion that killed five policemen near the Kumargunda stream in Andhra Pradesh. This event led to an intensive manhunt, prompting Shivanna to flee to Chhattisgarh where he continued to oversee Naxal activities. In 2006, Chhattisgarh Police received information that Shivanna was hiding out in Bhanupratappur. The ensuing police operation ended in a gunfight when Naxals opened fire. After the clash, Shivanna's lifeless body was discovered – the unceremonious end of a crime lord who had seventy-five cases lodged against him. Naxalite activity in Gadchiroli reduced considerably after his death, leading to discussions among top Naxal leaders about how best to revive operations.

The subsequent years, especially 2009, saw intensified Naxal offensives against the Gadchiroli Police, hindering elections. The rampant ambushes included major attacks in February and May 2009, leading to significant police casualties, including officers close to Krishipal who had spearheaded anti-Naxal operations. These continuous clashes prompted the government to launch Operation Green Hunt, while the Naxals continued their Tactical Counter Offensive Campaign, aimed at disrupting the electoral process. Meanwhile, peace initiatives couldn't progress due to mutual distrust.

The biggest blow to the Naxal movement came in April 2018, when forty alleged Maoists were killed in an encounter at Boriya–Kasansur, as described in Chapter 1. Krishipal, who had hung up his boots in 2015, couldn't hide his smile when he heard the news. The force he had created thirty-one years ago had nearly achieved its lofty goal.

In the afternoon of 19 December 2022, Deputy CM of Maharashtra Devendra Fadnavis told the Vidhan Sabha, 'Today the youth of Gadchiroli are not joining the Naxal dalams. They have to bring recruits from Chhatisgarh and Odisha.'[3] Upon hearing about this triumph, Krishipal's heart was filled with pride and satisfaction.

18

DETAINING BAL THACKERAY

Before Krishipal could complete his tenure as SP of Ahmednagar, he was suddenly transferred to the state police headquarters in Bombay in 1993, as the assistant inspector general (AIG), Establishments. He later learnt that a minister had wanted to post another officer at Ahmednagar, leading to his relocation. His new role did not involve much fieldwork, mostly signing files and attending meetings. However, by now, Krishipal had earned a reputation as an officer who performed well on the ground and had successfully handled tense law and order situations.

DGP Shivajirao Baraokar, impressed by Krishipal's laurels, wanted to utilize him for challenging cases. Hence, when Shiv Sena supremo Bal Thackeray announced that he was going to visit Aurangabad – an area that was simmering due to caste-based violence – the chief chose Krishipal, along with Mumbai Police DCP R. D. Gawande, to prevent Thackeray's arrival.

Bal Thackeray had long opposed the renaming of Marathwada University in Aurangabad. Several Dalit organizations wanted to name the university after Dr B. R. Ambedkar, which was unacceptable to the Shiv Sena. Krishipal had already seen the fallout of this conflict in Bombay in 1989, when he had to control an aggressive mob. Four years later, this issue persisted and violent clashes had broken out between Dalit organizations and Shiv Sainiks across Maharashtra.[1]

Aurangabad was already at a breaking point and Thackeray's announcement added to the stress of the police. They feared that Thackeray's visit and any speeches he gave in Aurangabad would aggravate the situation. The police decided to apprehend Thackeray before he reached Aurangabad. Krishipal and Gawande contemplated detaining him in Pune, where he was halting briefly,but the chief vetoed the idea, fearing that Shiv Sainiks would go on a rampage in the city. The route from Bombay to Aurangabad passed through Ahmednagar. Since Krishipal had served in Ahmednagar, the police chief thought that he would be the right man to restrain Thackeray there. However, this would not be an easy task.

Bal Thackeray left his bungalow in Bombay for Aurangabad with a substantial security convoy, along with numerous vehicles carrying Shiv Sainiks waving saffron flags. Krishipal and Gawande had reached Ahmednagar a day earlier and stationed themselves near the ancient Ranjangaon Ashtavinayak Ganesh temple on the Pune–Ahmednagar highway. When Thackeray's group reached the highway after taking the planned break in Pune, they found the road barricaded. When the supremo exited his car, DCP Gawande and Krishipal walked up to meet him.

'Saheb, you cannot go ahead from here,' Gawande said.

'Why can't I go? I can go anywhere I want in Maharashtra. Who are you to stop me?' Thackeray responded angrily. His workers came out of their cars and surrounded their leader.

'Sir, there are prohibitory orders in place. The situation in Aurangabad is not good, and we have been instructed to detain you,' Krishipal clarified, handing Thackeray a copy of the order in question.

With a calm expression, Krishipal dug his heels into the ground. He was face to face with one of the biggest political forces in Maharashtra. Fearing that Thackeray would order his men to create a ruckus, he had prepared his force for a lathi-charge. However, contrary to his expectations, Thackeray willingly complied. After a brief glance at the paper, Thackeray only said, 'Hmm. In that case I want to go to Pune.'

'Sure, Saheb. You can go there but in our company,' Krishipal told him firmly. He thought it prudent to keep Thackeray under his watch, to ensure he wouldn't try to enter Aurangabad some other way.

After an hour's journey, Thackeray, Krishipal and Gawande reached an apartment in Pune which was occupied by a Shiv Sainik. Thackeray was friendly with both the officers and offered them tea and snacks. He then called CM Sharad Pawar with a smile on his face and said, 'So, now your police has detained me. I am in Pune.'

That conversation with Pawar lasted for about five minutes, during which Thackeray laughed several times. To those present, it appeared the Shiv Sena supremo was a friend of Pawar's. Krishipal tried to make sense of what Thackeray was saying on the call and concluded that everything was scripted. He realized that, as a police officer, he was a mere pawn in a larger political game.

19

A MOLE IN THE CBI?

Krishipal's career had taken him everywhere from the forested depths of Gadchiroli to the historic Maharashtra Police Headquarters. In 1996, he faced a new challenge as he inadvertently became embroiled in the dealings of Mumbai's industrial giants.

After serving the Maharashtra Police in various roles, Krishipal's next goal was to diversify his expertise by joining a central law enforcement agency. Hence, when the opportunity arose, he opted for a deputation in the CBI in December 1994. For a brief time, he served at the agency's anti-corruption wing in Mumbai, before being sent to the CBI headquarters in Delhi. Krishipal had joined the CBI to turn over a new leaf and learn more about law enforcement. However, his experience in the CBI left him more wary than ever of the corruption ingrained in the system.

In 1992, the Government of India introduced a policy that offered some of its oil fields to private parties for development, as a joint venture with the state-owned Oil and Natural Gas Corporation (ONGC). After an auction, two oil fields were awarded jointly to Reliance India Ltd and Enron in 1994. As per the contract, the consortium was to receive 60 per cent of the proceeds and ONGC, 40 per cent. It was also agreed that the government would have the first option to buy 100 per cent of the oil produced at the international price.

A few newspapers reported that there were certain irregularities in the awarding of the contract to the Reliance–Enron consortium.[1] The comptroller and auditor general (CAG) also found in its investigation that this deal had led to losses for the government.[2] Although the CAG was yet to submit its report officially, the CBI took cognizance of the media reports and decided to conduct a preliminary investigation.[3] When the name of former petroleum minister Satish Sharma also cropped up during the inquiry, the matter was referred to the CBI headquarters for instructions. Senior officials reviewed the case files and recommended that the official report of the CAG should be consulted before proceeding further.

Meanwhile, in July 1997, an NGO filed a public interest litigation (PIL) in the Delhi High Court, challenging the decision to grant the oil fields to the Reliance–Enron consortium.[4,5] The petitioners alleged that the project had been awarded arbitrarily for collateral considerations and with mala fide intent. They argued that the oil fields had been given to the consortium for a paltry sum. Their contention was that the price at which the government had agreed to purchase the oil from the joint venture was above the market price. The petitioners sought a criminal investigation into the matter, for the contract to be cancelled and departmental action against the government officials who had played a role in awarding the contract.

The petitioners had presented a 'Part II' file of the case to furnish their argument, in which a superintendent rank officer had recommended filing a criminal case before he was sent out of the CBI. To verify the petitioners' claim, the court ordered the CBI to produce said file. Krishipal, who had been promoted to DIG only a few days earlier, couldn't recall any file marked Part II. On his instruction, the CBI told the court that no such file existed. However, the petitioners then put forward a photocopy of the purported file in which Krishipal had made a note: 'Let us wait for the [CAG] report.'

It was an embarrassing situation for Krishipal. Only after the petitioners challenged the CBI's claim did he remember what was being called the Part II file. It was a simple two-page note with a newspaper clipping attached to it. Since Krishipal had just taken up the charge of DIG when the note was presented to him, he was not aware of the details of the case. He elected to follow his superiors and wrote that the CBI should wait for the CAG report. But the worrying question remained: where was that file?

Despite a thorough search of the CBI office in Mumbai, the file couldn't be traced. This gave the petitioners a chance to cast aspersions on Krishipal's integrity and allege that he had connived with the Reliance–Enron consortium.

Krishipal, who attended several of the court hearings, was pained by such ignominy. All his achievements appeared to have been washed away by a case which he had never even investigated.

Eventually, the High Court found that the accusations of the petitioners were unsubstantiated and dismissed the PIL.[6] To Krishipal's relief, the court passed no strictures against him. The petitioners challenged the High Court's order in the Supreme Court. However, after hearing the arguments, the apex court also dismissed the appeal in October 2000.[7] In its judgement, the court observed that the grant of contract to the Reliance–Enron consortium was not unreasonable. It couldn't be established that Reliance had bribed the petroleum minister to get the contract and none of the other bidders had come forward to challenge the validity of the contract. The court, however, took a strict view on the disappearance of the file. Reprimanding the CBI, the court asked the agency to put 'its house in order before it is too late'.[8]

Krishipal had been spared prosecution and departmental action, but the stricture passed by the Supreme Court haunted him throughout his career.

One day, shortly after the Supreme Court's order, Krishipal was sitting in his chamber with a colleague when a clerk walked in.

'Sir, I want to confess something. I destroyed the file which the court sought from you.'

Krishipal jumped out of his chair. He was beyond enraged. Trying to regain his composure, he asked, 'Do you have any idea what you have done to me? You have robbed me of my honour, my dignity … my peace. Why are you telling me this now?'

'Sir, my conscience is not allowing me to sleep. I will tell you everything. Give me any punishment you want,' the clerk said, looking at the floor.

He then narrated the full story. He had acted on behalf of an officer subordinate to Krishipal, who was no longer working with the CBI. The officer had impressed upon the clerk that he was a crusader against corruption and that the hands of his fellow CBI officers were not clean. With the intention of helping the officer in his fight against corruption, the awestruck clerk had blindly followed his instructions. After being moved out of the CBI, the officer had contacted him and asked him to destroy Part II of the file. Accordingly, the clerk had torn up the file and thrown away the pieces – but not before taking a photocopy of it.[9]

As the clerk finished his narration, Krishipal was drenched in sweat. His mind went numb for a few minutes. Steadying himself, he asked the clerk to file an affidavit. He then wrote a letter to the CBI headquarters, supported by the affidavit, requesting permission to file a criminal case and initiate departmental action against the officer. However, the case had become infructuous after the Supreme Court's order. With time, it seemed that everyone had forgotten about the case. The only exceptions were Krishipal and the clerk, whose increment was stopped for two years as a punishment.

'Sir, Mr Dhirubhai Ambani wants to meet you. However, he can't come to your office as it is on the first floor and there is no lift. He has a problem with his knees that makes it difficult for him to climb stairs. Would you be able to come down to his office at Nariman Point?'

The request from Dhirubhai Ambani's office came to Krishipal years later, when he was heading the STF in 2002. Krishipal was divided on whether to meet Ambani. It seemed rude to decline an invitation from India's top industrialist but, on the other hand, he feared that this would add weight to the false allegations that he was Ambani's crony. Though Krishipal had never met Ambani or even spoken to him on the phone, the missing file incident had dented his upright reputation. After some careful contemplation, Krishipal decided to meet Ambani regardless of what his detractors might say. They had already done enough damage.

On the agreed upon day, Krishipal walked into the grand office located on the fourth floor of Maker Chamber IV. There, he found Dhirubhai Ambani waiting for him. He welcomed Krishipal warmly and led him to a wide table for tea. Dhirubhai's sons, Mukesh and Anil, also joined them.

'Sir, we are sorry that you have had to suffer so much because of us,' Dhirubhai said with a sympathetic look. 'We were also wondering why your name was dragged into the matter despite you having nothing to do with the case.'

'Why are you apologizing? It wasn't your fault. Sometimes things just happen due to misfortune. Thankfully, you and I have been exonerated by the Supreme Court.'

Dhirubhai, after an hour-long conversation, invited Krishipal to have dinner with him soon. However, that dinner could never happen. Not long after, on 6 July 2002, Dhirubhai fell ill and passed away.

20

A FURIOUS SONIA GANDHI

28 October 2000

Krishipal was in Agra for an official meeting when he received news that he was being transferred. It did not come as a surprise. During his previous visits to Mumbai, senior officers of the Maharashtra Police – including the DGP – had tried to convince him to return to his parent cadre. Although he still had eight months left of his tenure with the CBI, Krishipal had agreed to be repatriated early. The Maharashtra government promptly sent a request to the Government of India to release him from the CBI. Krishipal was eager to return to familiar ground and his superiors had hinted that he would be appointed the additional commissioner of the south region in the Mumbai Police Commissionerate – a prestigious position.

According to standard protocol, all cases of premature repatriation were referred to the Appointments Committee of the Cabinet. It took the committee over two months to deliberate on Krishipal's case. When news of his transfer reached him in Agra, it wasn't quite what he had expected. He had been appointed the chief of the STF to implement the Srikrishna Commission's recommendations. During his time at the CBI, Krishipal had lost touch with the political situation in Maharashtra. Through phone calls to his friends and well-wishers in Mumbai, he gathered information about the circumstances that had led to his sudden transfer.

Following the demolition of the Babri Masjid in Ayodhya, India was plunged into communal turmoil. Bombay bore the brunt of the violence between the Hindu and Muslim communities, unfolding in two harrowing phases. The initial eruption occurred on 6 December 1992 and persisted for over a week. Incidents of murders, arson and destruction of places of worship were reported from across the city. The second phase broke out on 6 January 1993, catalysed by the fatal stabbing of two Mathadi workers – manual labourers from western Maharashtra who were employed in the transport sector. The subsequent riots escalated and law enforcement officers were directly targeted, with firearms deployed in several instances. Even the city's police commissioner, Shrikant Bapat, had narrowly escaped death when a crude bomb exploded near him during an inspection of the riot-affected Masjid Bunder area.

After the situation stabilized, the Congress-led government in Maharashtra set up a commission, headed by Justice B. N. Srikrishna of the Bombay High Court, to investigate the 1992–3 communal riots in Mumbai. The commission was established in 1993. Two years later, Congress lost the state assembly elections and the Shiv Sena–BJP alliance came into power. The saffron government, led by Manohar Joshi of the Shiv Sena, discontinued the commission, sparking outrage from opposition parties, the media and civil rights groups. Prime Minister Atal Bihari Vajpayee intervened, and the commission was reinstated with certain conditions. The commission submitted its findings and recommendations in August 1998.

The Srikrishna report put forward damning observations against the incumbent Shiv Sena and Mumbai Police. It highlighted that the Shiv Sena had incited violent incidents in various areas of Bombay through its cadres and provocative editorials in its publication *Saamana*. Additionally, the report pointed out that the police had acted in a biased manner during the riots, targeting Muslims. The commission recognized that the violence perpetrated by Muslim rioters and the attacks on policemen were driven by the anger following the demolition of the Babri mosque.[1] As the authorities had failed to protect the disputed structure, the police had been attacked as representatives of that authority. It came as no surprise that the Shiv Sena, being part of the government, did not accept a report that implicated its leaders and cadres.

During their 1999 Vidhan Sabha election campaign, the Congress promised to implement the commission's recommendations in its manifesto.[2] At the time, the Samajwadi Party was gaining support in Muslim neighbourhoods and the newly formed Nationalist Congress Party (NCP) also had the potential to attract Muslim voters. To maintain its connection with the local Muslim community, the Congress successfully used the Srikrishna Commission as a key issue during the election. It emerged as the largest party in the elections and created a coalition with the NCP to form the government.

Vilasrao Deshmukh, a member of the Congress, was appointed chief minister. Once in power, Deshmukh was being pressured to fulfil his party's promises. Meanwhile, a group of social activists had petitioned the Supreme Court, requesting that the CBI be charged with implementing the commission's report.[3] The government convinced the petitioners that the CBI was not necessary. Instead, they proposed setting up an STF with an officer who had experience working in the CBI at its head. Krishipal's name was suggested, and he was assigned to lead the STF.

When Krishipal returned to Mumbai in October 2000, he was met with many surprises. The so-called STF that he was supposed to take charge of did not exist. He had to first establish the force and then assume the role of its chief. Technically, the STF was meant to operate under the crime branch of the Mumbai Police; in reality, it had to function independently without any support from the crime branch.

To match his rank, the position of DCP (Preventive) was upgraded to the rank of additional commissioner and re-designated as chief of the STF. Still, Krishipal was asked to use the office of the DCP (Preventive), located in an old government building next to a smelly fish market. The cramped office space was not appropriate for an additional commissioner. He had been provided with two DCPs, eight inspectors, ten sub-inspectors and a few constables, but there was no office space for them. Krishipal had to share a room with both his DCPs – Bipin Kumar Singh and S. M. Sayyad. With only two chairs between them, they often joked that they were playing musical chairs.

Krishipal expressed his predicament to Police Commissioner M. N. Singh and requested additional space for his staff. The commissioner simply responded, '*Dhoondh lo jagah.*' (You find a place.) On making inquiries, someone told Krishipal that the Anti-Narcotics Cell was moving its office from the annexe of the Azad Maidan police compound to Cuffe Parade. He was allowed to set up the STF office in the place they had vacated. Two air conditioners were rented and installed in the office. Once these basic requirements were sorted, it was time for Krishipal and his team to face the primary challenge: implementing the commission's recommendations.

The report was extensive and Krishipal realized that even reading it was going to be an enormous task. After contemplating the best strategy, he divided the STF into two units and the commission's report into two equal parts. DCP Sayyad was put in charge of Unit-1, while DCP Singh in charge of Unit-2. They were instructed to review their half of the report quickly and identify cases where action could be taken. In this context, 'action' would entail initiating investigations, registering offenses against the individuals named in the report and arresting and prosecuting them.

The STF was investigating riots that had occurred seven or eight years ago. Krishipal was concerned that, in that time, many witnesses may have died or left the city. He was sceptical about whether those who could be found would cooperate with the investigation. Additionally, gathering evidence that would hold up under legal scrutiny during the trial posed a challenge.

Among the many individuals against whom the commission had made extensive adverse observations were Ramdev Tyagi, former police commissioner of Mumbai, and Bal Thackeray. Tyagi had been accused of killing nine innocent bakery workers in cold blood after mistaking them for terrorists and Thackeray, of inciting riots against Muslims.[4] Thackeray was a political rival of the incumbent Congress–NCP alliance and Tyagi had demonstrated his affinity for the Hindutva ideology by joining the Shiv Sena after his retirement and the government was inclined to put both of them behind bars. The onus fell on Krishipal to fulfil these expectations.

Meanwhile, the Supreme Court, after hearing multiple

petitions filed by social organizations, issued a notice to the state government asking what action it had taken over the commission's report. The government asked Krishipal to respond to the notice. When he visited the Supreme Court, the lawyers of the petitioners lambasted the STF and Maharashtra government for not acting on the recommendations and demanded the case be transferred to the CBI. Krishipal was surprised to see Arif Naseem Khan, a minister of the state, among the petitioners. Khan was criticizing his own government and alleging that the Mumbai Police wasn't making sincere efforts to arrest the culprits.[5] Krishipal tried to placate the court by saying that work was in progress and would soon provide results. He filed a detailed affidavit stating that the Srikrishna Commission's report was being examined so that the action could be initiated against the accused.

Krishipal was under pressure from all corners. The press, social activists and his own political bosses were all accusing him of laxity and not doing enough to nail the culprits. CM Deshmukh and Deputy CM Chhagan Bhujbal frequently began summoning Krishipal to the Mantralaya for updates. Krishipal dreaded these meetings. Bhujbal, in particular, often spoke to him curtly and made him feel that he like was not doing his job sincerely.

One day, in July 2001, CM Deshmukh asked Krishipal to accompany him to Delhi to brief some people about the progress of the STF's work. They were joined by Kripashankar Singh, minister of state of the Home Department. The trio spent the night at the Maharashtra Sadan and in the morning, the CM took Krishipal to the bungalow of Arjun Singh, who was a Congress parliamentarian and union minister. Singh sat on a grand chair in a spacious, beautifully decorated hall as Deshmukh introduced Krishipal to him.

'Arjun ji, Raghuvanshi is a bright officer and has worked with the CBI. He is heading the STF and investigating the Mumbai riots.'

At Deshmukh's instruction, Krishipal began explaining the progress that had been made by the STF. Singh didn't look impressed. After hearing him out, Singh whispered something in Deshmukh's ear. Krishipal was then asked to wait outside the hall while the CM and Singh spoke privately. After two minutes, a visibly perplexed Deshmukh exited the hall and ushered Krishipal towards their vehicle.

Once they reached the Maharashtra Sadan, Deshmukh stopped Krishipal from checking into his room. 'Come immediately. We have to leave,' he urged in a rushed tone. 'Madam has called for us.'

The 'Madam' in question was Sonia Gandhi. She was the leader of a political party, not a minister. Krishipal was unsure of how to proceed. How could he meet and brief someone who held no position in the government? Would it be inappropriate for him to discuss his work with Mrs Gandhi? However, refusing to meet her would have disastrous consequences. Krishipal contacted his boss, M. N. Singh, to seek his counsel. The police commissioner advised him to brief Gandhi, since he would be meeting her with the CM.

According to Deshmukh's sources in the party, a group of social activists had met with Sonia Gandhi two days before Krishipal's visit to Delhi. They had accused the Congress party of deceiving them by making false promises in their election manifesto. Their complaint was particularly aimed at Deshmukh; they believed that he was not taking any action to bring the accused to justice. In their view, the establishment of the STF was merely a facade and no concrete steps had been taken. They even went so far as to allege that the government was protecting the accused, especially Thackeray and Tyagi. Gandhi was infuriated.

Deshmukh and Krishipal reached Gandhi's residence – 10, Janpath – around 1 p.m. They were asked to wait in a grand meeting hall. Around ten minutes later, Sonia Gandhi appeared. Dressed in a sari, she took her place on a chair around 12 feet away from the sofa on which they were sitting. Deshmukh stood up and introduced Krishipal to her, before Gandhi signalled for them to sit. For the first time, Krishipal witnessed the power that Sonia Gandhi wielded in her party.

At Deshmukh's instruction, Krishipal started to brief her. 'Ma'am, we are going through the Srikrishna Commission's report thoroughly and soon the results will be there for everybody to see. We want to make legally sound cases, so that they stand up to the scrutiny of the court. We are taking extra precautions; that is why it is taking time.'

Gandhi listened to his explanation but, like Arjun Singh, her facial expressions displayed dissatisfaction and disappointment. She kept looking over at Deshmukh in dismay while Krishipal spoke. When he finished, Deshmukh reminded Gandhi of a cautionary tale from a year earlier. The Mumbai Police had arrested Bal Thackeray in an old case, only for him to be discharged by the court within minutes. To avoid a repeat of such an embarrassment, he explained, the STF required more time.

The whole interaction made Krishipal feel that he and Deshmukh were the accused in Gandhi's court. He was very aware that she could snatch away the CM's chair from Deshmukh in a second; that he too could be transferred again to some place like Gadchiroli. Gandhi left the hall with a brief instruction delivered in a commanding tone. 'Vilasrao ji, I want the report to be implemented in both letter and spirit.'[6]

After they left the meeting hall, Deshmukh was in sombre mood. 'Raghuvanshi, you have to show results soon. Everybody is looking at me. You have no idea of what I am going through. Madam is unhappy with us.'

Krishipal returned to Mumbai that night. The few hours of sleep he got were far from restful. This trip had been a reality check as to the burden of expectations on his team – and the consequences of failing to deliver. He woke up to a call from the deputy CM's office. Bhujbal wanted Krishipal to brief him about what had transpired in Delhi.

21

YOU ARE UNDER ARREST, SIR

'Yes, Jitendra. We have arrested Tyagi sir.'

Krishipal's demeanour, usually stoic was now perturbed, as he relayed the news of Ramdev Tyagi's arrest to the author, then a television journalist. It was 14 August 2001, and Krishipal had reached his residence after a trying day as chief of the STF. After he had done his due diligence informing the media, he poured a drink and pondered the strange turns that life was prone to take. Tyagi had once been his mentor and now Krishipal had been tasked with bringing him into custody.

On 9 January 1993, the communal riots in Bombay had reached their peak. The events of that day were later recounted to the Srikrishna Commission by the police officers who were on the ground.

At 9:30 a.m., Inspector Anant Ingale was patrolling a riot-stricken area that fell under the jurisdiction of Pydhonie Police Station. Constables stationed at the Minara mosque junction had reported being fired upon by assailants positioned atop the adjacent Suleman Bakery. Renowned for its sweet delicacies like nankhatai and aflatoon, the confectionary was managed by workers from UP and was nestled next to the Chunabhatti Masjid. This locale was renowned for being a culinary haven during Ramadan, drawing food enthusiasts of all faiths to relish an array of delights. Even celebrities frequented the area for street food during these nights. Now, it was embroiled in communal strife. The typically bustling streets were eerily deserted that morning due to the imposed curfew, so the gunshots were heard loud and clear.

As Ingale strategized with his constables, additional shots rang out. Rallying a small contingent, he ascended to the terrace of Taj Book Depot, situated opposite the bakery. From this vantage point, Ingale observed eight to ten individuals taking cover behind the building's water tank, one holding an automatic weapon and two others wielding revolvers. Despite Ingale's demands for surrender, the armed group remained defiant. He discharged two rounds from his service revolver, but the assailants were beyond its effective range.

Ingale swiftly called the control room for reinforcements; the urgent message pulsated through the police's wireless communication system. Among those who intercepted the transmission was Tyagi, then serving as the joint commissioner of the Mumbai Crime Branch. He was already patrolling the riot-torn area with his Special Operations Squad (SOS) and promptly responded. By 12:30 p.m., Tyagi had arrived on the scene with his team and assumed command of the operation.

Despite the presence of Tyagi and the SOS, gunfire persisted from the bakery rooftop. All attempts to coax cooperation from those inside were met with resistance; glass bottles and acid bulbs were hurled in response to Tyagi's demands. Tear gas shells were deployed in an effort to quell the rioters yet they remained unyielding. In response, Tyagi ordered his men to breach the bakery's entrance.

Upon reaching the terrace, the squad encountered a hostile mob armed with choppers, iron bars and knives. Ignoring demands for their surrender, they charged at the officers. One individual wielded a Sten gun-like weapon, prompting retaliatory fire from Tyagi's team. Amidst the chaos, eight to ten individuals managed to evade capture, fleeing through a gutter passage between the bakery and Chunabhatti Masjid. Subsequently, seventy-eight individuals were apprehended, while the nine people had been fatally shot. Later investigations revealed that five of the deceased were bakery workers, one hailed from a nearby mosque and three were identified as outsiders, who were not employed by the bakery.[1]

However, the Srikrishna Commission's inquiry cast serious doubts on the credibility of the Mumbai Police's account, uncovering numerous inconsistencies. It highlighted the absence of any reported injuries among police personnel, whether from gunfire or the projectiles allegedly thrown by the assailants. Furthermore, no weapons were recovered from the scene, undermining the narrative that there had been an imminent threat. Post-mortem examinations revealed that the victims had sustained gunshot wounds to their backs, indicating they had been shot while attempting to flee. Contrary to claims of urgency, the wireless communication between Tyagi and the control room failed to suggest a fast-approaching crisis.

Justice Srikrishna criticized the conduct of the SOS as 'utterly trigger-happy', characterizing the police firing as a disproportionate response to the alleged gunfire incident. The commission concluded that the officers had been gripped by 'fear psychosis', leading to excessive and unwarranted action.[2] Tyagi became the face of atrocities, excesses and anti-Muslim behaviour exhibited by the city's police force.

Upon his return from Delhi, Krishipal convened a meeting with both of his DCPs, instructing them to expedite their review of the commission's report and propose actionable cases. Though he endeavoured to conceal his distress, DCP Singh discerned the shift in Krishipal's demeanour.

A couple of days later, during a tea break, Singh tactfully broached the subject. 'Sir, you seemed unusually tense after your trip to Delhi. Is there anything you wish not to share, or that we should remain unaware of?'

The discreet inquiry prompted Krishipal to open up about his ordeal. He recounted his unsettling experience in Delhi; how individuals in positions of authority were eager for swift results, particularly regarding the arrests of Tyagi and Thackeray.

Though troubled by this information, Singh managed a smile. 'Sir, the good news is that the scrutiny of paragraphs pertaining to the role of Bal Thackeray is almost complete. I will submit my report in a day or two.'

Soon, Krishipal received reports from his DCPs on both Thackeray and Tyagi, highlighting preliminary evidence that might prove useful. An elated Krishipal updated Police Commissioner M. N. Singh. Commissioner Singh, along with Krishipal and his two DCPs, then rushed to the STF's legal adviser, P. R. Vakil. After perusing the reports, Vakil opined that the evidence against Bal Thackeray was feeble and wouldn't stand up to legal scrutiny. However, in his view, a criminal case could be registered against Tyagi after analysing the circumstances mentioned in the commission's report and fetching more evidence.

Krishipal asked Vakil to provide his opinion about Bal Thackeray's case in writing, but the counsellor's stenographer wasn't available. Hence, Commissioner Singh called his stenographer Ramani for the job. Krishipal and Ramani then sat late into the night with Vakil to prepare a detailed opinion letter.

The next day, Krishipal brought the letter to the CM's

official bungalow, accompanied by Commissioner Singh. Deputy CM Bhujbal was also present for their meeting with Deshmukh.

'So, Raghuvanshi saheb, when are you registering a case against Bal Thackeray?' Deshmukh asked.

Just as Krishipal was about to reply, Commissioner Singh raised a hand, signalling for him not to speak. He interjected, 'Sir, P. R. Vakil is taking some time to opine on Thackeray. However, a case can be registered against Tyagi straightaway.'

Krishipal was surprised. No preparation had been made to arrest Tyagi, but Commissioner Singh had suddenly proposed the move to the CM. Glad to see progress on the STF's investigation, Deshmukh asked Krishipal to go ahead and register a case against Tyagi.

On the journey back from the CM's bungalow, Krishipal cautioned Commissioner Singh that it would be hasty to arrest Tyagi. Singh dismissed his concerns and said that the process to file a case against Tyagi must be expedited. Krishipal was left wondering why Singh had made such a proposition to the CM. To avoid another reprimand for Deshmukh and Bhujbal, or show that the STF had finally done some concrete work? Or had it been an impulsive statement?

Regardless, the STF collected all available material pertaining to the firing incident and submitted it to Vakil for his legal opinion. After a careful review, Vakil had a detailed discussion with Krishipal, DCP Sayyad and the investigating officer of the case. He opined that Tyagi, being in charge of the operation, had been aware that an AK-47 was a deadly weapon. It had the potential to kill a large number of people and shouldn't have been used in a case related to civil policing. Generally, police may use non-automatic rifles to disperse a violent mob if other measures like lathi-charge and tear gas have failed. Automatic weapons are used only in operations against armed terrorists or gangsters. Hence, Vakil opined that a case of murder could be registered against Tyagi and the SOS members who had opened fire in the bakery.

Based on Vakil's advice, an FIR was registered under Indian Penal Code (IPC) sections 302 and 307, for murder and attempt to murder respectively. Tyagi applied for anticipatory bail in the Bombay High Court as soon as he learnt of the case registered against him. However, his plea was rejected and he was asked to surrender before the STF. As a last resort, Tyagi submitted a Special Leave Petition in the Supreme Court. This was rejected as well.

Meanwhile, the STF expedited the investigation and approached the Home Department to get sanction to prosecute Tyagi. This was mandatory since the incident pertained to a period when Tyagi was in the service, and the case was related to his official duty.

Shortly after the Supreme Court rejection, the STF received a message from Tyagi, stating that he was coming to the STF to surrender. At 11 a.m. on 14 August 2001, Tyagi left his home in Worli for the STF office. En route, he complained of chest pain and was driven to Bombay

Hospital. Around noon, he was admitted to Intensive Care Cardiac Unit.[3]

Krishipal was in a dilemma. Was it justified to arrest a man in his sixties who had been hospitalized? He sought P. R. Vakil's opinion. The counsellor reverted that since Tyagi had intimated the STF about his surrender, they were duty-bound to arrest him. Hence, Tyagi was placed under arrest that very day, while he was still admitted in the hospital. An armed police guard was deployed outside his ward and nobody except the medical staff was allowed to visit him.

In 1984–5, Tyagi was the police commissioner of Thane. As a DCP, Krishipal reported to him. Although Tyagi was Krishipal's boss in Thane, in later years they had developed a friendly relationship. Krishipal saw Tyagi as his well-wisher and often sought his guidance on professional matters. Once, when Krishipal was posted at the CBI's Delhi headquarters, Tyagi – then director general of the National Security Guard – had invited him for lunch at his residence. When Krishipal had asked about his retirement plans, Tyagi had laughed and said, 'Let me retire peacefully first. I can't say anything right now because they [the Maharashtra government] can put me in jail.' At the time, Krishipal had no idea that he would be the one to arrest Tyagi, just a few years later.

On 28 August 2001, the STF filed a chargesheet against Tyagi in court.[4] After a few days, he got bail. In April 2003, he was discharged from the case without a trial.

22

CHHAGAN BHUJBAL VS BAL THACKERAY

'Not just Mumbai, but the whole of India will burn if I am arrested.'

Bal Thackeray issued this threat to Police Commissioner M. N. Singh over a phone call on 23 July 2000. Despite being aware of the ramifications for Mumbai's law and order, Singh went ahead and arrested Thackeray two days later. Singh had to bend to the 'obstinacy' of Chhagan Bhujbal – then Maharashtra's home minister as well as deputy CM. Bhujbal was allegedly driven by a 'personal vendetta' against his former mentor Thackeray and with the reins of the city police in his hands, he wasn't prepared to miss the opportunity.[1]

Bhujbal's feud with Thackeray dated back to December 1991, when he led a rebellion in the Shiv Sena and joined the Congress along with eighteen MLAs. Once a staunch supporter and confidant of party supremo Thackeray, Bhujbal had started to feel sidelined in the party. Bhujbal's rebellion – engineered with the help of Sharad Pawar, who belonged to the rival Congress – not only weakened the Shiv Sena's presence in the Vidhan Sabha but also tarnished Thackeray's reputation. The supremo ruled the party with an iron fist and none of its members dared to stand against him. In a fit of rage, Thackeray labelled Bhujbal a traitor and publicly referred to him as Lakhoba, a conman from a popular Marathi play.[2]

In 1997, two years after the BJP–Shiv Sena alliance formed the government, Thackeray decided to punish Bhujbal for his rebellion in a more tangible way. Despite being the Leader of the Opposition in the Vidhan Parishad and having been allocated an official bungalow at Nariman Point, Bhujbal suddenly had his Z-category security withdrawn. On the morning of 13 July 2000, hundreds of Shiv Sena workers attacked his bungalow. They search the entire structure for Bhujbal, who had locked himself in a room. Failing to locate him, the enraged workers proceeded to vandalize the bungalow, destroying furniture, official documents and computers.

Five years later, the tides had turned. Thackeray's party had been ousted from power as a new era began with the formation of the Congress–NCP government. Bhujbal had aligned himself with Sharad Pawar following the latter's departure from the Congress to establish the NCP. This led to his appointment as deputy CM along with the coveted charge of home minister.

Under the previous saffron government, nearly all cases against Bal Thackeray had been withdrawn. However, during a review of old cases, Bhujbal had stumbled upon one that remained unresolved. Dating back to 1993, the case accused Thackeray of penning inflammatory articles aimed at sowing discord between religious groups under Section 153A of the IPC. Notably, such cases required sanction from either the central or state government for the prosecution to proceed. Ironically, despite the offense occurring during the Congress's tenure, no decision had been made.

Seven years later, in July 2000, Bhujbal now had significant authority. He granted the Mumbai Police the necessary sanction, thereby clearing a path for Thackeray's arrest.[3] However, the case against Thackeray was dismissed on grounds of it being time-barred, since it had been over seven years since the incident in question.[4]

Soon, he found that the Srikrishna Commission's report might provide another opportunity to arrest Thackeray.

While indicting Bal Thackeray, the commission had heavily relied upon an affidavit filed by Marathi journalist Yuvraj Mohite. As per Mohite, when the riots were in full swing on 8 January 1993, he met with Chandrakant Handore, then mayor of Bombay. The journalist suggested that a memorandum be signed by the leaders of political parties and Bombay's Muslim community to appeal for the restoration of peace. Accordingly, a handwritten memorandum was prepared. Handore then asked Mohite to accompany him while meeting the leaders to get the memorandum signed. After getting the signature of smuggler-turned-politician Haji Mastan, they went to Bal Thackeray's bungalow. The mayor had asked Mohite not to reveal that he was a journalist in front of Thackeray.

According to the affidavit, while Handore was persuading Thackeray to sign the memorandum, the Shiv Sena leader received several phone calls. Mohite overheard Thackeray instructing his party workers to attack Muslims. During one of the calls, Thackeray allegedly ordered that not a single Muslim should survive to give oral evidence. In his words, the riots had begun in Muslim areas and the arrogance of the Muslims had to be put to an end. On another call, he said that A. A. Khan – an IPS officer posted as additional commissioner (Western Mumbai) – should be eliminated. During the meeting, other party leaders like Madhukar Sarpotdar and Ramesh More also allegedly arrived at the bungalow and briefed Thackeray about the situation in their respective areas. He gave similar instructions to them as well. In a call to a party functionary in Mazgaon, Thackeray specified that Bohri Muslims residing in a particular building must not be harmed.

After much persuasion, Thackeray agreed to sign the peace memorandum. However, he was irked to see Haji Mastan's signature on the document and refused to sign, lambasting Handore for approaching him.[5]

Based on Mohite's narration of the meeting, the commission concluded, 'From 8th January 1993 at least there is no doubt that the Shiv Sena and Shiv Sainiks took the lead in organizing attacks on Muslims and their properties under the guidance of several leaders of the Shiv Sena from the level of *Shakha Pramukh* to the Shiv Sena *Pramukh* Bal Thackeray who, like a veteran General, commanded his loyal Shiv Sainiks to retaliate by organised attacks against Muslims.'[6]

These were the details brought forward by the STF when they discussed the case with P. R. Vakil. Justice Srikrishna's conclusion had been solely based on the affidavit filed by Mohite about a conversation that had happened in a closed room where only three people were present – Thackeray, Handore and Mohite himself. Vakil opined that if Mohite's affidavit was treated as an FIR, Handore's statement as an independent witness was vital. Without Handore verifying the version of events narrated by Mohite, the FIR wouldn't hold up to legal scrutiny. He advised that, before registering an FIR, Handore's statement should be recorded.

On Vakil's advice, the STF approached both Mohite and Handore to record their statements. However, Mohite immediately refused and insisted that whatever he had to say had been captured by the Srikrishna Commission in his affidavit. Perhaps he was not eager to get embroiled in the hassle of court processes. On the other hand, Handore kept dilly-dallying about his response. With neither of the witnesses willing to go on record, it was difficult for the STF to proceed.

Around the same time, some social activists approached the Supreme Court and complained that the STF was not doing its job diligently. The court directed the Maharashtra government to file an affidavit detailing the action that had been taken. Krishipal filed the affidavit – over 100 pages long – with details about the procedure being followed and its results. He was personally present in the courtroom during the hearing. The court was satisfied with the STF's progress and didn't make any adverse remarks.

Despite the Supreme Court taking note of the STF's efforts, Krishipal had to face the heat from his political bosses back home in Maharashtra. One day, DGP Subhash Malhotra summoned him to discuss the progress made by the STF. During the meeting, Krishipal kept his phone on silent mode. An hour later, he checked his phone only to see two missed calls from Chhagan Bhujbal's office. He immediately called back and the operator connected him to Bhujbal.

The deputy CM's tone was curt. 'What kind of Raghavanshi, Suryavanshi ... whatever ... are you? Why are you scared of arresting Bal Thackeray? Why are you not filing the case? Are you above a High Court judge? If a judge has indicted Thackeray, what is stopping you?'

Krishipal explained that Handore's statement was vital for the case, but he wasn't cooperating. Bhujbal was not satisfied by this explanation and demanded, 'Why are you so afraid of arresting of Bal Thackeray when the whole government is behind you?'

'I am not afraid, sir. There are 100 policemen posted at his residence. I just have to go there and announce that he is under arrest. I don't want the government and police to be embarrassed like last year when Thackeray was arrested,' Krishipal said firmly.

'People are asking me: Tyagi has been arrested, but what about Bal Thackeray?'

'Sir, please get me the statement of Chandrakant Handore. Once I have that, a case will be registered and Bal Thackeray arrested the very next moment.'

Krishipal found himself astounded by Bhujbal's apparent disregard for official police protocol for the sake of prompt action. The city had been ensnared by the menacing underworld. Blood stained its streets almost daily due to relentless gang activity and rivalries. Numerous film personalities and businessmen had been targeted for extortion, adding to the atmosphere of fear and insecurity. Given this dire state of affairs, Krishipal couldn't help but question the wisdom of engaging in actions that risked further destabilizing law and order in Mumbai and potentially sparking riots. He felt as if there was no room for prudence and the decisions he was being pressured to carry out threatened to exacerbate the already precarious situation.

Bhujbal said that he would ask CM Deshmukh to arrange a meeting between Handore and the STF. Accordingly, a few days later, Deshmukh called a meeting at his office which was attended by Handore, Bhujbal, Kripashankar Singh, M. N. Singh, Subhash Malhotra and the additional chief secretary (Home). Krishipal briefed the attendees about the case and explained why Handore's statement was necessary to nail Thackeray. After Krishipal spoke his turn, the CM asked Handore to give his statement to the STF. He reluctantly agreed and said that he would record his statement soon. The meeting ended on a happy note. However, looking at Handore's body language, Krishipal was doubtful that he would appear before the STF.

Krishipal waited for about two weeks, but there was no communication from Handore. Finally, one afternoon, his personal assistant came to the STF office to deliver a letter written by him. In the brief note, Handore only said that no such incident had taken place on 8 January 1993.

Vakil advised that, in light of the negative statement by Handore, it would be imprudent to register an FIR against Thackeray. It would only meet the same fate as the earlier case against him. Vakil warned that even if the STF registered a case suo moto, it would be quashed in the first hearing. The same was conveyed to Deshmukh and Bhujbal, and the plan to arrest Bal Thackeray was dropped.

23

TERRORISM, BOLLYWOOD AND ABU SALEM

Beyond the borders of Jammu and Kashmir and the north-eastern states, Mumbai stands out as a part of India that has weathered a significant number of terrorist onslaughts. Among these, the serial bombings on 12 March 1993 marked a dark chapter in the city's history – the most devastating terrorist attack on Indian soil in terms of casualties, duration and geographical reach at the time. Orchestrated by Pakistan's intelligence agency Inter-Services Intelligence (ISI) in collaboration with the notorious gangster Dawood Ibrahim Kaskar, the mayhem claimed the lives of 257 individuals, leaving nearly 700 injured. These brutal acts were perceived as a grim aftermath of the 1992–3 communal riots that were ignited by the demolition of the Babri Masjid in Ayodhya.

Following a brief interlude, terror resurged in Mumbai from December 2002. A series of harrowing attacks plunged the city into a state of constant apprehension.

Mumbai often bore the brunt of events unfolding in distant corners of the country and this was no exception. On 27 February 2002, fifty-nine Hindu pilgrims died and several others were injured in a tragic train fire in Godhra, Gujarat. Anti-Muslim riots ensued, which have since been attributed to the alleged inaction of the ruling BJP government in Gujarat and its purported complicity in the violence against the minority community.[1]

In a bid to avenge the Gujarat carnage, radical Muslim groups targeted Hindu Gujaratis residing in Mumbai, exploiting the sizable Gujarati population scattered across its suburbs. Their primary modus operandi was striking public transport and crowded locales within these areas. The initial salvo occurred on 2 December 2002, when a bomb detonated aboard a BEST bus outside Ghatkopar railway station. Subsequent blasts unfolded in rapid succession: at a McDonald's outlet in Mumbai Central station on 5 December 2002, a bustling Vile Parle market in January 2003 and aboard a local train in Mulund in March 2003.

On 28 July 2003, the city witnessed yet another bomb explosion aboard a BEST bus in Ghatkopar. The horror reached a crescendo with twin blasts on 25 August 2003. These were coordinated attacks that targeted taxis parked at the iconic Gateway of India and the bustling Zaveri Bazar, claiming the lives of sixty individuals and injuring over 100 more. These events now serve as poignant reminders of Mumbai's resilience in the face of adversity, but at the time, they underscored the city's vulnerability to ripples of violence emanating from afar.

Thus, it became clear that in the new century, the foremost challenge for the Mumbai Police was resisting terrorism. Indian intelligences agencies reported that the grand plan of the ISI was to spread terror in the hinterland of the country.[2] Hence, the central government advised various states to set up their own counter-terror forces. The crime branch of the Mumbai Police had evolved to combat underworld activities, but terrorism was a totally different ball game. Gangsters killed for money, while terrorists were radicalized youngsters filled with hatred and a desire for vengeance. A need was felt to raise a specialized unit which could deal with cases related to terrorism.

In the early 1990s, a team was raised under additional commissioner Aftab Ahmad Khan, named the Anti-Terrorism Squad. The unit had conducted a few successful operations against Khalistani militants and Dawood Ibrahim's infamous D-Company gang. However, it was shortly disbanded. Now, once again, the top brass of Mumbai's police and political establishment were looking to come up with a terror-fighting team along similar lines.

One afternoon in 2004, Krishipal received an unexpected call from his friend Ahmad Javed, then serving as the joint commissioner of Law and Order in the Mumbai Police. Javed disclosed that Police Commissioner Anami Roy had expressed a keen interest in appointing Krishipal to head the newly proposed counter-terrorism unit. Caught off guard by this sudden proposal, Krishipal felt unprepared for such a significant responsibility. After navigating two stressful years with the STF, he had been relishing a more tranquil tenure as IGP, Konkan Range since March 2002.

His time as head of the STF had highlighted the immense challenges inherent to establishing a completely new unit, starting from the lengthy process involved in acquiring even the most basic resources. Javed clarified that the position would hold the rank of joint commissioner within the Mumbai Police Commissionerate, offering Krishipal an enticing opportunity to be part of one of India's most esteemed law enforcement agencies. Still, Krishipal couldn't ignore the daunting nature of the appointment. Although this would be his third time leading a nascent unit – after the C-60 and the STF – this would be an entirely new level of responsibility. Considering the number of bureaucratic and political hoops he had had to jump through for the first two, Krishipal wasn't sure he wanted to repeat the experience.

He requested time to deliberate and discussed the proposal with Sarita and their children after returning home that evening. Garima and Abhijeet staunchly advocated for the new posting, encouraging their father to seize the opportunity. 'Dad, you love challenges. Say yes,' Garima cheered.

Reflecting on his daughter's counsel, Krishipal had to acknowledge that the new role would present him with an entirely different set of challenges. While he had previously navigated the complexities of handling rioters and Naxals, terrorism posed a novel threat, one that would involve safeguarding India's internal security. Recognizing the chance to confront this formidable adversary head-on, he made the decision to accept the offer. In due course, the transfer order arrived, marking his transition to the hallowed halls of the Mumbai Police Commissionerate.

Upon meeting Commissioner Roy, Krishipal was entrusted with his new responsibilities, accompanied by a two-page government resolution (GR) outlining his mandate. As he emerged from Roy's office and perused the contents of the GR, a sense of apprehension washed over him. It dawned upon Krishipal that he once again had to confront the immense task of building something from the ground up. The GR stipulated the allocation of a few key resources: two DIGs or additional CPs, two SPs or DCPs, eight inspectors and eight sub-inspectors. Yet conspicuously absent were provisions for any additional staff, including constables or clerical support. Not even a stenographer had been designated.

Amidst this shortage of manpower, Krishipal grappled with the pivotal question of where his squad would be headquartered. The predicament echoed the challenges he had faced when tasked with establishing the STF four years prior. Commissioner Roy instructed the crime branch to allocate a hall for Krishipal's temporary use until a permanent office could be established. However, the reception from the crime branch personnel was less than welcoming. They perceived the new force as a potential rival, evident in their aloof behaviour towards Krishipal and his team. This sense of isolation left Krishipal feeling marginalized. He found himself reliant on others for even the most basic necessities, resorting to borrowing stationery items from Ahmad Javed's office.

The situation was unsustainable and Krishipal soon began scouting for a place to set up a permanent office. Other police units proved reluctant to share their facilities. The traffic police headquarters in Worli initially seemed promising, but Krishipal's request to utilize the vacant space was refused by the joint commissioner of traffic, who cited plans for its future use as a traffic control room. Another potential location Krishipal explored was within the premises of the DCP office in Bandra Kurla Complex. However, his hopes were dashed when the DCP expressed concerns about the unit's functionality due to the space already being shared with the BKC police station. Despite numerous setbacks, Krishipal's perseverance ultimately paid off when Commissioner Roy intervened, issuing an order permitting the unit to establish its office within the Traffic Training Institute in Byculla.

The ground floor of the building housed the additional commissioner (South), while half of the first floor was dedicated to the office of the DCP, Zone-2. The remaining space was allocated for the Traffic Training Institute. Manoeuvring around these constraints, Krishipal established his office. The interiors were revamped and wooden partitions were erected to create functional cabins. The retiring room of DCP, Zone-2 was repurposed into an office for the DCP attached to Krishipal's team.

Recognizing the need for essential resources,

Commissioner Roy allocated funds from the Secret Service Fund, enabling Krishipal to procure the necessary equipment and supplies to ensure the operational effectiveness of his team. To fortify the unit's capabilities, Krishipal strategically recruited officers renowned for their stellar performance and sharp detective skills from other police units to fill vacant positions. He also inducted twenty new recruits from the headquarters to serve as constables within his team.

Though several 'encounter specialist' cops expressed interest in joining the team, Krishipal remained steadfast in his refusal, mindful of their controversial reputations and political affiliations. These encounter specialists often behaved like members of organized crime syndicates and extortionists themselves. Some of them had been accused of killing people in cold blood for selfish motives. Krishipal believed that killing a criminal should be the last resort for cops, only when it becomes necessary to save the lives of oneself and others. Intent on maintaining the integrity and credibility of his squad, Krishipal opted to keep such officers at arm's length.

With the logistical hurdles of office space and staffing successfully navigated, Krishipal now faced the formidable task of delivering tangible results for the newly established organization, dubbed the Anti-Terrorism Squad.

In alignment with the directives outlined in the GR, Krishipal meticulously structured the ATS into two distinct units. The first unit was designated to handle cases within Mumbai, while the second unit assumed responsibility for the remainder of Maharashtra. Each unit was to be overseen by an officer holding the rank of additional commissioner, with a deputy commissioner positioned under their command – a hierarchical structure conducive to efficient operations and streamlined coordination.

Krishipal reached out to specialized counter-terrorism units in other states, such as the Gujarat ATS, the Special Cell of the Delhi Police and the STF of the Uttar Pradesh Police, seeking insights and cooperation. While he received support and collaboration from officers in other states, the atmosphere within his own commissionerate remained frosty. The general feeling of the crime branch officials was that the ATS was a potential competitor. So far, the crime branch had occupied the limelight and been romanticized by the press and Bollywood. The personnel attached to the crime branch had a sense of superiority over other wings of the Mumbai Police. This divide became evident when Krishipal attempted to access the telephone surveillance unit of the crime branch, only to be met with avoidance and excuses from its officials.

Fortunately, DCP Jai Jeet Singh, assigned to the ATS, proved to be a valuable asset due to his technological know-how. In a remarkably short span of time, he established an independent surveillance unit for the ATS, thus ending its dependency on the crime branch for intercepting telephonic communications of suspects. This development was significant, given the ATS officers' concerns about the crime branch potentially compromising their information or appropriating credit for cracking cases.

Krishipal further bolstered his team by bringing on board Additional CP Subodh Jaiswal, renowned for his investigation of the high-profile Telgi scam. Jaiswal had succeeded Krishipal as SP, Gadchiroli in 1992. He also recommended the induction of an officer returning from a deputation in the esteemed spy agency, Research and Analysis Wing (RAW). With the customary ritual of breaking a coconut to signify the commencement of their endeavours, Krishipal and his team were ready to embark on their mission and confront the challenges ahead with resolve.

However, in an ironic twist of fate, terrorist activities in Mumbai seemed to come to an unexpected halt shortly after the establishment of the ATS. In stark contrast to the preceding year, which had witnessed five separate bomb explosions claiming the lives of approximately eighty individuals, the sudden lull left the ATS seemingly without purpose.

A full year after its inception, the ATS was struggling to demonstrate significant achievements. In its initial operations, the ATS had managed to intercept a carbine smuggled into Mumbai, followed by similar instances where locally manufactured weapons were confiscated and minor offenders apprehended. However, these incidents raised concerns regarding the delineation of the ATS's role. Hadn't the ATS been envisioned as a specialized agency tasked with countering terrorism? Its involvement in routine policing tasks raised doubts about its effectiveness in fulfilling its designated mandate and its distinctiveness from conventional police units like the crime branch.

In November 2005, Commissioner Roy called Krishipal for an evening meeting at his office. Senior officers from the crime branch were also present. Roy revealed that finally, after a long legal battle, the Portuguese government had agreed to repatriate the infamous gangster Abu Salem. Out of the nine cases registered against him in various cities of India, three were related to Mumbai. He was one of the conspirators in the 12 March 1993 serial blasts in Mumbai which led to terror charges being files against him.[3] The others were murder cases – of Ajit Dewani, who was the secretary of actress Manisha Koirala, and a builder named Pradeep Jain.[4,5] The CBI was the prosecuting agency on the serial bombings case, but the prosecuting agencies for the killings of Dewani and Jain were yet to be fixed. Since Salem had been booked under TADA in the Jain murder case, the commissioner suggested that the ATS would be the right agency to handle the case. Krishipal readily agreed. At last, the ATS was going to handle a case worth its brief.

Abu Salem, whose real name was Abdul Qayyum Ansari, hailed from Azamgarh in Uttar Pradesh. He had first arrived in Mumbai in search of employment but found a different calling instead. While switching between different jobs, he got in touch with Dawood Ibrahim's brother, Anees Ibrahim. Soon he was inducted into the D-Company and rapidly climbed the ranks due to his ability to recruit hitmen from UP. He became the representative of the gang in Bollywood. He extorted money, organized *filmi* shows in Dubai where actors and singers were summoned to dance and sing and settled disputes among the film fraternity. One of the most sensational crimes he orchestrated was the murder of T-Series baron Gulshan Kumar in broad daylight, outside a temple in Mumbai.[6]

During his interactions with Bollywood personalities, Salem was introduced to actress Monica Bedi in Dubai. Salem and Bedi soon started living together. The author of this book got the opportunity to visit Monica Bedi's parental home in Norway in November 2005. Her father Premkumar Bedi told the author that Salem had visited them once and introduced himself as Sanjay. In 1997, Salem separated from the D-Company and started running his own gang. He and Bedi began shuttling across the world, while he ran his operation over the phone.

Killings and extortion calls from Salem to film personalities and builders became frequent. In 2002, Interpol issued a Red Corner Notice for him at the behest of Mumbai Police. Such a notice is an alert and request by Interpol to law enforcement agencies worldwide, to detain an accused wanted for serious crimes. Ultimately, Salem was apprehended in Portugal alongside Monica Bedi in September of that year.

Salem vigorously contested his extradition to India. However, his legal battle ended in defeat as the court in Lisbon ruled in favour of handing him over to Indian authorities, albeit subject to certain conditions. These included safeguards against capital punishment, a maximum prison sentence not exceeding twenty-five years and prosecution solely for the eight cases that had been presented before the court. In November 2005, Salem was extradited to India, marking a significant victory for law enforcement in their relentless pursuit of justice.

After the CBI remand in the Mumbai blast case ended, the ATS took over Salem's remand in the Pradeep Jain murder case. Salem had demanded a part of the builder's property at the behest of Anees Ibrahim. Over the telephone, Jain abused Ibrahim. An enraged Ibrahim then ordered Salem to kill him. On 7 March 1995, Jain was gunned down at his office in Andheri. Salem was finally being prosecuted for the case a decade later. Krishipal realized that this would not be an easy task – his team would be required to trace witnesses from ten years ago and convince them to testify in court against a formidable gang leader. Fortunately for the ATS, the brother of the deceased, Sunil Jain, was standing his ground and supporting their case against Salem.

The menacing reputation of Salem cast a palpable shadow over the ATS officers tasked with investigating his case. One senior officer confided in Krishipal that the sub inspectors had experienced noticeable intimidation during Salem's interrogation. Apparently they were so unnerved by his presence that they couldn't even muster the courage to meet his gaze while questioning him.

The interrogation room where Salem was brought in for questioning was adjacent to Krishipal's own cabin. One fateful day, as Krishipal was settling into his office, he caught a glimpse of the interrogation room since its door was slightly ajar. What he witnessed left him incensed. Salem sat on the floor while the interrogating officer, though positioned directly in front of him, refused to meet his eyes. Instead their gaze was focused on the wall throughout the interrogation. This stark display of apprehension only confirmed Krishipal's concerns. He retreated into his cabin and later called upon the officer to give them a piece of his mind.

'Tell me, how much has this bastard vomited?'

'Sir, he is too smart. He is speaking about the other cases for which he is not being prosecuted but not about our case.'

As Krishipal was about to reprimand the officer, his peon entered the room and informed him that the brother of one of Salem's victims wanted to meet him. With Krishipal's permission, the timid-looking, slim man of middling height was allowed in. He pleaded, 'Sir, I beg you to let me see the face of that man who killed my brother. I know you will do your best to get him punished but seeing him just once will give me peace and a sense of closure.'

Since the man had to appear as the prosecution's witness in court, Krishipal couldn't refuse his request. On

Krishipal's instruction, two constables brought Salem into the room and stood in the corner. The victim's brother lost his cool after seeing Salem and pounced towards him, shouting, '*Madarchod*! *Kayar*! *Begunaah aadmi ko maar kar don banta hai*?' (Motherfucker! Coward! You claim to be a don by killing innocents?) He was about to slap Salem, but the constables overpowered him with great difficulty. The victim's brother then took off his shoes to strike Salem but was held back by the constables before he could do so. He continued to shout expletives while being pushed out of the ATS's office.

Once Salem had been escorted out of the cabin, a solemn atmosphere settled within the room. Krishipal's gaze shifted towards the officer seated before him. 'A common man could summon the courage to confront a notorious criminal yet police officers shrink away from meeting the gaze of those they interrogate,' he remarked in a tone of sober reproach. 'It is a shameful state of affairs.'

The officer understood who the remark was directed towards and looked towards the floor, ashamed. His point made, Krishipal asked the officer to sit beside him and take notes. 'Now I will interrogate Abu Salem,' he said.

Krishipal was struck by the stark disparity between Salem's appearance and the fearsome reputation that preceded him. Contrary to expectations, Salem possessed the demeanour of a Hindi film hero; soft-spoken in a way that belied his notorious image. Yet there was an unmistakable aura of confidence about him, devoid of remorse, as he faced Krishipal.

In response to Krishipal's inquiries, Salem offered a candid account of his journey from Azamgarh to Mumbai in the early eighties, recounting his humble beginnings in menial jobs before he delved into the underworld. With remarkable transparency, he detailed his ascent within the ranks of the D-Company, pulling back the curtain on his dominance in Bollywood and the profound influence he wielded over the industry's elite. Salem didn't shy away from revealing his associations with prominent Bollywood figures, boasting of friendships with several A-list stars, including one of the esteemed 'Khans' of the film fraternity. He confidently claimed that this Khan would respond to his messages within a mere twenty-four hours, underscoring the depth of their relationship.

Salem made everyone in the room laugh when he narrated his encounter with film star Sanjay Dutt. According to him, Anees Ibrahim had smuggled a consignment of weapons into Mumbai and asked Salem to deliver a few guns to Dutt. '*Vo ek-ek rifle ko utha kar aise dekh raha tha jaise ki log ganna khareedte hain.*' (He was examining each and every rifle, just like people examine sugarcanes before buying them.) A special TADA court later convicted Dutt under the Arms Act, 1959 for illegal possession of firearms and sentenced him to six years of imprisonment.[7]

During his interrogation, Salem disclosed the names of actresses whom he had helped get jobs in the film industry. He also revealed those film personalities whom he had targeted for extortion. Among his victims was Rakesh Roshan, a prominent Hindi film producer. Roshan had been injured by shooters hired by Salem days after the release of his movie *Kaho Na ... Pyaar Hai* (2000), his son Hrithik's debut.[8] Salem claimed that he had extorted a large amount of money from Roshan.[9]

Based on Salem's confession, Krishipal thought of contacting his victims to ascertain the veracity of his claims and check whether fresh cases could be filed against him. Accordingly, many film personalities were asked to give statements to the ATS, but they were too scared to cooperate. Rakesh Roshan reluctantly agreed to meet Krishipal under the condition that he would only talk inside his vanity van. Perhaps he didn't want to be seen interacting with a cop. Krishipal drove to the set of Roshan's upcoming movie in Film City and was directed to the vanity van, where Roshan was already waiting for him.

When Krishipal asked Roshan to narrate how Salem had harassed him, he pleaded with folded hands, 'Sir, a long time has passed. I don't want any turbulence in my life. I don't want to pursue the matter.'

Krishipal returned empty-handed, realizing that although Salem was behind bars and would remain there for many years, his terror was still pervasive in the film industry. He spoke to Monica Bedi too, who told him that Salem was very violent and often used to beat her. She admitted that proximity with Salem had destroyed her career in the film industry and soured her relationship with her family.[10]

On 12 January 2006, when the ATS produced Salem

before the special court to extend his custody, he created a sensation by alleging torture. He told Judge P. V. Bavkar, '*Sahab, in logon ne mujhe* belt *se maara. Peet-peet kar confession likhwaya.*' (Sir, these people hit me with a belt and beat me until I wrote a confession.) Salem alleged that the ATS officers had mentally tortured him and subjected him to 'third degree' – coercive, unlawful – methods of interrogation. He complained of dizziness and requested a chair in the witness box to sit on during the hearing.[11]

Ujjwal Nikam, the special public prosecutor, contested Salem's allegations and called him a 'cunning wolf' who had been tutored to lie.[12] Salem's claims of coercion and torture were widely reported by the media, forcing Krishipal to issue a statement. In it, he called Salem a compulsive liar and his allegations, an afterthought. 'The ATS is committed to professionalism and upkeep of human rights of all accused in its custody,' the statement clarified.[13]

The Abu Salem case catapulted the ATS into the spotlight, a stark departure from its previous obscurity. Ironically, the notorious criminal they had apprehended helped the organization gain recognition. There was renewed sense of purpose and morale among the ATS officers, who had previously lamented the lack of substantive work. The case not only restored faith in the organization but also attracted informants to its ranks, leading to a surge in actionable intelligence regarding various criminal activities such as counterfeit currency operations, arms smuggling and narcotics trafficking. Operating within a vast domain, the ATS's responsibilities encompassed a wide array of tasks, ranging from gathering intel and conducting counter-terrorism operations to investigating cases of terror financing and narco-terrorism. This multifaceted approach emphasized the agency's pivotal role in safeguarding national security and combatting threats posed by terrorism and organized crime.

A colleague of Krishipal's once told him in jest, 'Abu Salem *ne toh* ATS *ka udghatan kar diya*.' (Abu Salem has inaugurated the ATS.) All the publicity and praise was not in vain – while at the ATS, Krishipal ensured that a watertight case was made against Salem. He convinced relevant witnesses to depose fearlessly before the trial court and expose the truth. Holding frequent discussions with the prosecutors, he kept himself updated about the progress of the trial. Another decade later, in February 2015, Abu Salem was convicted and sentenced to life in prison for the Jain murder case.[14]

24

OPERATION AMANAT

After nabbing Abu Salem, the ATS was all over the news. Team morale was high and the police establishment started looking at theirs as a unit with great potential.

Gradually, the initial hurdles that had plagued the squad began to dissipate, paving the way for smoother operations. As 2005 drew to a close, the ATS witnessed a surge in allocation of manpower and resources, signifying a new-found support for its endeavours. Concurrently, Indian intelligence agencies began actively collaborating with ATS officers, sharing valuable insights and information crucial for counter-terrorism efforts.

In October 2005, Krishipal received a call from Pratap Kulkarni, a retired officer from a central agency who had been his friend for over three decades. Kulkarni gave him a mobile number and instructed, 'Keep a track of this. You will get something.'

The number was immediately put under surveillance.

A monitored conversation revealed that it belonged to an apple businessman named Irfan Dar who lived in Budgam, Kashmir. Dar and his employee Naved (name changed) often came to Navi Mumbai to sell their produce. In another conversation, it became apparent that the businessman was in touch with Syed Salahuddin, a dreaded Kashmiri terrorist.

Born in Budgam, Salahuddin's real name was Mohammed Yusuf Shah.[1] In the early 1980s, he had become affiliated with terrorist organizations in the region. In time, he became a leader of the Hizbul Mujahideen, a Pakistan-affiliated militant organization responsible for several violent incidents in Jammu and Kashmir. Salahuddin operated from Pakistan Occupied Kashmir (PoK) and headed the United Jihad Council, a conglomeration of terrorist groups based in Pakistan.[2]

While talking to Dar, Salahuddin had mentioned Mumbai numerous times, which alarmed the ATS. Krishipal feared that something sinister was being planned and decided to personally pursue the case. Irfan had described his plan to travel to Mumbai by train, while Naved would come to the city via the truck transporting their goods. They were set to attend the Agricultural Produce Market Committee's market in Navi Mumbai. Krishipal realized that it was crucial to track Irfan and Naved in order to pre-empt the conspiracy.

He swiftly devised a plan to gather more intel, utilizing one of his inspectors to establish a rapport with Naved, who was oblivious to his employer's sinister connections.

The inspector, in the guise of a potential customer, initiated a dialogue with Naved, gradually cultivating a friendly relationship. Naved, a towering figure with a fair complexion and distinctive long nose, eventually warmed up to these overtures, especially since the inspector consistently purchased substantial quantities of apples from him.

As their acquaintance deepened, the inspector subtly hinted at a business opportunity for Naved. He disclosed that his 'boss', who had sampled and appreciated the quality of Naved's apples, had expressed an interest in placing a significant order. Intrigued by the prospect of securing a lucrative deal, Naved eagerly accepted an invitation to meet this potential client. The inspector led Naved to a guest house in Navi Mumbai, where he was introduced to Krishipal.

'I need 20 kilos of apples but they should be of the best quality. I have to gift them to some guests at my home,' Krishipal said.

'Don't worry, sir. No other Kashmiri brings the kind of apples that I do. Our apples don't just shine; they are very tasty, too. Don't pay me if you are not satisfied with the quality.'

'Okay. If they really are as good as you say, I will even consider ordering more.'

After the deal was struck and an advance of ₹2,000 paid, Krishipal enquired about life in Kashmir and Naved's family. The next stage of their plan had been put into motion.

Over the course of around three months, Krishipal effectively nurtured his friendship with Naved, fostering a sense of trust and camaraderie between them. Through regular interactions whenever the merchant visited Mumbai, he successfully earned Naved's confidence. After biding his time, during one of their meetings, Krishipal disclosed his true identity as a senior police officer.

Initially taken aback, Naved soon recognized the potential benefits of having an ally within law enforcement. Having such a connection could potentially alleviate the challenges he faced as a trader, like the extortionate practices of the local traffic police. Krishipal assured Naved of his support with a reassuring smile. 'In case you encounter any trouble in Mumbai, don't hesitate to reach out to me,' Krishipal affirmed, cementing their burgeoning alliance.

Naved was pleasantly surprised by the warm and respectful treatment he received from Krishipal, a stark contrast to his previous experiences with law enforcement, both within and outside of J&K. He was accustomed to encounters marked by scepticism and hostility. Krishipal's genuine kindness and consideration towards him, despite his humble occupation as a fruit vendor, left Naved feeling gratified and valued. It was a rare for a senior police officer to extend such cordiality to someone in his position, prompting Naved to reconsider his preconceptions about the police.

The merchant began to turn to him for help with legal matters, which Krishipal was able to solve quite easily. These favours built so much trust between them that Naved even invited the cop to his sister's wedding in Kashmir. And this very trust would help Krishipal get the information he required.

After some time had passed, Krishipal went to Srinagar. He phoned Naved and told him that he was in the valley for some official work and would like to meet. It was a difficult decision for Naved. Though he didn't want to say no, the prospect of being seen with a police officer in Srinagar – even one from Mumbai – filled him with apprehension. He was well-aware of the dangers inherent in being perceived as a police informant by militant sympathizers.

Ultimately, Naved reasoned that Krishipal's relative anonymity in Kashmir would provide some measure of safety. Convinced that their meeting would likely go unnoticed amidst the hustle and bustle of the city, Naved cautiously agreed. He instructed Krishipal to come to an inconspicuous coffee shop near a designated gate of Dal Lake later that evening. It was a calculated but necessary compromise, as Naved navigated the precarious landscape of trust and suspicion that defined his existence in Kashmir.

Krishipal dressed innocuously for their meeting, in a polo T-shirt, jeans and a funky hat that made him look like a tourist. On reaching at the location, he found Naved waiting for him at a corner table. The merchant ordered two cups of kahwa, a traditional Kashmiri tea. When the steaming cups arrived, Krishipal knew the time had come to reveal his true purpose. Disclosing Irfan's terrorist connections to Naved was risky – Krishipal couldn't predict how his unlikely ally would react. Despite the looming threat of Naved tipping off his employer, Krishipal found himself leaning towards trust. It was a gamble fraught with uncertainty but one that Krishipal deemed necessary.

The coffee shop was not very crowded. Still, Krishipal leaned forward before asking Naved softly, 'Do you know of Syed Salahuddin?'

'Yes, sir. He is a very dangerous man. He now stays on the other side of Kashmir but often comes here,' Naved whispered, after looking around to check that nobody was looking at them.

'Hmm. Your boss Irfan is in touch with him.'

'I always had my suspicions that he had some hidden motive,' Naved admitted.

'See, Naved, Salahuddin is planning something in Mumbai. I don't know what it is. I suspect it might be another conspiracy to attack Mumbai. If you help me, many innocent lives will be saved.'

'I will do whatever I can to help you, sir. I am fed up with the gun culture in the valley. I don't support this whole fraud of *azadi*. Real azadi is to live without fear of guns and honestly earn your livelihood. The enemy country is using our gullible Kashmiri youngsters as scapegoats for its selfish motives.' Naved's emotions took a hold of him; he didn't realize that he wasn't whispering anymore. Krishipal's eyes immediately scanned the other tables. He was relieved to see that everybody was too engrossed in their own conversations to notice theirs.

After sitting together for another half hour, the two left the coffee shop. The sun had set by then; it was dark outside. The houseboats anchored at Dal Lake had switched on their bright lights and their colourful reflections on the water resulted in a mesmerizing view. Krishipal couldn't resist the temptation to take a short stroll along the promenade, observing the nightly grandeur of the historic lake. Naved accompanied him but maintained a distance of a few steps. After ten minutes, Krishipal left for the hotel where his SP friend in the J&K Police had arranged a room for him.

'Let me know if you come across anything of my interest,' was Krishipal's parting request to Naved before he got into a cab.

In the first week of December 2005, after his sister's wedding, Naved returned to Navi Mumbai with a truckload of apples. He visited Krishipal's office with a few baskets of fruit in tow. Krishipal picked up an apple and took a bite. 'This time you have brought really good apples. What else do you have for me?'

'Sir, I recently overheard Irfan speaking to Salahuddin. Although I'm not sure exactly what Salahuddin said, from Irfan's response I assume that he is planning to send some *amanat* (consignment) to Mumbai. Salahuddin asked Irfan to ensure that the consignment will be delivered safely to people who have already reached Mumbai. I don't know whether the consignment will be sent along with me on the truck or by some other means.'

'Do you have any other number of Irfan's?' Krishipal asked in a tense voice.

'No, sir.'

'Okay, try to find out if he has any other number.'

Krishipal patted his back and paid him for the apples. Naved left the office after promising to reach out if he came across anything else.

Around a week later, Naved called Krishipal from a public phone in Budgam. 'Sir, I have not been able to find Irfan's other number, but I do have some very important information,' he said. 'The boys that Salahuddin has sent are to be accommodated at the Haj House in Mumbai.' He also gave Krishipal the mobile number of Salahuddin's contact in Mumbai. He had overheard Salahuddin dictating it to Irfan and jotted it down on a piece of paper.

Krishipal asked the telephone surveillance unit to track the number after following the due procedure. He was shocked to learn that the number belonged to a maulana from the Haj House mosque. An analysis of the maulana's calls revealed that he too was in touch with Salahuddin. In one wiretapped conversation, he complained to Salahuddin that the two men he had sent for the 'mission' hadn't met him yet.

Later, Salahuddin called a number in Mumbai to reprimand an unidentified man. 'Why are you people not meeting maulana sahab? He has made all the arrangements for your stay at the Haj House.'

'Janab, we went there as soon as we reached Mumbai but found that place very unsafe. There was heavy police presence in the area.'

Both the police commissioner's office and Mata Ramabai Ambedkar Marg police station were located adjacent to the Haj House. The road was a hotspot for police vehicles, which had scared the men.

'We have booked a room at Hotel Zamzam near Mumbai Central station. This area seems less risky.'

Salahuddin updated the maulana and, at his request, shared a contact number for the group. The maulana then called the number and asked for a meeting.

'Maulana sahab, we have come to Mumbai for the first time. Let us tour the city. Two days from now, Bada Seth from Srinagar will also reach. We will meet you then. For now, we'll enjoy,' replied the man who had received the call.

After listening to these conversations between Salahuddin, the maulana and the suspected men, Krishipal panicked. It was the last week of December – it was likely that the terrorists were planning something sinister on New Years Eve. Based on the information gathered by intercepting their calls, Krishipal drew some preliminary conclusions. The maulana was likely part of the sleeper cell of Hizbul Mujahideen, while the two men had been tasked with planting the bombs that Irfan would transport from Kashmir along with his goods. Perhaps those explosives were the amanat which Salahuddin had mentioned in his phone call with Irfan. But one detail didn't make sense: Irfan had not yet left Kashmir. Confused, Krishipal instructed an ATS inspector to book a room at Hotel Zamzam, pretending to be a tourist. The inspector was able to reserve a room next to the one booked by the suspects.

On the night of 31 December, the telephone surveillance unit diligently monitored the movements of the suspects, providing real-time updates to Krishipal. Around 10 p.m., the two suspects were observed leaving their hotel. Their mobile signals indicated their trail: they went to Girgaon Chowpatty in South Mumbai, then lingered for some time at Hotel Oberoi before proceeding to the iconic Haji Ali Dargah. Following an hour-long sojourn, they returned once again to Girgaon Chowpatty.

Recognizing the potential gravity of the situation, Krishipal contacted Commissioner Roy to apprise him of the suspects' movements around 1 a.m. Roy, alarmed by the possibility of a looming conspiracy, urged Krishipal to detain the suspects immediately. However, Krishipal, expressed reservations about immediate detention. The suspects were frequenting areas that were known to be crowded and bustling. He proposed an alternative, safer approach: apprehending the suspects from their hotel, where they had yet to check out with their belongings. The inspector posted at the hotel discreetly revealed his identity to the management, garnering their trust and cooperation in facilitating the apprehension of the suspects.

At 3 a.m., when the men unlocked the door and entered their room, the inspector barged in along with two constables in plainclothes. Holding a revolver in his right hand, he caught one of the accused, while the constables pounced on the other. The man held by the inspector pushed away from him and rushed towards the door, only to find five armed cops waiting outside. Ultimately, they gave up their efforts to escape and chose to cooperate with the ATS. The officers sat with them in their hotel room where they revealed about themselves and their role in the conspiracy. They were not arrested at that point of time. The officers convinced them they would not be treated harshly if they helped them bust the whole terror module.

The duo, Amjad and Haroon, were both residents of Baramulla, Kashmir in their twenties. They revealed that their plan was to set off multiple bombs on Republic Day, not New Year's. They had been assigned to do reconnaissance and plant the bombs, whereas Irfan had been asked to provide the detonators. Two more men were expected to reach Mumbai to support their scheme. The common points of contact between them were the maulana and Salahuddin. After their confession, the suspects were made to talk with Irfan and Salahuddin over call. They were told to maintain a normal tone and do nothing to reveal that they were sitting with ATS officers. Krishipal instructed his officers to behave softly with them and closely monitor their conversations.

On 5 January 2006, Salahuddin informed the maulana that Irfan had left Kashmir with the amanat and would reach Mumbai via the Firozpur Janta Express the next day. This conversation was intercepted by the telephone surveillance unit and promptly reported to Krishipal. He planned to apprehend Irfan once he disembarked at Mumbai Central Station, where the train terminated. However, a simple issue emerged: who would identify Irfan?

Neither Krishipal nor his officers had seen Irfan, merely listened to his voice while intercepting his telephonic chats. There was only one person who was up for the task – Naved. Krishipal asked him to take the first available flight from Srinagar to Mumbai. However, Naved expressed his inability to do so since Irfan had sent him to Baramulla for some work. Naved also feared that he might come face to face with Irfan, thus putting his life in jeopardy. Krishipal was disappointed by this response; it seemed that the operation was stuck.

Thankfully, while Krishipal was thinking over an alternate solution, he received a call from Naved. 'Sir, I have found a way out. My brother-in-law Hussain also knows Irfan. Please arrange his flight ticket. He will be able to help you.'

Krishipal's friend in the J&K police immediately booked and delivered a flight ticket to Hussain at his request. The man soon arrived in Mumbai.

On the evening of 6 January 2006, a team of plain-clothed ATS officers accompanied Hussain to platform four of Mumbai Central station, where the Firozpur Janta Express was set to arrive. Before entering the station, Hussain had told the officers that he did not want to face

Irfan and would identify him from a distance, using a signal. By the time the train reached the Mumbai Central, only a handful of passengers remained. Most travellers had deboarded at Borivali station.

Once the train halted, the remaining passengers disembarked in rapid succession, but Hussain couldn't spot Irfan. The ATS officer leading the team was worried. Had Irfan alighted at some other station? Perhaps he had got a whiff of the ATS's presence at Mumbai Central. Had he dropped the plan to come to Mumbai midway and returned to Kashmir? Had he changed his appearance? An impatient Krishipal was calling the officer every five minutes for an update, but there was none.

Suddenly, Hussain whistled, attracting the officer's attention. The man scratched his left ear, pointing one finger towards a man in his early sixties with a grey beard, wearing a dark coloured jacket and carrying a bag. This was the gesture they had decided upon to identify Irfan! The team pounced on the bearded man. He tried to free himself and flee but was swiftly overpowered by ATS constables who had spread themselves across the platform strategically.

Irfan was taken to the ATS office, where his luggage and clothes were checked. To Krishipal's disappointment, nothing incriminating was found. Had the maulana and Salahuddin deliberately misled them?

'Tell me, where have you kept the consignment? If you tell us the truth we will be lenient with you. Otherwise ...' Krishipal poked Irfan's large belly with his stick to intimidate him – it was abnormally hard. 'Is this a layer of fat on your belly or a sheet of metal?' Krishipal poked his stomach again.

He asked his constables to remove Irfan's clothes. Irfan protested but was silenced with a fierce look from Krishipal. The officers were aghast when they saw what lay underneath – five different electronic circuits had been hidden by his undershirt. Having secured concrete evidence of the conspiracy, Irfan was thoroughly interrogated until he confirmed that two more men were coming to Mumbai with explosives. He revealed that the bombs were to be planted at five popular locations across Mumbai on 26 January.

Krishipal told Irfan to speak normally to Salahuddin until then, if he called. In order to catch the two additional men who were carrying explosives, it was necessary to keep Salahuddin in the dark. The mastermind had to remain oblivious to the fact that his conspiracy had been exposed and most of his co-conspirators arrested.

While Irfan was still sitting in the interrogation room, his mobile rang with a call from Salahuddin. Krishipal asked him to answer with the speaker on. Irfan told Salahuddin in Urdu that he had reached Mumbai and would shortly meet the maulana. He confirmed that everything was on the track and that work should go smoothly on 26 January. Suddenly, he said something in Kashmiri which the officers couldn't understand. Salahuddin abruptly disconnected the phone and a cunning smile appeared on Irfan's face. Krishipal realized that he had revealed his arrest to Salahuddin. From that moment onwards, the fugitive terrorist's number went dead.

It was clear that the two men with explosives would not come to Mumbai now, thus evading arrest. However, Krishipal was satisfied that his team had been able to avert multiple bomb blasts on Republic Day. Irfan, Amjad, Haroon and the maulana were booked under sections of the stringent Unlawful Activities (Prevention) Act (UAPA). Krishipal later learnt from intelligence agencies that, after the failed operation in Mumbai, the ISI had taken away the assignment from Syed Salahuddin and assigned it to Azam Cheema, another terrorist.

This operation was the first major achievement of the ATS against terrorism and justified the need for the organization. However, Krishipal sometimes missed the delivery of fresh apples from Kashmir that he had come to associate with Naved. The two lost touch after a few years.

25

CONSPIRACY TO ASSASSINATE CHIEF MINISTER NARENDRA MODI

Thee names of all those accused in this case, except Fayaz Kagzi, have been changed.

Though the Republic Day bombing conspiracy had been foiled through 'Operation Amanat', the ordeal served as a stark reminder of Mumbai's continued vulnerability to cross-border terrorism. The city remained a prime target, and the ATS found itself propelled into a heightened state of vigilance and preparedness for future threats. Buoyed by the early success of 2006, Krishipal and his team were imbued with renewed enthusiasm and confidence.

With a collective commitment to safeguarding the city, every member of the ATS – regardless of rank – wholeheartedly engaged in gathering intelligence and cultivating an extensive network of informants. Krishipal directed his focus towards unravelling the threads of past terrorist incidents across Maharashtra. Amidst this relentless pursuit, a disturbing tip-off surfaced in the first week of May 2006. An informer told Krishipal that a large cache of arms and ammunition was likely to be transported from Karnataka to Gujarat via the Marathwada region in Maharashtra.

The intelligence was very vague and urgent efforts would be required to trace the suspects. Krishipal asked DCP Jai Jeet Singh to dig up more information on the case, while he formed two teams to work on it. One would be headed by ACP Kisan Shengal, the other by Inspector Vasant Tajne. It was decided that they would intercept any suspicious vehicles at different locations. The teams left Mumbai in two separate Bolero cars carrying around half a dozen armed constables.

After four to five hours, both teams reached their destinations. Dusk had taken over by then. Krishipal had also left Mumbai and camped at Nashik to supervise the operation. While Tajne's team was positioned at the Niphad junction of the Mumbai–Agra highway in Nashik, Shengal's went further out to the Yeola junction of Manmad–Aurangabad road. Throughout the night, any vehicle which was even slightly suspicious was stopped and thoroughly checked; its occupants frisked. The personnel took turns having quick naps.

The exhausting task of checking vehicles persisted over the following days, gradually wearing down the morale and patience of Shengal, Tajne and their team members. Stationed outside Mumbai, they grappled with frustration and boredom, uncertain when they would be able to return home. Despite their growing weariness, fear of appearing insincere dissuaded them from reaching out to Krishipal to request relief. Under the scorching heat of the summer sun, though their physical and mental exhaustion compounded, they persisted – driven by a sense of duty and responsibility.

Finally, around 4 p.m. on 9 May, Shengal reached his breaking point. Concluding that the operation had likely been triggered by a false alarm, he was just about to ask Krishipal for permission to conclude their mission when a speeding Tata Sumo emerged on the road. Seeing three individuals squeezed onto the front seat, Shengal and his constables signalled for the vehicle to halt. Though the driver initially slowed down, he sped away after one of the passengers whispered something into his ear. With adrenaline surging through his veins, Shengal swiftly rallied his constables into the Bolero. And with that, a high-octane pursuit of the suspicious Tata Sumo was on.

The thrill of the chase eclipsed the stress and fatigue that had burdened them only moments before. Though the Sumo was speeding ahead, it remained within their sights, fuelling their determination to apprehend the perpetrators. In the middle of the action, Shengal dialled Krishipal to update him and seek guidance.

'Sir, we are chasing a suspicious Tata Sumo – I believe that those bastards are sitting in it. We signalled for them to stop but they sped away,' Shengal enthusiastically relayed.

'This is good news but be careful. These guys can do anything. We must capture them alive but don't hesitate to use your weapon if the need arises. Keep me updated.' Having given these instructions, Krishipal disconnected the phone.

The occupants of the Sumo attempted to outmanoeuvre the ATS team by employing deceptive tactics at junctions along the route: falsely signalling a right turn before veering sharply to the left. Undeterred, the seasoned police driver behind the wheel of the Bolero remained steadfast, recognizing and countering the criminals' tactics. With a wealth of experience in chasing suspicious vehicles, he was able to expertly navigate the lanes and maintain a relentless pursuit of the Sumo.

However, skill alone was not enough. As the chase stretched over 80 kilometres, the driver glanced at the dwindling fuel gauge. With no opportunity to refuel mid-pursuit, the team faced the daunting prospect of an empty tank. Moreover, overtaking the Sumo proved challenging, as its reckless speed posed a threat not only to the passengers but to other road users as well. Tension mounted, and the Bolero's fuel gauge hovered dangerously close to empty. The ATS team had to face the grim reality of a potentially failed operation.

Suddenly, fate intervened in a most unexpected manner. As the Sumo hurtled past the Grishneshwar Shiva temple near Aurangabad, it was faced with a bizarre obstacle: a herd of cattle, meandering across the road. Caught off guard by this unforeseen impediment, the Sumo's driver slammed on the brakes, bringing the vehicle to a screeching halt. Seizing the opportunity presented by this fortuitous turn of events, the ATS team sprang into action. With resolve etched upon his face and a loaded revolver clutched firmly in his right hand, Shengal advanced towards the halted Sumo. His voice cut through the air as he shouted in Marathi, '*Aye, thamb*!' (Hey, stop!)

Shengal's constables followed close behind. He instructed, '*Dhara hyana*.' (Catch them.)

The occupants of the Sumo abandoned their vehicle and fled into the nearby woods, ignoring Shengal's warnings to surrender. Shengal and his team wasted no time in following them into the dense foliage. Joined by a parking attendant from the temple grounds and fuelled by the curiosity of local villagers, who thought the police were chasing the dacoits who had been plaguing the area, the ATS team pressed on. After a gruelling chase spanning approximately a kilometre, the ATS personnel managed to apprehend one of the suspects. Despite their best efforts, the driver and third suspect managed to elude capture.

With the arrested suspect confined to the Tata Sumo under the watchful eye of a constable, the team embarked on an exhaustive search of the surrounding area with the help of the locals. Despite hours of scouring the rugged, hilly landscape, their efforts proved fruitless. As darkness descended, Shengal made the difficult decision to call off the search, realizing that they were unlikely to catch the accused under the cover of night.

Back at the seized Sumo, Shengal noticed that the

middle and rear seats were occupied by brown boxes. After an impromptu interrogation, the arrested man revealed that his name was Mohammad Inzmam and the boxes contained weapons and explosives. Perturbed, Shengal thought it prudent to report the incident to the nearest police station so that explosives experts could be sent for. Inzmam, along with the Sumo, was taken to the Khultabad police station in whose jurisdiction the vehicle was seized. Another officer of the ATS, Inspector Sunil Deshmukh, also reached the police station to assist Shengal.

At the request of the ATS, the Bomb Detection and Disposal Squad (BDDS) was called upon. As the BDDS personnel started their work, clad in blast-proof jackets, the power went out. The outer premises of the police station, including the spot where the Tata Sumo was parked, were plunged into darkness. The villagers helped arrange a few lanterns and work could resume. Boxes were unloaded from the vehicle and inspected, one by one. The inspection rattled everybody present at the scene. Each box contained a computer server, inside which there was an AK-47 rifle, four magazines, 200 live cartridges and a packet of a sticky, black explosive substance, which was identified as RDX. Overall, ten AK-47 rifles, forty magazines, 2,000 live cartridges and approximately 3 kilograms of the RDX were found. After all the boxes had been unloaded and inspected, the Sumo was searched. The cops recovered a mobile phone that had fallen below the seats.

Meanwhile, Mohammad Inzmam revealed the names of the two persons who were with him in the Sumo: Akram and Qasim. He also confessed that there was another car – a Tata Indica – transporting arms and explosives. Two men named Noor Jamal and Zamiruddin Ansari, aka Jaki, were in charge of the other car. Finally, Inzmam gave the police the phone numbers of his co-conspirators. Krishipal immediately asked the telephone surveillance unit to intercept the numbers and trace the suspects. He then sought help from the Khultabad Police to hunt down the absconders.

Noor Jamal was located at a relative's home in Aurangabad and taken to the Khultabad police station. Shortly after, Akram was detained from a house in Khultabad. A case was registered against the three accused under various sections of the UAPA, Arms Act and Explosive Substances Act. Through the night, the panchnama of the seized articles and paperwork for the case were completed. On the morning of 10 May, the accused were brought to the ATS headquarters in Mumbai along with the recovered Sumo.

At the Mumbai office, the arrested suspects were rigorously interrogated. Krishipal's intuition hinted that these arrests had merely scratched the surface of a larger, more ominous scheme to rock the nation. Urgently seeking answers, he pressed for critical information – not only to advance the investigation, but also to pre-empt any further acts of terror. Where were Qasim and Jaki, the other occupants of the implicated vehicles? What had become of the Indica loaded with weaponry and explosives? Who had orchestrated this sinister operation?

And most crucially, where were these arms intended to wreak havoc?

Time was of the essence as Krishipal raced against the clock to uncover the truth. He formed different teams to trace the fugitives and the Indica. Simultaneously, a message was sent to DG control rooms across Maharashtra to trace the car. Three days later, on 12 May, a patrol of the Malegaon Police found an Indica abandoned on Sayane Road. As the car didn't have a number plate, the cops suspected that it might be part of some crime. They immediately informed the ATS and seized the car. When the Indica was searched, its registration papers were recovered. The owner of the car was traced and summoned to a police station in Malegaon. Meanwhile, Krishipal had also reached Malegaon. The terrified owner admitted that the Indica was his but told the cops that he wasn't aware it was being used for terrorist activities. Noor had borrowed the car on the morning of 9 May, citing personal reasons.

The investigation began gaining momentum. Information extracted from the accused revealed that, on 9 May, Noor and Jaki had taken the boxes containing arms, ammunition and explosives to an Unani medical college in Malegaon. Jaki had wanted to store the boxes in the college, but the watchman was reluctant to allow them to enter the premises. A man named Dr Farid, who worked for the hospital, was called. He instructed the watchman to allow the boxes to be stored in the resident medical official's room, explaining that the car had broken down and the occupants were known to him.

Late in the night, Dr Farid and the others had returned to the hospital. The boxes were taken out of the RMO room and loaded onto an autorickshaw that Dr Farid had brought along. The rickshaw transported some of the boxes to an electrical appliances shop in Azad Nagar, run by the brother-in-law of one of the accused. The rest were taken to a different location. As they couldn't find a safe place to hide the Indica, they abandoned it on Sayane Road after removing its number plate. However, they forgot to remove the registration papers from the car.

The interrogation of the accused led the ATS to a small bridge behind Gorakshnath Hill on Yeola–Manmad road. From underneath the bridge, two boxes were recovered. One of them was labelled 'ATX'. This time, the unboxing led to no surprises. They found another computer unit which concealed an AK-47 rifle, 200 live cartridges, magazines and pouches. The second box was made of wood and contained fifty hand grenades. All the seized material was brought to the ATS office in Mumbai.

Another ATS team went to the electrical shop in Azad Nagar, where some of the boxes had been kept. After breaking the lock, the shop was searched and five boxes were recovered. Five AK-47 rifles, twenty magazines, 1,000 cartridges, and 13 kilograms of RDX were seized. Krishipal was aghast – were the accused planning to wage a war?

Meanwhile, a series of arrests advanced the ATS investigation. The Aurangabad Police arrested Abdul Qasim, who had driven the Tata Sumo, and handed him over to the ATS. He and Jaki had hired the car on 8 May. Dr Farid was also picked up by the ATS and revealed during his interrogation that he had helped Jaki at the behest of a person named Billu. Soon, Billu was arrested.

The accused individuals in custody also disclosed the involvement of one Sayyed Mehraj who lived in Aurangabad. On 19 May, a team was dispatched to Aurangabad to detain Mehraj. When questioned, Mehraj revealed that he was in touch with a Pakistani national named Juned through two email accounts. The cops took him to a cyber cafe, where he was made to log into the accounts. After scanning the sent and received emails from both accounts, printouts of twenty-six emails were taken. In one email dated 25 February 2006, Mehraj had written:

> *Hum sab khairiyat se hain aur ummeed karte hain ki aap bhi khairiyat se honge. New business chalu kiya hai. 19 tareekh ko Arsalan bhai ke haathon se opening hua hai. 25 se 30 log aaye thei. Sab ko refreshment diya. Sab acche se ho gaya. Dua kijiye ke business acche se chale. Bye bye.*
>
> (We are fine here and hope you are fine, too. We have started a new business. It was inaugurated by Arsalan bhai on the 19th. Around twenty-five to thirty people had come. I gave refreshments to everybody. Everything went well. Pray that the new business flourishes. Bye bye.)

Mehraj admitted to the cops that this was a coded message pertaining to an IED blast at Kalupur railway station in Ahmedabad on 19 February that year.

Within a month, authorities managed to apprehend ten individuals linked to the case based on the information they had received from Mehraj. While some of the suspects confessed voluntarily, others required rigorous interrogation to divulge pertinent information. As Krishipal sifted through the confessions and analysed technical evidence, a coherent narrative of the conspiracy emerged.

The genesis of the sinister design was the Godhra train fire incident. On 27 February 2002, the Sabarmati Express went up in flames near the railway station of Godhra, Gujarat. Two of the bogies of the train, occupied by karsevaks returning from Ayodhya, were allegedly torched by a violent mob.

The news that around sixty people had burnt to death triggered a massive outbreak of communal violence between Hindus and Muslims across Gujarat. The state had a BJP government at the time, led by CM Narendra Modi. Several media outlets, social organizations and an IPS officer attached to the Gujarat Police claimed that Modi's administration deliberately didn't take any effective steps to contain the riots. According to them, this emboldened workers of Hindu outfits like the VHP and

Bajrang Dal to organize large-scale killings of minorities.[12] More than 1,000 people were killed during the riots, which continued for months after the Godhra incident. In the aftermath, Modi came to be seen as a mascot of the aggressive Hindutva ideology.[3]

Extremist organizations operating out of Pakistan with the support of the ISI, such as the LeT and Jaish-e-Mohammed, saw the Gujarat tragedy as an opportunity to advance their malevolent agenda within India. With Mumbai's significant population of Hindu Gujaratis, the city became a prime target for these groups. Between 2 December 2002 and 25 August 2003, Mumbai witnessed six devastating terror attacks in areas predominantly inhabited by Gujaratis. Bomb explosions claimed the lives of approximately 100 individuals. These coordinated plots were orchestrated by terrorist factions bearing names like the Gujarat Muslim Revenge Force.[4]

Although the twin blasts at the Gateway of India and outside Mumbadevi temple on 25 August were deadliest in the series, resulting in the deaths of over sixty people, the terrorist organizations had planned more such attacks in future. Many members of the banned organization Students' Islamic Movement of India (SIMI) had been contacted by LeT operatives to execute their conspiracies.[5]

It was around this time that Fayaz Kagzi, a resident of Beed and former member of SIMI, was approached by Juned, a Pakistan-based member of LeT. Kagzi travelled to Pakistan via Iran and was trained in making bombs. After returning to India, Kagzi began to further the cause.

He would show videos of the Gujarat riots and alleged atrocities against Muslims to the youngsters to radicalize them.[6] He introduced Juned to another Beed resident, Jaki. A graduate of the Industrial Training Institute, Jaki had become radicalized after the Gujarat riots. He gave provocative speeches at religious gatherings called Dars and distributed books with inflammatory content. Kagzi and Juned instructed him to form a terror module consisting of other radicalized youths like him. They told him that soon, a big mission would be executed, and the members should prepare for Jihad.[7]

One of the persons in the module was Mohammed Inzmam, who got acquainted with Jaki through SIMI. The two often met to discussed religion and their plans to wage Jihad. Once, Jaki told Inzmam that Juned had planned a mission to kill Modi, who was still CM of Gujarat. A large cache of arms and ammunition had been dispatched by Juned for the mission. Apart from Modi, the target was Pravin Togadia – a VHP leader who was often in the news for his provocative speeches.

On the morning of 9 May, Jaki asked Inzmam to bring a four-wheeler to Ozar on the Dhule–Nashik highway. Inzmam then spoke to Noor, telling him that he needed a car to attend a friend's wedding. Noor arranged for the Tata Indica and joined him. Soon Inzmam, along with Noor and Zuber, headed to the location given by Jaki. They found Jaki waiting near a petrol pump in a Tata Sumo. He told them that the consignment of arms and explosives had arrived and instructed them to follow the Sumo.

After driving around 20 kilometres, they reached a dark green Eicher truck parked beside the road. Inside were fifteen brown boxes with the letters 'ATX' painted on them. The boxes were unloaded: ten were placed in the Sumo and the remaining five in the Indica. Jaki then told Inzmam to head for Aurangabad in the Sumo, while he would follow in the Indica. Since the backseat rows were full of boxes, Inzmam and Akramsat in the front beside Qasim as he drove.

Everything was going as per plan until the ATS team led by ACP Shengal intercepted the Sumo and the chase began. Inzmam called Jaki and alerted him that the cops were pursuing their vehicle in a Bolero. Jaki insisted that they reach Beed with the boxes regardless of the circumstances. However, after the timely intervention near Grishneshwar temple, most of the accused were detained by the ATS one by one and the whole conspiracy was unearthed.

Although Jaki failed to execute his mission of killing Modi and Togadia, he managed to escape India and go to Pakistan. After relocating to Pakistan, he frequently travelled to Saudi Arabia using fake documents. He was deported to India from Saudi Arabia in June 2012. Fayaz Kagzi also escaped to Pakistan via Iran. It was reported that he blew himself up outside the US consulate in Saudi Arabia in July 2016, killing four policemen.[8]

The case of the ATS was largely based on the recovered evidence, witness testimonies and confessional statements given by the accused. Some of the suspects alleged that they had given these statements under duress, even torture.[9,10] The ATS refuted these allegations, stating that such accusations were a tactic to get away from the clutches of law. Twenty-two accused were put on trial in a special court of Mumbai. The judgement was delivered in August 2016, ten years after the consignment was seized. The court acquitted eight of the accused. Jaki and six others were given life imprisonment whereas the others convicted received lesser sentences.

26

2006 MUMBAI TERROR ATTACK

On 19 February 2006, the Karnavati Express, arriving from Mumbai, pulled into Ahmedabad's Kalupur railway station around 9:30 p.m., marking the end of its journey. Within minutes, the passengers had disembarked and the cleaning crew took over, readying the train for its return trip. In one of the chair cars, a vigilant sweeper discovered a suitcase tucked beneath a seat. Assuming that someone had left behind their luggage, the sweeper relocated it to platform two. The Karnavati Express then proceeded to the shunting yard, neatly slotted into the station's routine rhythms.

The tranquillity was shattered at approximately 1:43 a.m. by a deafening explosion, engulfing the station in smoke and chaos. Panic ensued as people scrambled to flee the scene; the force of the blast tore a portion of the roof asunder. While around twenty-five individuals sustained injuries, the explosion's impact was mitigated by the absence of a train at the platform. The investigation eventually yielded a chilling revelation: the suitcase, laden with explosives, had originated in Mumbai and it seemed that the bomber's intended target was the Karnavati Express itself. A timing error in the explosive device had caused it to detonate only after the train had been vacated, averting catastrophic casualties.

In Mumbai, a grim routine emerged whenever bombs detonated elsewhere in India: a barrage of phone calls flooded the police control room. Vigilant citizens were quick to dial in upon spotting unattended bags or suspicious behaviour. Given Mumbai's unfortunate history of terrorist attacks, the authorities treated each call with utmost seriousness. However, more often than not, these were false alarms.

The police also had to contend with the nuisance of pranksters. Hoax calls claiming an imminent bomb threat at a specific time and location had become an all-too-common occurrence. Some individuals seized upon the heightened alertness to settle personal scores. They would fabricate stories, alleging that their adversaries were engaged in suspicious activities suggestive of terrorist involvement. As a result, the accused would promptly be detained and subjected to rigorous interrogation, only to be released after a thorough investigation cleared them of any wrongdoing.

After the Karnavati Express incident, the ATS also received such calls on daily basis. One evening, on 11 July 2006, Krishipal was reviewing the Aurangabad Arms Haul case with his team in his office when a journalist called him.

'Sir, has a bomb exploded on some local train?' the journalist asked in a panicky voice.

'No. We don't have any such information. Every day we are getting such calls. They turn out to be fake.'

When Krishipal disconnected the call, his phone rang again. This time the caller was Police Commissioner Roy. 'KP, information is coming in that a blast has happened on the Western Railway line. Check the TV. You guys need to get into action,' he directed.

The TV on the wall opposite Krishipal was on mute. He switched on the audio and called DCP Jai Jeet Singh to his cabin. Initially, the 'Breaking News' band on the screen reported only one blast at Lower Parel station. Within minutes, the number increased. Two blasts ... four ... six ... seven ... ten ... twelve blasts.

Krishipal was astounded that so many explosions had happened in a span of fifteen minutes. According to the news report, all the blasts had happened between the Lower Parel and Bhayandar stations in first-class coaches of the local trains. The visuals of damaged coaches shared by the media indicated the intensity of the blasts. Krishipal's conclusion was simple: 'This is clearly a terrorist attack.'

DCP Singh offered to immediately rush to the targeted spots to assess the situation. However, Krishipal advised that he could not do so single-handedly, as the blast sites were far from each other. Since the ATS had a dearth of officers – only seven or eight at the time, all of whom were already working on different cases – Krishipal instructed DCP Singh to visit three to four spots while he would cover the rest.

Although Krishipal had intended to leave for the spots immediately, he first had to field numerous calls from senior police officers and media personnel. Nearly thirty minutes later, he reached out to DCP Singh for an update. Singh was still en route to the closest site, Lower Parel station – a mere 4 kilometres away from the ATS office in Nagpada. The DCP had become gridlocked near Mahalaxmi due to the chaos wrought by the explosion.

The blast had thrown the entire local train network – particularly the Western line – into disarray, leading to an overflow of commuters spilling onto the streets during rush hour. As road transport became the only viable option, Mumbai's arterial roads clogged with colossal traffic jams, reducing the pace of movement to a crawl. Sudden heavy rainfall added to the turmoil, raising fears that crucial evidence at the blast sites might be washed away. Krishipal, who had considered 2006 a fortunate year given that ATS had successfully thwarted two terrorist attacks, now felt a sense of foreboding.

As Krishipal pondered how to navigate these challenges, he got a call from DGP P. S. Pasricha, who asked him to take over the investigation. 'KP, I think that all these blasts are part of a single conspiracy,' the DGP opined. 'There seems to be only one group of conspirators which has planted the bombs in all seven trains. So, only one FIR should be registered and the investigation must be done based on that.'

'Sir, I beg to differ. Registering separate FIRs will be advantageous for us. Even if the group of conspirators is the same, we can keep suspects in our custody for a longer period by registering seven different cases. When the remand ends in one case, we can seek their custody in another from the court,' Krishipal explained. 'The blasts have taken place across 30 kilometres and in the jurisdictions of different railway police stations. There is no legal barrier in registering seven cases. Later, we can club them and file a single chargesheet.'

With Pasricha's approval, Krishipal directed the inspectors in charge of the railway police stations to register cases against the blasts that had happened in their respective jurisdictions. He also requested the railway police commissioner to ensure that the crime scenes were protected. Since the ATS had a strength of only about half a dozen officers, the DGP temporarily provided use of a few inspectors of the Railway Police. Pasricha wanted to ensure that the staff crunch wouldn't hinder a speedy investigation.

The initial confusion over the number of blasts was cleared by 9 p.m. Seven local trains had been bombed, not ten or twelve as a few news channels had reported. All the explosions had happened in a span of eleven minutes, from 6:24 p.m. to 6:35 p.m., in trains originating from Churchgate and heading towards the northern suburbs. The bombs had gone off when the trains were at or around the Matunga Road, Mahim, Bandra, Khar, Jogeshwari, Borivali and Mira Road stations. Around 200 people were thought to have been killed and over 700 wounded. The injured victims had been taken to various hospitals by railway policemen and fellow civilians.

Krishipal called Commissioner Roy and requested him to implement the Standard Operating Procedure (SOP) which he had formulated after the Karnavati Express blast in Ahmedabad. As per the SOP, the police officer nearest to a blast location would reach the spot, while the local police station would set up a temporary help desk in hospitals within their jurisdiction and record the number of deaths and injuries. Another team of cops would record statements from the victims and eyewitnesses. The zonal DCP would supervise relief arrangements at the hospitals. In this case, swift application of the SOP prevented disorder in the hospitals. At Krishipal's request, Commissioner Roy also ordered police stations to check hotels and lodges in their area and collect details of the guests.

While Krishipal was busy directing his men, Roy dropped a bombshell over the phone. 'Tonight, Congress president Sonia Gandhi, Home Minister Shivraj Patil and Railway Minister Lalu Prasad Yadav are landing in Mumbai. They will be visiting the blast sites and local hospitals.'

'Oh no! Sir, please can you tell them not to come? Their security arrangements will cause a big mess,' Krishipal pleaded. Though he had the same concern, it was beyond the commissioner's capacity to restrain the movements of VVIPs.

Late in the night, Gandhi, Patil and Yadav visited Bhabha Hospital in Bandra, where some of the injured passengers had been admitted. They were followed by L. K. Advani, who was the Leader of the Opposition at the time. However, they all limited their visits to one bomb site, at Matunga, and returned to Delhi a few hours later.

Senior politicians, particularly those in power, face a complex dilemma when it comes to visiting sites of tragedy. If they opt not to visit, they risk being criticized as insensitive by opposition parties and the media. Conversely, if they do, they may be accused of exploiting the situation for publicity. It's a lose-lose situation that demands a delicate balance between demonstrating empathy and avoiding accusations of opportunism. For law enforcement, the presence of such VIPs may add an additional dimension of difficulty to an already fraught situation.

Three days later, Prime Minister Manmohan Singh also arrived in Mumbai and visited a few hospitals to talk to the patients and their families. After speaking to some of the victims whose arms or legs had been amputated, Singh said with teary eyes, 'Pakistan in 2004 had solemnly given an assurance that Pakistani territory will not be used to promote, encourage, train and abet terrorist elements directed against India. That assurance has to be fulfilled before the peace process or other processes can make progress.'[1] Singh had called a meeting of senior police officers at the airport where he was told about the suspected role of Pakistan-based terrorists in the blasts, prompting him to make such a comment.[2]

Singh, along with National Security Adviser (NSA) M. K. Narayanan, spoke with senior law enforcement officers about the progress of the investigation. All the officers had bloodshot eyes and dark circles – nobody had slept for several days. A high-ranking officer introduced Krishipal to them as the one in charge of the investigation.

'How were the terrorists able to plant bombs in crowded trains?' Prime Minister Singh asked.

Krishipal was about to answer when the officer who had introduced him jumped in to impress the PM. 'Sir, they might have hidden the bombs in the train toilets.'

Astounded at the officer's reply, Krishipal thought, 'This person has been in Mumbai throughout his career in the police, yet he doesn't know that there are no toilets in the local trains.'

Noticing Krishipal's confounded look, NSA Narayanan realized that the officer might be bluffing. He stepped in with a snub to the man. 'Please allow Mr Raghuvanshi to brief the PM, since his team is investigating the case.'

Grateful for his intervention, Krishipal took over. 'Sir, we suspect that the bombs were placed on the overhead luggage racks. The initial evidence seems to suggest that the explosives were kept in pressure cookers. The impact of the blasts reveals that some high intensity explosive was used.'

'Has there been any breakthrough in the case?' the prime minister asked.

'Till now, nobody has been arrested. However, we have identified some people who visited Pakistan recently and called them in for questioning. Hopefully we will crack the case soon,' Krishipal replied confidently.

'How are you proceeding with the investigation?' NSA Narayanan prompted.

'Sir, we have procured dump data from mobile towers located near the blast spots. Technical teams have been formed to analyse them. We are also working with forensic science experts to examine the evidence recovered from the crime scenes.'

Both PM Singh and NSA Narayanan expressed their satisfaction over the progress that had been made. Before he left, Narayanan told Krishipal, 'I expect some good news from the ATS soon.'

This remark further stressed out Krishipal; would he be able to live up to Narayanan's expectations?

The investigation stretched on for nearly a month and Krishipal was subjected to relentless pressure from both the media and politicians. Day in and day out, he found himself fielding uncomfortable questions and weathering criticism from various quarters. Some lambasted the ATS for failing to prevent the blasts, while others decried its failure to apprehend the perpetrators in the weeks that followed.

Unbeknownst to these critics, the ATS was toiling tirelessly behind the scenes, enduring round-the-clock operations and sleepless nights. Each morning, newspapers and TV news channels would deliver headlines that stung Krishipal and his team: 'Cops groping in the dark in 7/11 case' or 'ATS still clueless about the train bombers'.[3] Krishipal attempted to buoy the morale of his men by dismissing such criticism as a professional hazard but inwardly, his frustration was mounting.

The first insight that set the investigation into motion came from the forensic laboratory in Kalina. The lab report revealed that the explosive used in the blasts was a mixture of RDX and ammonium nitrate. Another key lead was the pressure cooker trail. Immediately after the bombings, the BDDS had retrieved a pressure cooker handle from the Jogeshwari blast site. This was followed by the recovery of charred aluminium and remnants of pressure cooker handles and lids from the six other locations as well. Krishipal concluded that the explosives had been stored in pressure cookers. Soon, his team identified the store from which the cookers had been purchased and took statements from the shop owner and salesmen.

This initial evidence ignited hope in the ATS officers With the help of the local police, over 400 people who had a history of radical or communal behaviour were brought in for interrogation. Scores of suspicious mobile numbers were put under surveillance. Intelligence agencies like the Intelligence Bureau (IB) and RAW were simultaneously pursuing the case and assisted the ATS with their inputs.

While conducting phone surveillance, the IB noticed frequent calls between a man named Jameel Ansari, who lived in Bihar near the Nepal border, and Navi Mumbai resident Parvez Chowdhary. While Chowdhary did not have a criminal history, Ansari was on the IB's radar. The IB had information that Ansari had earlier gone to Pakistan for training at a terrorist camp. After receiving a tip off from the IB, two ATS teams were formed. One went to detain Parvez Chowdhary in Navi Mumbai while another went to Bihar in a special aircraft of the Indian Air Force to retrieve Ansari. A shoe shop owner, Navid Shaikh, was also arrested on suspicion of arranging meetings between Ansari and members of LeT at his shop.[4]

Interrogating the suspects in custody led to more arrests by the third week of August 2006. Meanwhile, the ATS received an input that two men had landed in Mumbai to execute another attack. A hunt was launched for them. In no time, a Pakistani national named Mohammad Nawabuddin was arrested with 2 kilograms of RDX, detonators, a timer device, pistol and $50 in his possession.[5]

Nawabuddin told the interrogators that he and his accomplice, Abu Osama, had reached Mumbai two days earlier but were unable to contact their handler. Hence, they hid in an unoccupied building of the Central Government Servants colony in Antop Hill. They chose to hide there because, as Pakistanis, they found it difficult to get accommodation in a hotel or lodge.

Krishipal dispatched a team of his men to pick up Osama from the hideout. Around 4:30 a.m., the cops surrounded the building and asked the fugitive to surrender. However, Osama allegedly responded with a volley of bullets fired from an AK-47 rifle. He was killed in the retaliatory fire.[6]

27

ATS VS CRIME BRANCH

In a press conference on 29 September 2006, around three months after the train blasts, Commissioner Roy announced that the case had been cracked. He revealed that the conspiracy had been designed by the ISI and executed under the supervision of LeT commander Azam Cheema, who lived in Bahawalpur. Eleven Pakistani nationals were involved in the blasts and had executed the conspiracy with the assistance of their Indian contacts. 'It was a professional, precise, and well-planned operation,' the commissioner described.[1]

The eleven Pakistanis had reached Mumbai in May. Some of them had infiltrated the porous border with Gujarat while others came via Nepal and Bangladesh. LeT's Mumbai contact, Faisal Shaikh, had rented flats for them in Malad, Borivali, Bandra and Mumbra. On 10 July, the bombs were prepared in a slum in the Govandi area of north-eastern Mumbai. Twenty kilograms of RDX were combined with 4 kilograms of ammonium nitrate to make an even more lethal explosive. Each of the seven pressure cookers was stuffed with 2.5 kilograms of the explosive and equipped with a Quartz timer. The cookers were placed in bags and covered with newspaper.

The conspiracy had been executed by seven different teams, comprising of one Pakistani and one Indian operative each. After the bombs exploded, the Pakistani suspects had escaped the city – except for one who was killed in the blast between the Khar and Santacruz stations.[2] The ATS had successfully tracked down the Indians who were involved over the next few months. In all, thirteen people were arrested, including a few members of the banned organization SIMI.

In February 2008, when Krishipal completed his tenure, his conscience was satisfied. In the last four years, he had not only raised an organization from scratch but also helped avert two terror strikes. He felt guilty that the train blasts couldn't be prevented but was consoled by the fact that he had successfully unearthed the conspiracy and apprehended most of the accused. After handing the ATS over to his successor, IPS officer Hemant Karkare, Krishipal was transferred as the additional DG of the Railway Police.

In the last week of September 2008, the then chief of the Mumbai Crime Branch held a highly anticipated press conference. He was set to share the significant progress that had been made in investigating the spate of bombings that had plagued several cities across India that year. The event was broadcasted live, drawing the attention of reporters and police officers alike.

The chief informed the gathered media that the Mumbai Crime Branch had made a breakthrough, arresting five individuals from Mumbai and UP who were affiliated with the terrorist organization Indian Mujahideen. According to him, these five accused had been implicated in numerous bombing incidents across India, dating back to 2005. This included the heinous serial explosions on Mumbai's local trains in July 2006.

The crime branch's theory relied heavily on the confession allegedly made by one of the accused, Murtuza Shaikh (name changed). They concluded that the group had falsely introduced themselves as Pakistani to the others accused and arrested earlier by the ATS, and were instrumental in making and planting the train bombs.[3] Murtuza claimed that he and his co-conspirators were acting at the behest of the Indian Mujahideen's co-founder Riyaz Bhatkal (name changed), who had escaped to Pakistan. As per Murtuza's version of events, the bombs were created in a flat in Sewri.

The Crime Branch chief's statement deviated significantly from the narrative put forth by the ATS. According to the ATS's investigation, the plot was orchestrated by the LeT in collaboration with former members of SIMI, with

Azam Cheema as the mastermind. Moreover, the ATS had claimed that the bombs were manufactured in a hut located in the Govandi slums. These discrepancies further fuelled the confusion surrounding the investigation. The media was eager to frame the situation as a clash between the Mumbai Crime Branch and the ATS, igniting speculation about the innocence of the thirteen individuals held in custody for the past two years.

Following the press conference, crime reporters wasted no time in reaching out to Krishipal for his reaction to the claims made by the crime branch, seeking clarification on the disparities between the two agencies' accounts of the events. With the Crime Branch's revelations, it seemed imperative for the ATS to swiftly demand custody of Murtuza to verify his claims. However, Krishipal found himself in a powerless position, as he was no longer with the ATS.

Seeking solace and validation, Krishipal reached out to his former teammates Subodh Jaiswal, Jai Jeet Singh and Naval Bajaj, wanting to know their thoughts on the crime branch's pronouncement. To his relief, they stood firm in their support of the ATS investigation and affirmed its accuracy. Even Anami Roy, now the DGP, echoed their sentiments. He suggested that the conflicting narratives might have been a tactic employed by terrorists to sow confusion among investigators.

Despite the reassurances from his colleagues, Krishipal battled with depression and insomnia that night. The weight of ensuring that no innocent individual had been wrongfully imprisoned was immense. He was haunted by the need to clear his conscience of any potential injustice.

Two months later, a series of coordinated terrorist attacks conducted over four days shook Mumbai – and the entire nation. ATS Chief Hemant Karkare was killed in an ambush on the first day of the onslaught, 26 November 2008. Krishipal was asked to take the additional charge of chief of the ATS. Later, he was relieved of his responsibility as additional DG, Railways and given full-fledged charge of the ATS. Despite the tragic circumstances, he was happy to be back in the organization he had fathered.

One afternoon, a reporter from a prominent morning newspaper visited the ATS office to interview Krishipal about Mumbai's preparedness to avert another attack like 26/11. During their conversation, she asked an unexpected question which stumped Krishipal for a moment. 'What do you have to say about the Mumbai Crime Branch's claim that they have arrested the man responsible for the train blasts? Their story is different from yours. Who is speaking the truth?'

Krishipal thought for a while and answered, 'I stand by the ATS investigation. The crime branch may have informed the media about the arrest but as far as the ATS is concerned, we have not received any official communication from them. Hence I can't comment further.'

The next morning, the newspaper highlighted the fact that the crime branch hadn't officially informed the ATS about Murtuza's arrest. A few hours later, the crime branch sent a letter to the ATS officially intimating the same. Immediately, Krishipal sought Murtuza's remand. The suspect was moved from judicial custody to the ATS's custody. Krishipal now had another problem to face. The officers who had investigated the train blasts were no longer with the ATS two and half years later. Most of the ATS personnel had been transferred to various police units across Maharashtra.

Krishipal, determined to excavate the truth, decided to personally interrogate Murtuza. Seated on the floor with folded legs, Murtuza's expression remained impassive as his involvement in the train blasts was questioned. Even when Krishipal presented the evidence gathered during his investigation, Murtuza steadfastly stuck to the narrative he had shared with the crime branch. Krishipal assigned a team of officers renowned for their adept interrogation tactics to continue questioning Murtuza the following day. Hours passed and as the day drew to a close, the exhausted officers reported that, despite their efforts, Murtuza had remained unwavering in his claim that he had been a part of the conspiracy.

Recognizing that Murtuza might be following a predetermined script, Krishipal opted for a different approach during his next interrogation session. Setting aside questions related to the blasts, Krishipal spoke to the accused about unrelated topics, such as his family and native village. He spent hours patiently building a rapport with Murtuza and establishing a sense of trust. Krishipal even ordered biryani for them to share. As they dined together, Krishipal subtly steered the conversation towards Murtuza's acquaintances and connections.

It was during this exchange that he recalled Murtuza's affiliation with Riyaz Bhatkal, who was reportedly operating from Pakistan after fleeing India. This realization sparked a new line of questioning.

'Are you making this claim because you are afraid of Riyaz Bhatkal?'

'No, why should I be scared of him?'

'I know that you are scared of him. But let me tell you that your Riyaz Bhatkal is a dead man now. He was killed in a police encounter,' Krishipal lied.

Murtuza's expression changed into one of shock after listening to these words. 'Is this true, sir?'

'Yes. I can show you the newspaper clippings. His game is over.' Krishipal sold the lie with confidence.

Murtuza began reciting a prayer for the dead with teary eyes. '*Inna lillahi wa inna ilayhi raji'un.*' (Indeed we belong to Allah, and indeed to him we will return.)

As Krishipal stood up to leave the room, Murtuza called him back. 'Sir, I will tell you everything.'

Murtuza eventually admitted that he had falsely claimed involvement in the train bombing conspiracy. He revealed that Riyaz Bhatkal had instructed all Indian Mujahideen members to meticulously monitor the investigations into terror incidents across India since 2005. Operatives were tasked with collecting newspaper clippings containing detailed accounts of the investigations. This preparation was intended to bolster their credibility in the event of police questioning, providing them with a fabricated background to support their claims.

'Bhatkal ordered us to own up to other blasts if we were caught. This would confuse the police and courts as well as weaken the charges against our Jihadi brothers who are languishing in jail in various cases,' Murtuza told Krishipal, wiping his tears. 'I was just following his instructions. In the future, if any Indian Mujahideen men are arrested, they will also make similar claims.'

With Murtuza's confession, Krishipal was vindicated. He called up the then home minister of Maharashtra and narrated the whole story. At his suggestion, the minister came to the ATS office and spoke to Murtuza. Afterwards, he patted Krishipal's back and congratulated him on unearthing the truth.

A special Maharashtra Control of Organised Crime Act (MCOCA) court was set up and commenced the trial. Murtuza's account in court differed greatly from Krishipal's version of events. The accused alleged that crime branch officials had forced him to confess to participating in the train blasts under threat.[4] He also refuted the statement given to the ATS. In September 2015, the MCOCA court announced its verdict. Twelve of the thirteen individuals arrested by the ATS were convicted. Public prosecutor Raja Thakare had sought death penalty for the accused, calling them 'merchants of death'. The court announced capital punishment for five convicts whereas the remaining seven were sentenced to life in prison.[5]

Krishipal was content with the judgment of the court, satisfied that the trial had been completed right before he hung up his boots. However, a major twist in the tale came ten years later, on 21 July 2025. The Bombay High Court overturned the MCOCA court's verdict, acquitting all twelve individuals who had been convicted. The ATS's evidence was found insufficient to prove the charges. The judges dismissed key witness testimonies as unreliable and opined that the confessional statements of the accused were obtained through torture. The court also highlighted some procedural lapses during a police line-up conducted during the investigation. The court ordered the immediate release of the exonerated men, after nineteen years of languishing in different jails.[6]

Krishipal was on a pilgrimage to Puri, Odisha, when he received the news from a journalist who had called for his reaction. He was aghast at the order. In that moment, he mentally revisited the entire case – the pains he and his team had taken to unearth the conspiracy. All of that had been wiped away by the High Court's judgement.

One of the parametres to gauge a police officer's worth is the number of his cases that have withstood judicial scrutiny. A depressed Krishipal called Anami Roy, who was Mumbai's police commissioner at the time of the blasts. Roy, too, was equally shocked. However, both of them were retired now and could do nothing more than hope that the state government would challenge the High Court's order in the Supreme Court.

To Krishipal's relief, the Maharashtra government filed an appeal in the Supreme Court the very next day. Accepting the argument that the Bombay High Court's remarks in the order could potentially impact other MCOCA cases, the apex court stayed the order but did not deem it necessary for the accused to be taken back in custody.[7] Krishipal was confident that the ATS would be vindicated whenever the Supreme Court delivered its verdict.

28

26 NOVEMBER 2008

Krishipal was eagerly anticipating a lovely dinner on 26 November 2008. A friend of his from Delhi, who worked as an income tax officer, was visiting Mumbai. Along with a common friend who lived in the city, they had decided to indulge in a spicy Chinese fare at Golden Dragon in the iconic Hotel Taj Mahal.

However, as the evening approached, Krishipal developed a sore throat and started feeling feverish. Concerned about his health, he rang his friend to inquire about the possibility of postponing their dinner. Surprisingly, his friend too was feeling unwell and suggested rescheduling for his next visit to Mumbai. With the change of plans, Krishipal settled for a simple meal of khichdi, took a paracetamol and retired for the night in his residence in Malabar Hill.

Just as Krishipal was about to drift off to sleep around 9:30 p.m., a reporter from an English tabloid called his mobile phone. 'Sir, is there a gang war happening at CSMT railway station? Shots have been fired on the premises.'

'No, I don't have any such information,' Krishipal responded groggily, assuming it was a mere rumour. If the news had been accurate, he would have received official intimation by then. Having been transferred from the ATS in January 2007, Krishipal now held the position of additional director general of police (ADG), Railways. It was his responsibility to ensure the safety of rail passengers and property throughout Maharashtra. The law mandated that his force investigate any crimes committed on railway premises.

After ending the call, another reporter contacted Krishipal with the same question. Unable to provide an answer, he turned on the TV to find some news channels reporting gunfire at CSMT station. However, no visuals or detailed information were available. Feeling alarmed, Krishipal dialled Mumbai's Railway Police Commissioner A. K. Sharma, who lived close to the station.

Sharma, too, wasn't aware about the incident. Krishipal instructed him to go to CSMT station and assess the situation. Meanwhile, dressed in the same plain shirt he had worn all day, Krishipal set off to join him there. Since he was likely to be targeted by Pakistani terrorists due to his involvement in unearthing several conspiracies, the Government of India had directed the Mumbai Police to provide him with Z+ security. This involved more than ten armed police officers accompanying him in two vehicles for protection and surveillance when he was on the move.

During the brief 5-kilometre journey, Krishipal's phone was constantly buzzing with inquiries about the gunfire at CSMT. He wanted to speak to the Mumbai Police commissioner and A. K. Sharma but was unable to do so due to the influx of incoming calls. An irritated Krishipal would struggle to end one call only to have another ringing immediately after. After a few minutes, he finally managed to get through to Sharma.

In a panicked tone, Sharma informed him, 'Sir, *yahan toh laashon ka dher laga hua hai.*' (Sir, there is a heap of dead bodies here.) It was at that moment that Krishipal realized the incident was not a gang conflict but a terrorist attack.

As Krishipal's car approached the southern exit of the J. J. Flyover, near Haj House, a crowd halted his retinue and cautioned him against proceeding further due to ongoing gunfire. The CSMT railway station was just 300 metres away and Krishipal could clearly hear shots being fired. The realization that he had left his AK-47 rifle at home was a humbling one, but it was his duty to continue on.

He got out of his vehicle and began walking towards the station. At the same time, he finally managed to get through to DGP Anami Roy after several attempts. Krishipal urgently requested that the Quick Response Team (QRT) be dispatched immediately to CSMT to neutralize the criminals. The QRT had been established in 2003 to handle situations where an armed confrontation was likely. However, Roy informed Krishipal that sending a QRT was not possible, as the commandos were being deployed to multiple locations.

It was then that Krishipal was informed that CSMT wasn't the only target of the attackers. The terrorists had not only massacred people at CSMT but also struck several other prominent locations in the city simultaneously: multiple two-star hotels, a Jewish cultural centre and even a hospital. There had also been two explosions in Wadi Bunder and Juhu, where bombs had been planted in taxis.

When Krishipal arrived at CSMT, the terrorists responsible for the carnage had already moved to a new location near the Times of India building, which was across the road. Krishipal and Sharma took charge of clearing dead bodies, helping the injured and collecting the passengers' luggage. Suddenly, a sub-inspector ran towards them, shouting that Ashok Kamte had been injured in the gunfire. Additional Commissioner Kamte was known for his bravery and had rushed to CSMT upon hearing about the attack. Krishipal followed the sub-inspector to the police station to check the TV coverage and was shocked to learn that Kamte, ATS Chief Hemant Karkare and Inspector Vijay Salaskar had all been killed. The three officers had been sitting together in a police car. There was an exchange of fire with the same two terrorists who had opened fire indiscriminately at CSMT.

As they watched the TV broadcast in shock, Sharma told Krishipal, 'Sir, be prepared to resume your role as the ATS chief. The government can't leave the position vacant, and there is no one else but you who can fill it.'

Sharma's prediction came true. About half an hour later, Krishipal received a call from DGP Roy, who asked him to immediately take temporary charge as ATS chief. He was summoned to the police headquarters, where he spent the entire night discussing strategies to deal with the terrorists with DGP Roy, the additional chief secretary (Home) and other senior officers. In the meantime, one of the terrorists named Ajmal Kasab was captured alive during an encounter with the local police on Girgaon Chowpatty. Kasab revealed the entire conspiracy to the police and admitted that he and nine other associates had arrived in the city from Pakistan via the sea route.

Privately, Krishipal wondered what might have happened if he had gone to Hotel Taj Mahal with his friends for dinner.

Circumstances had led Krishipal to return to the organization he had founded after eleven months. Everything had changed, except the office furniture. The original team members – both officers and constables – had either retired or been transferred to other police agencies. When Krishipal had established the ATS, he had made sure to only onboard individuals with clean records and a passion for participating in counter-terror operations. However, in the new team, Krishipal noticed that there were a few officers with tainted pasts. One senior officer had faced an inquiry for planting drugs in a businessman's home to extort money. Another had been arrested for extorting money from a tradesman while he was an inspector. A few others had been suspects in the disappearance of a witness in the Malegaon blast case that same year. Despite the team's shortcomings, Krishipal had no choice but to work with them.

On the night of 26 November, Ajmal Kasab was taken into custody by the Mumbai Crime Branch, who were tasked with overseeing the investigation. Krishipal found this absurd. On the third day of the attacks, he called a meeting with the ATS officers at their headquarters. To them he said, 'The ATS was established to investigate incidents related to terrorism. So, when we are facing the biggest terrorist attack in the city's history, don't you think it is our responsibility to carry forward the investigation? Shouldn't the ATS bring those responsible for killing its chief to justice? I want to know your opinions before I try to convince the government to transfer the case to us.'

Krishipal's words were met with silence. After a few moments, an IPS officer spoke up. 'Sir, our hands are full. The ATS is already burdened with the Malegaon blast investigation. We shouldn't bite off more than we can chew.'

Though he had wanted to take over the case, Krishipal's charge of the ATS was temporary. He decided to abandon the idea of persuading the government to transfer the case. After all, it was pointless to take over a case of such magnitude when his team members were disinterested and lacked enthusiasm.

The crime branch's investigation gained widespread publicity as the media covered every development in the case. A few days later, the dissenting ATS officers too realized that they had made a mistake.

29

A DRUG-DEALING IPS OFFICER

'Sir, please think about the reputation of the Indian Police Service. Arresting an IPS officer like this will damage our image,' the man in front of him said, without showing any remorse.

Krishipal exploded after hearing his words. He couldn't control himself and slapped the man. 'You shameless person! Why didn't you think about the reputation of IPS when you got involved in all of this? You are a disgrace to the uniform!'

In January 2009, an inspector told Krishipal about a major drug deal that was set to take place at a club in Bandra. One of the prime responsibilities of the ATS was to monitor narco-terrorism. The team had several informants who provided information about illegal drug transactions happening across the state. Based on the intel the inspector had received, the ATS set up a trap and arrested two individuals in possession of over two kilograms of heroin. One of the accused was a police constable. During the interrogation, the perpetrators revealed that a big-time drug trafficker was going to be travelling from Delhi to Mumbai to deliver more goods.

Around a week later, the suspect arrived in Mumbai. He went to Raheja Club in Andheri to carry out the deal, only to be apprehended by ATS personnel stationed at the club. He tried to intimidate them by claiming to be an IPS officer, but the police were undeterred. A search of his bag revealed twelve 1-kilogram packets of heroin. Further questioning led the ATS to a flat in Naigaon where they found an additional 25 kilograms of heroin. The man identified himself as Sammohan Kumar (name changed), an IPS officer from the batch of 1995. As a member of the J&K cadre, Sammohan had held prestigious positions such as zonal director of the Narcotics Control Bureau (NCB) and joint director of the Enforcement Directorate (ED).

Under Krishipal's stern interrogation, Sammohan revealed his modus operandi. While working in the NCB, he had conducted numerous operations against drug cartels. However, he would steal half of the seized drugs and only record the remaining half. He would then mix clay with the stolen drugs and sell them back to the cartels. A constable from the Haryana Police had assisted him in this scheme. Since no one could complain about buying adulterated drugs, Sammohan earned crores of rupees while the authorities remained oblivious.

Krishipal contacted O.P.S. Malik, the director general of the NCB, to inform him about Sammohan's arrest. Malik was shocked by the allegations against Sammohan and promptly flew to Mumbai to meet Krishipal. Following their meeting, Malik ordered an investigation into all the drug cases that Sammohan had handled during his twenty-three-month tenure as the zonal director of the Chandigarh NCB unit. Ironically, Sammohan had been the one to uncover a nexus between the Chandigarh Police and local drug dealers while working for the NCB. The revelations about Sammohan finally explained why he had requested a transfer to Cochin after only two years with the NCB – though officers typically served an additional two years – despite his success in the role.

A few days after Sammohan's arrest, his father, a retired army officer, visited Krishipal in his office. He claimed that Sammohan was an upright officer, citing the fact that he had received the President's Police Medal for bravery. 'Mr Raghuvanshi, my son has become a victim of politics. While working for the NCB, he exposed several drug rackets and made many enemies as a result. Your ATS officers colluded with those people and trapped Sammohan. Please help him.'

Moved by the man's advanced age, Krishipal sympathized with him but explained that the law would take its own course – he couldn't offer any assistance.

In March 2009, the Chandigarh Police filed another case against Sammohan for pilfering seized drugs based on the NCB's findings. Three of his subordinates at the NCB were also arrested. In 2015, Sammohan was convicted under the Narcotic Drugs and Psychotropic Substances Act and sentenced to fifteen years in prison by a special court in Mumbai. The constable who had aided him received a thirteen-year sentence, while the third accused was released after he turned approver.

30

FINAL ENCOUNTERS

'He deserves this. He should rot in jail for the rest of his life,' Krishipal thought as he watched the news coverage about a former union minister being arrested by the CBI. The minister had been accused of misusing his position of power in collaboration with his son to obtain illegal financial benefits.

During Krishipal's second innings with the ATS, the minister had made his life extremely difficult, ultimately leading to his unceremonious exit from the organization. Seeing the bespectacled man, clad innocuously in a white shirt and dhoti, being pushed into a police car reaffirmed Krishipal's belief in karma. Although he had retired from the police service on 28 February 2015, the arrest of the minister brought back those bitter memories four years later.

When Krishipal took charge of the ATS again in November 2008, the investigation into the Malegaon blast was ongoing. Malegaon, a town in the Nashik district of Maharashtra, had been rocked by twin blasts on 29 September 2008, caused by explosive devices planted on a motorcycle. The explosions at the busy Bhiku Chowk, near a mosque, had resulted in the deaths of seven people and injured around 100 others. Hemant Karkare – Krishipal's successor and now predecessor – oversaw the investigation, which concluded that a Hindutva organization named Abhinav Bharat was behind the blasts.

It was alleged that members of Abhinav Bharat and other Hindu extremist groups had conspired to carry out violent acts against Muslims in Malegaon, among other places. The ATS had arrested over a dozen individuals, including Lt. Col. Prasad Purohit, a serving officer of military intelligence; Sadhvi Pragya Singh, a religious preacher; Major (Retired) Ramesh Upadhyay and Dayanand Pandey, a self-proclaimed godman. They had been charged under various sections of the UAPA and the IPC.[1]

The case took on a political character when saffron parties like the BJP and Shiv Sena accused the Congress government at the centre and in Maharashtra of using the ATS to harass supporters of the Hindutva ideology. One particular minister in the union cabinet had taken a keen interest in the case. He had been pleased with the progress made when Karkare was overseeing it but became suspicious after Krishipal took over.

One of the reasons for the minister's distrust was the controversy surrounding Krishipal's past interaction with one of the accused, Lt. Col. Prasad Purohit. Krishipal had invited Purohit to lecture the ATS on intelligence gathering techniques during his previous term. No money had been paid to Purohit, but Krishipal had written a letter of gratitude to him for his time. The letter was leaked to the media after Purohit's arrest, along with a picture supposedly showing Krishipal welcoming him with a bouquet of flowers.

Interestingly, Purohit was the only suspect in the bombings who was still in the ATS's custody when Krishipal took charge. Wanting to confront Purohit for betraying his trust, Krishipal ordered the investigating officer to bring the man before him.

'You don't practice what you preach. You've caused me so much embarrassment,' Krishipal said angrily.

'Sir, believe me, I've been framed in this case. I haven't done anything wrong. Politicians are using me as a scapegoat,' Purohit tried to convince him.

'Almost every accused individual I've dealt with has made similar claims. The ATS has strong evidence against you.'

'Sir, the evidence has been fabricated to silence me.'

While Krishipal was talking to Purohit, the union minister called on his mobile phone. Krishipal signalled for the constables to take the suspect away before accepting the call.

'Why haven't you arrested Indresh Kumar yet? Are you

waiting for some auspicious time?' the minister demanded rudely. There had been some speculation that Indresh Kumar, an RSS leader, had been involved in the Malegaon conspiracy.

'Sir, we don't have any evidence against him. We can't arrest him.'

'Don't try to fool me. Hemant Karkare had told me that the ATS has evidence against Indresh. Why are you protecting him?'

Though intimidated by the minister's loss of temper, Krishipal replied firmly. 'Sir, I can arrange for you to speak to the investigating officer and the public prosecutor.'

The minister abruptly ended the call. Krishipal wanted to call back and confront the man regarding his humiliating behaviour. However, his political party was in power, both at the state and central level. It wouldn't be prudent to be at odds with the ruling politicians, Krishipal realized.

Instead, he called a meeting with the public prosecutor and investigating officer to analyse the evidence against the suspects already in custody and recheck if there was any proof of Indresh Kumar's involvement. After reviewing all the evidence and statements from the accused, it was concluded that there was none. The only mention of Kumar in the case papers was that he had attended a meeting of around 100 people. 'How can someone be prosecuted for conspiring in a meeting with so many people present?' the prosecutor pointed out.

A few days later, Krishipal received another call from the minister. This time, the man claimed, 'I've been told that there are photos of Indresh Kumar with some of the accused.'

'Sir, all such materials have already been examined. We can't consider these as evidence against Kumar. I can send the DIG, who has been supervising the investigation since the beginning, to meet you and present all the evidence if you're not convinced.'

The minister once again ended the call without responding to Krishipal's offer. Days later, he summoned Krishipal to Delhi and reprimanded him. 'You haven't arrested any additional accused in the Malegaon case after taking over as ATS chief. Indresh Kumar is also moving around scot-free.'

'I resubmit, sir, that we have no evidence against him. I can't arrest anyone without evidence. As far as fresh arrests are concerned, the ATS is chasing the one who planted the bombs. Our team has been sent to Uttarakhand to catch him, based on a tip-off.'

The chargesheet for the Malegaon blast case was filed in court not long after. Indresh Kumar's name was absent, much to the minister's dismay.

Meanwhile, a PIL was filed in the Bombay High Court, alleging that the government wasn't taking terrorism seriously. The petitioner cited the lack of a full-time ATS chief as evidence of their claim, since Krishipal only held the position as an additional charge. The Government Pleader's response was surprising: 'My Lord, after Shri Hemant Karkare was martyred, the post of ATS chief is considered to be cursed by the officers, and no one is willing to take the charge.'[2]

After receiving stern remarks from the court, the Maharashtra government upgraded the post of the ATS chief from IG rank to additional DG rank. Krishipal was appointed as the full-time chief of the ATS.

Krishipal had a feeling that his actions would not be well-received and that the minister would try to find an excuse to harass him. However, he believed that he had already experienced the worst in his policing career, from serving in Gadchiroli to the rocky formation of the STF. Any appointment seen as a punishment had turned out to be a blessing in disguise for him. Once again, Krishipal mentally prepared himself for the unexpected.

In March 2010, the ATS arrested two suspects who had conspired to plants bombs in the ONGC office in Bandra and several shopping malls. It was a significant achievement for Krishipal's team, and reporters began calling him for details. Seeing an opportunity to showcase his team's efforts and boost their morale, he called for a brief press conference at his office and shared the details of the operation. All these particulars were part of the FIR, a public document.

After briefing the reporters, Krishipal went straight to Pune to oversee the ongoing investigation of the German Bakery blast case, which had happened a month prior. To his surprise, within forty-eight hours of the press conference, his phone was flooded with calls from reporters again. News channels began flashing sensational headlines, like 'Raghuvanshi shunted out from the ATS' and 'Rakesh Maria to replace KP Raghuvanshi as ATS

Chief'. According to their reports, the central government was angry about the press conference.[3]

Krishipal suspected that the minister had taken the opportunity to target him. He may have objected to Krishipal's media briefing and alleged that he had disclosed too much information, thus jeopardizing the investigation. Due to the pressure, the state government removed Krishipal as the ATS chief and transferred him to the position of additional DG (Law and Order).

Hurt by the sudden transfer, Krishipal met with Chief Minister Ashok Chavan. Chavan held Krishipal in high esteem, as he had witnessed his father Shankarrao Chavan appreciating his bravery and professionalism.

'Sir, I have been requesting a transfer from this stressful position in the ATS for so long but to no avail. Now, with the way I have been removed, how will I face my colleagues?'

Chavan consoled him. 'You should not feel bad about this, Raghuvanshi saheb. The position of additional DG (Law and Order) is the second most powerful in the state police after the DGP. You should be happy instead.'

Time is a great healer. After a few days spent feeling dejected, Krishipal gradually overcame his negative thoughts and refocused on his work. Now in charge of maintaining law and order across Maharashtra, he once again had the opportunity to oversee policing in

Gadchiroli. He was pleased to see that the C-60 unit he had established was successfully combatting the Naxal presence in the region and being recognized for its efforts. Dressed in a commando uniform, Krishipal occasionally visited Gadchiroli and ventured into the jungle – not so much for operational reasons, more for nostalgia. He enjoyed sharing stories of his time as SP in Gadchiroli with the new recruits of C-60 and providing them with tips on effectively policing the area.

Ten months later, the additional chief secretary (Home) called Krishipal in his office, bearing shocking news. He had been transferred to the position of additional DG (Thane). Krishipal couldn't help but view this as a demotion, given his prior tenure in the region a decade ago. Moreover, he had never heard of an additional DG (Thane) … had a new post been created? Recognizing his mistake, the bureaucrat swiftly corrected himself, clarifying that Krishipal had, in fact, been appointed as the police commissioner of Thane. Relief washed over Krishipal as the true nature of his new role dawned on him.

Shortly thereafter, Krishipal was summoned by Home Minister R. R. Patil. In a tone tinged with regret, Patil acknowledged the perceived injustice done to Krishipal. His decision to elevate Krishipal to the coveted position of police commissioner of Thane was a form of restitution. The minister emphasized its significance as the second most powerful post in Maharashtra, trailing only the police commissioner of Mumbai. Krishipal politely conveyed that he was content with his present position, but Patil insisted that he take up the offered posting.

After serving as Thane's police commissioner for three years, Krishipal was transferred to the Maharashtra Security Force (MSF) as its director general. Although this position is sometimes seen as low-profile in police circles, it is equivalent to being the police chief of a state. The MSF's responsibility is to provide security for government installations, banks and public transport systems such as metro rails and monorails, as well as supplement the police force. After an uneventful tenure with the MSF, Krishipal retired from the police in 2015.

Like most IPS officers of the Maharashtra cadre, Krishipal had nurtured the desire to become Mumbai's commissioner of police – a role that earned the call sign 'King'. With his brilliant performance at all the posts he had been assigned, Krishipal had hoped that he was meritorious enough for the government to consider him for the coveted post. Unfortunately, he didn't get the chance.

When Patil was admitted to Mumbai's Lilavati Hospital after being diagnosed with late-stage oral cancer, Krishipal went to visit him. From his bed, the home minister said with tears in his eyes, 'Raghuvanshi, you didn't come to see me earlier.'

'I'm sorry, sir. I was very occupied with official work,' Krishipal replied.

'I know you are unhappy with me, as I didn't make you the Mumbai police commissioner. Anyway, we will meet at my bungalow soon. We will talk about it then.'

Patil was hopeful that he would recover and resume his work. However, he died soon after, in February 2015.

A year before his retirement, a national political party offered Krishipal the opportunity to contest the Lok Sabha election from the North Central Mumbai seat. However, he considered himself unsuited for politics – he lacked the funds and cunning needed to win elections. He requested time to discuss the proposal with his close relatives but by the time Krishipal made up his mind to give politics a try, the party had already chosen another candidate. In retrospect, the missed opportunity was not a source of regret for Krishipal.

Throughout his career, Krishipal was rarely given the prestigious posts that most IPS officers strive for. Often, he was placed in positions that others disliked or where he had to struggle to succeed. However, Krishipal was satisfied that each of these assignments had made him stronger and allowed him to leave his mark. Among his cherished memories, his posting in Gadchiroli continues to hold a special place. If Naxal activity has decreased in Gadchiroli, it is in large part due to the efforts of his C-60 force, which continues to achieve results three decades after its establishment.

During a conversation with the author, Krishipal expressed his pride and contentment with his life as a police officer. Despite the trials and tribulations, he said, 'Given the choice, I would become a police officer again in my next life.'

NOTES

Preface

1. Nazia Sayed, 'Encounter specialist Angre, acquitted by court, but dismissed by DGP for extortion', *Mumbai Mirror*, 2 June 2014. Available at: https://mumbaimirror.indiatimes.com/mumbai/cover-story/encounter-specialist-angre-acquitted-by-court-but-dismissed-by-dgp-for-extortion/articleshow/35934177.cms.

1. A Gunfight in the Forest

1. Uttam Kumar Sharma, 'Tendu Leaves: Trade and management practices in India', Indira Gandhi National Forest Academy. Available at: https://www.ignfa.gov.in/document/biodiversity-cell-ntfp-related-issues15.pdf.
2. PTI, 'Gadchiroli encounter: Killed Maoists had come to enjoy a marriage party', *New Indian Express*, updated 24 April 2018. Available at: https://www.newindianexpress.com/nation/2018/apr/23/gadchiroli-encounter-killed-maoists-had-come-to-enjoy-a-marriage-party-1805405.html.
3. PTI, 'Gadchiroli Naxal encounter: Maharashtra police identify 11 of 16 insurgents killed, two were 17-year-old girls', *FirstPost*, 23 April 2018. Available at: https://www.firstpost.com/india/gadchiroli-naxal-encounter-maharashtra-police-identify-11-of-16-insurgents-killed-two-were-17-year-old-girls-4443207.html.
4. Vivek Deshpande, 'Police harassment turned Sainath into a Maoist', *Indian Express*, 5 May 2018. Available at: https://indianexpress.com/article/india/police-harassment-turned-sainath-into-a-maoist-5163991/.

5. Interview with Dr Abhinav Deshmukh.
6. FIR no. 12/2018, filed at Bhamragarh Police Station, 24 April 2018.
7. Arunima, 'Maharashtra Police's Gadchiroli Naxal Encounter One of the Most Successful in Recent Times', *News18*, 23 April 2018. Available at: https://www.news18.com/news/india/maharashtra-polices-gadchiroli-naxal-encounter-one-of-the-most-successful-in-recent-times-1726235.html.
8. Interview with Dr Abhinav Deshmukh.
9. '39 Naxals Killed: Two Encounters in Two Days in Maha's Gadchiroli', *The Quint*, 22 April 2018. Available at: https://www.thequint.com/news/india/naxal-operation-in-gadchiroli-maharashtra#read-more.
10. Soumitra Bose, 'Missing villagers, poisoning claim add to Maoist intrigue', *Times of India*, 30 April 2018. Available at: https://timesofindia.indiatimes.com/india/missing-villagers-poisoning-claim-add-to-maoist-intrigue/articleshow/63966109.cms.

2. Timid Boy Becomes a Cop

1. 'Mission Statement', Sardar Vallabhbhai Patel National Police Academy. Available at: https://www.svpnpa.gov.in/static/gallery/docs/7747d5204f2d4367a172c699957c3476.pdf.
2. Ibid.
3. Parth Shastri, 'Cop pens history of mounted police', *Times of India*, 15 July 2018. Available at: https://timesofindia.indiatimes.com/city/ahmedabad/cop-pens-history-of-mounted-police/articleshow/64992422.cms.

3. The Challenge of Communal Violence

1. As told to the author by K. P. Raghuvanshi (KPR).
2. 'For Sangh, it's a "homecoming"', *Telegraph India*, 10 December 2014. Available at: https://www.telegraphindia.com/india/for-sangh-it-s-a-homecoming/cid/1577232.
3. J. Kumar, 'Maharashtra: Why and how Shiv Sena's relationship with Muslims is changing', *Moneycontrol*, 12 April 2024. Available at: https://www.moneycontrol.com/elections/lok-

sabha-election/maharashtra/maharashtra-why-and-how-shiv-senas-relationship-with-muslims-is-changing-article-12625151.html.

5. Bombay Burns Over a Book

1. M. Rahman, 'Civic poll battle in Aurangabad inflames communal passions', *India Today*, 15 June 1988. Available at: https://www.indiatoday.in/magazine/indiascope/story/19880615-maharashtra-civic-poll-battle-in-aurangabad-inflames-communal-passions-797337-1988-06-14.
2. Violette Graff and Juliette Galonnier, 'Hindu-Muslim Communal Riots in India II (1986-2011)', SciencesPo, 20 August 2013. Available at: https://www.sciencespo.fr/mass-violence-war-massacre-resistance/en/document/hindu-muslim-communal-riots-india-ii-1986-2011.html.
3. 'Civic poll battle in Aurangabad', *India Today*.
4. Khushwant Singh, *The End of India* (New Delhi: Penguin Random House, 2003), pp. 26–7.
5. Sharad Pawar, *On My Terms: From the Grassroots to the Corridors of Power* (New Delhi: Speaking Tiger, 2016), pp. 81–2
6. Years later, Bal Thackeray said that he was not against renaming the university – he only wanted the word 'Marathwada' to be retained, with Ambedkar's name added alongside it. Source: 'I never opposed giving Ambedkar's name to Marathwada University: Bal Thackeray', *DNA India*, 18 May 2011. Available at: https://www.dnaindia.com/mumbai/report-i-never-opposed-giving-ambedkar-s-name-to-marathwada-university-bal-thackeray-1544871.

7. From Germany to Gadchiroli

1. Dandakaranya, *Britannica*. Available at: https://www.britannica.com/place/Dandakaranya.
2. Omar Rashid, 'Celebrating Ravan', *The Hindu*, 24 October 2015. Available at: https://www.thehindu.com/features/magazine/omar-rashid-on-ravan-worship/article7799972.ece.
3. Dr Sachidanand Das, 'Dandakaranya and the Legend of

Its Origin', *Sanskriti Magazine*. Available at: https://www.sanskritimagazine.com/dandakaranya-and-the-legend-of-its-origin.

4. Rahul Pandita, *Hello Bastar: The Untold Story of India's Maoist Movement* (New Delhi: Tranquebar, 2011), pp. 20–1.
5. Sumanta Banerjee, 'Once Upon a Time in Naxalbari', Indian History Collective. Available at: https://indianhistorycollective.com/once-upon-a-time-in-naxalbari/.
6. '1967: Naxalbari movement', *FrontLine*, 12 August 2022. Available at: https://frontline.thehindu.com/politics/india-at-75-epochal-moments-1967-naxalbari-movement/article65721597.ece.
7. M Rajivlochan, '50 years of Naxalite movement: What happened at Naxalbari on May 25, 1967?', DailyO, 26 May 2017. Available at: https://www.dailyo.in/politics/naxalite-naxalbari-may-25-1967-charu-mazumdar-kanu-sanyal-17404.
8. Ibid.
9. Ibid.
10. B. Upadhyay, 'On the Thoughts of Charu Mazumdar', Marxists Internet Archive. Available at: https://www.marxists.org/subject/india/cpiml/charu-thought.pdf.
11. Devendra Gawande, *Nakshalwadache Aavhan*, 4th ed., (Pune: Sadhana Prakashan, 2016).
12. Pandita, *Hello Bastar*.
13. Ibid.
14. Committee for the Protection of Democratic Rights (Bombay), *Peddi Shankar – Death by encounter: A CPDR Fact-finding Report*, 1981.
15. This conversation has been recreated based on the writings of Charu Mazumdar and inputs from the author's sources in Gadchiroli.

9. A Deep-Rooted Problem

1. As told to the author by KPR.
2. Gawande, *Nakshalwadache Aavhan*.
3. Jan Myrdal, *Red Star Over India: As the Wretched of the Earth are Rising* (Kolkata: Setu Prakashni, 2012).

4. Harsh Thakor, '40th anniversary of police firing on tribals in Indravelli', Countercurrents, 20 April 2021. Available at: https://countercurrents.org/2021/04/40th-anniversary-of-police-firing-on-tribals-in-indravelli/.
5. As told to the author by Ashok Biswas.
6. Ibid.
7. Ibid.

10. Thinking like a Naxalite

1. As told to the author by KPR.
2. Gawande, *Nakshalwadache Aavhan*.
3. As told to the author by KPR.

11. The C-60 Comes to Life

1. PTI, 'Maharashtra Gives Rs 5 Lakh To Prisons As "Secret Service Fund"', *NDTV*, 19 July 2018. Available at: https://www.ndtv.com/india-news/maharashtra-gives-rs-5-lakh-to-prisons-as-secret-service-fund-1886297.

12. The Saga of Kamala Alaam

1. As told to the author by Kamala Alaam.

13. The Abduction of Baba Atram

1. As told to the author by KPR.
2. 'MLA Abduction May Hit Congress', *Times of India*, 29 April 1991.
3. 'Govt ready for talks with captors', *Times of India*, 3 May 1991.
4. 'AP Congress MLA Shot Dead by Naxals', *Times of India*, 8 April 1991.

14. The Enemy Inside and Outside

1. M. Rahman, 'Charges of underworld links jolt Pawar but he tries to ride out the crisis once again', *India Today*, 15 September

1994. Available at: https://www.indiatoday.in/magazine/special-report/story/19940915-charges-of-underworld-links-jolt-pawar-but-he-tries-to-ride-out-the-crisis-once-again-809617-1994-09-14.
2. Article 311, Constitition of India. Available at: https://www.constitutionofindia.net/articles/article-311-dismissal-removal-or-reduction-in-rank-of-persons-employed-in-civil-capacities-under-the-union-or-a-state/#:~:text=Article%20311%2C%2-0Constitution%20of%20India,by%20which%20he%20was%20appointed.
3. As told to the author by KPR.

17. Fighting Raktabeej

1. Letter from V. K. Saraf to KPR, 1 July 1992. Shared with the author by KPR.
2. As told to the author by KPR.
3. PTI, 'Youth From Gadchiroli Not Joining Naxal Movement Anymore: Maharashtra DyCM Fadnavis', *Outlook India*, 18 January 2024. Available at: https://www.outlookindia.com/national/youth-from-gadchiroli-not-joining-naxal-movement-anymore-maharashtra-dycm-fadnavis-news-246293.

18. Detaining Bal Thackeray

1. Dhaval Kulkarni, 'Explained: The high-stakes renaming politics of Maharashtra', *Hindustan Times*, 29 May 2022. Available at: https://www.hindustantimes.com/cities/mumbai-news/explained-the-high-stakes-renaming-politics-of-maharashtra-101653843720814.html.

19. A Mole in the CBI?

1. R. Padmanabhan, 'A deal questioned', *FrontLine*, 7 March 1998. Available at: https://frontline.thehindu.com/the-nation/article30160998.ece.
2. Y. K. Sabharwal, *Centre For Public Interest Litigation ... vs Union Of India (Uoi) And Ors. on 1 January, 1999*, Delhi High Court. Available at: https://indiankanoon.org/doc/494219/.

3. 'Govt Gets Clean Chit In Mukta Panna Deal', *Business Standard*, 3 February 1998. Available at: https://www.business-standard.com/article/specials/govt-gets-clean-chit-in-mukta-panna-deal-198020301079_1.html.
4. Petition number: W.P.(C) 3020/1997.
5. 'Cbi, 3 Others Served Notices In Mukta-Panna Case', *Business Standard*, 19 February 1998. Available at: https://www.business-standard.com/article/specials/cbi-3-others-served-notices-in-mukta-panna-case-198021901036_1.html.
6. Y. K. Sabharwal, *Centre For Public Interest Litigation ... vs Union Of India (Uoi) And Ors. on 1 January, 1999.*
7. S. S. M. Quadri, *Centre For Public Interest Litigation & ... vs Union Of India & Ors on 19 October, 2000*, Supreme Court of India. Available at: https://indiankanoon.org/doc/99072131/.
8. Ibid.
9. As told to the author by KPR. Confessional affidavit available.

20. A Furious Sonia Gandhi

1. Full Srikrishna Report, Sabrang Communications. Available at: https://www.sabrang.com/srikrish/vol2.htm.
2. Lyla Bavadam, 'A probe and proceedings', *FrontLine*, 23 June 2001. Available at: https://frontline.thehindu.com/other/article30251096.ece.
3. Jyoti Punwani, 'How three brave men put Mumbai ex-police commissioner in the dock on murder charges after '93 riots', Scroll.in, 23 October 2020. Available at: https://scroll.in/article/976512/how-three-brave-men-put-mumbai-ex-police-commissioner-in-the-dock-on-murder-charges-after-93-riots.
4. Ibid.
5. Nirbhay Bano Andolan, *The Srikrishna Commission Report – Too hot to handle*, 2000. Available at: https://www.unipune.ac.in/snc/cssh/humanrights/04%20COMMUNAL%20RIOTS/A%20-%20%20ANTI-MUSLIM%20RIOTS/06%20-%20MAHARASHTRA/n.pdf.
6. Nishit Dholabhai, 'Minority hurt seeps out on delayed action', *Telegraph India*, 14 August 2007. Available at: https://www.

telegraphindia.com/india/minority-hurt-seeps-out-on-delayed-action/cid/1569442.

21. You Are Under Arrest, Sir

1. Full Srikrishna Report, Sabrang Communications.
2. Ibid.
3. 'Tyagi arrested for 1993 killings', *Times of India*, 15 August 2001. Available at: https://timesofindia.indiatimes.com/city/mumbai/tyagi-arrested-for-1993-killings/articleshow/1630138397.cms.
4. 'Tyagi, 17 others chargesheeted', *Times of India*, 28 August 2001. Available at: https://timesofindia.indiatimes.com/city/mumbai/tyagi-17-others-chargesheeted/articleshow/1584329038.cms.

22. Chhagan Bhujbal Vs Bal Thackeray

1. Jyoti Punwani, 'Ajit Pawar's regret and NCP's politics', *Mumbai Mirror*, 14 October 2019. Available at: https://mumbaimirror.indiatimes.com/maharashtra-assembly-elections/news/ajit-pawars-regret-and-ncps-politics/articleshow/71571814.html.
2. Dhaval S. Kulkarni, 'Chhagan Bhujbal: How Shiv Sena's original rebel turned a corner', *India Today*, 5 July 2023. Available at: https://www.indiatoday.in/india-today-insight/story/chhagan-bhujbal-how-shiv-senas-original-rebel-turned-a-corner-2402220-2023-07-05.
3. V Shankar Aiyar, 'Did the Shiv Sena chief elude imprisonment simply because he is Bal Thackeray?', *India Today*, 14 August 2000. Available at: https://www.indiatoday.in/magazine/nation/story/20000814-did-the-shiv-sena-chief-elude-imprisonment-simply-because-he-is-bal-thackeray-778950-2000-08-13.
4. Syed Firdaus Ashraf, 'Court throws out case against Thackeray', Rediff, 25 July 2000. Available at: https://m.rediff.com/news/2000/jul/25sena4.htm.
5. Full Srikrishna Report, Sabrang Communications, 9.3–9.10.
6. Ibid, 1.27.

23. Terrorism, Bollywood and Abu Salem

1. PTI, 'Gujarat HC Raps Modi Govt for 'Inaction' during Post-Godhra Riots.' *The Hindu*, 8 February 2012. Available at: https://www.thehindu.com/news/national/gujarat-hc-raps-modi-govt-for-inaction-during-postgodhra-riots/article2871891.ece.
2. As told to the author by KPR.
3. Purnima Sah, 'Have spent 25 years in prison, deserve remission: Bombay blasts convict Abu Salem tells High Court', *The Hindu*, 19 February 2025. Available at: https://www.thehindu.com/news/cities/mumbai/have-spent-25-years-in-prison-deserve-remission-bombay-blasts-convict-abu-salem-tells-high-court/article69238759.ece.
4. PTI, 'Abu Salem chargesheeted in Ajit Dewani murder case', *The Times of India*, 15 April 2006. Available at: https://timesofindia.indiatimes.com/india/abu-salem-chargesheeted-in-ajit-dewani-murder-case/articleshow/1491466.cms.
5. Rashmi Rajput, 'How the Pradeep Jain murder case was cracked', *Hindu*, 28 November 2021. Available at: https://www.thehindu.com/news/cities/mumbai/How-the-Pradeep-Jain-murder-case-was-cracked/article60331660.ece.
6. Jyoti Kanyal, 'The Gulshan Kumar Murder Case: A Recap', *India Today*, 1 July 2021. Available at: https://www.indiatoday.in/movies/celebrities/story/gulshan-kumar-murder-case-a-recap-1821531-2021-07-01.
7. Ankita Chaurasia, 'Sanjay Dutt Arms and Ammunitions case: Chronology of events', *Times of India*, 16 January 2017. Available at: https://timesofindia.indiatimes.com/entertainment/hindi/bollywood/news/sanjay-dutt-arms-and-ammunitions-case-chronology-of-events/articleshow/50464222.cms.
8. 'Sharpshooter who worked for Abu Salem, "shot at" Rakesh Roshan, arrested in Delhi', *Hindustan Times*, 16 June 2017. Available at: https://www.hindustantimes.com/delhi-news/sharpshooter-who-worked-for-abu-salem-shot-at-rakesh-roshan-arrested-in-delhi/story-s2Uxy56e7fbY7zloYG813H.html.
9. As told to the author by KPR.

10. 'Monica Bedi admits her past with Abu Salem has affected her dating and professional prospects', *Times of India*, 18 July 2023. Available at: https://timesofindia.indiatimes.com/entertainment/hindi/bollywood/news/monica-bedi-admits-her-past-with-abu-salem-has-affected-her-dating-and-professional-prospects/articleshow/101851060.cms.
11. 'Salem: Confession was beaten out of me', *Times of India*, 13 January 2006. Available at: https://timesofindia.indiatimes.com/india/salem-confession-was-beaten-out-of-me/articleshow/1370175.cms.
12. PTI, 'Abu Salem alleges torture by ATS', Rediff, 13 January 2006. Available at: https://www.rediff.com/news/2006/jan/13salem.htm.
13. PTI, 'Abu Salem: Mumbai police go online', *Times of India*, 13 January 2006. Available at: https://timesofindia.indiatimes.com/india/abu-salem-mumbai-police-go-online/articleshow/1371577.cms?from=mdr.
14. 'Abu Salem gets life term in Pradeep Jain murder case', *Hindu BusinessLine*, 24 January 2018. Available at: https://www.thehindubusinessline.com/news/abu-salem-gets-life-term-in-pradeep-jain-murder-case/article62317593.ece.

24. Operation Amanat

1. Individual Terrorists Under UAPA, Ministry of Home Affairs. Available at: https://www.mha.gov.in/en/page/individual-terrorists-under-uapa.
2. Kunwar Khuldune Shahid, 'Time for Pakistan to Cut Ties With Hizbul Mujahideen', *The Diplomat*, 30 May 2017. Available at: https://thediplomat.com/2017/05/time-for-pakistan-to-cut-ties-with-hizbul-mujahideen/.

25. Conspiracy to Assassinate Chief Minister Narendra Modi

1. Mahesh Langa, 'Gujarat IPS officer who took on Modi after 2002 riots dismissed', *The Hindu*, 17 November 2021. Available at: https://www.thehindu.com/news/national/Sanjiv-Bhatt-dismissed-from-IPS/article60305522.ece.

2. '"We Have No Orders To Save You": State Participation and Complicity in Communal Violence in Gujarat', Human Rights Watch, 30 April 2002. Available at: https://www.hrw.org/report/2002/04/30/we-have-no-orders-save-you/state-participation-and-complicity-communal-violence.
3. 'The riots singe Modi, again', *New Indian Express*, updated 16 May 2012. Available at: https://www.newindianexpress.com/opinions/editorials/2009/Apr/30/the-riots-singe-modi-again-45250.html.
4. 'Killed Mumbai blast suspect had a Yemeni father', *Times of India*, 13 September 2003. Available at: https://timesofindia.indiatimes.com/india/killed-mumbai-blast-suspect-had-a-yemeni-father/articleshow/180857.cms?from=mdr.
5. 'Ministry of Home Affairs extends ban imposed on Students Islamic Movement of India for 5 years', *The Hindu*, 29 January 2024. Available at: https://www.thehindu.com/news/national/simi-banned-for-five-more-years/article67788794.ece.
6. Charul Shah, 'Fayaz Kagzi may be Madina suicide bomber: ATS', *Hindustan Times*, 15 December 2016. Available at: https://www.hindustantimes.com/mumbai-news/ats-believes-madina-suicide-bomber-was-fayaz-kagzi/story-jojSwSgRWfCzrGwVXS0nLI.html.
7. Mateen Hafeez, 'Fayyaz Kagzi, a terror suspect, is suspected to have taken shelter in Saudi Arabia', *Times of India*, 29 June 2012. Available at: https://timesofindia.indiatimes.com/fayyaz-kagzi-a-terror-suspect-is-suspected-to-have-taken-shelter-in-saudi-arabia-/articleshow/14508216.cms.
8. Shah, 'Fayaz Kagzi may be Madina suicide bomber'.
9. 'Innocent youths were falsely implicated by ATS in 2006 terror cases, allege Jamiat', *DNA India*, 4 May 2016. Available at: https://www.dnaindia.com/mumbai/report-innocent-youths-were-falsely-implicated-by-ats-in-2006-terror-cases-allege-jamiat-2208879.
10. 'Acquitted innocent Muslims speak out at Peoples Tribunal', *Milli Gazette*, 31 October 2016. Available at: https://www.milligazette.com/news/4-national/14958-acquitted-innocent-muslims-speak-out-at-peoples-tribunal/.

26. 2006 Mumbai Terror Attack

1. Reuters, 'India leader meets Mumbai bomb victims', NBC News, 15 July 2006. Available at: https://www.nbcnews.com/id/wbna13861655.
2. As told to the author by KPR.
3. 'Cops Still Clueless about Two 7/11 Bomb Planters.' *The Times of India*, 20 October 2008. Available at: https://timesofindia.indiatimes.com/city/mumbai/cops-still-clueless-about-two-7/11-bomb-planters/articleshow/3616268.cms
4. Prerana Thakurdesai, '2006 Mumbai serial blasts: Inside story of how Mumbai Police cracked the conspiracy', *India Today*, 16 October 2006. Available at: https://www.indiatoday.in/magazine/cover-story/story/20061016-how-2006-mumbai-serial-blast-case-was-cracked-784466-2006-10-15.
5. Ibid.
6. 'Month after 7/11 Mumbai blasts, a controversial encounter at Antop Hill', *Hindustan Times*, updated 13 September 2015. Available at: https://www.hindustantimes.com/mumbai/month-after-7-11-mumbai-blasts-a-controversial-encounter-at-antop-hill/story-uwqpuoAhL6lkdBCqZPbqTP.html.

27. ATS Vs Crime Branch

1. Thakurdesai, '2006 Mumbai serial blasts'.
2. 'A Joint Operation', *Outlook India*, 30 September 2006. Available at: https://www.outlookindia.com/national/a-joint-operation-news-232669.
3. Stavan Desai, Presley Thomas and Debasish Panigrahi, 'Five terror suspects nabbed for Ahmedabad, Delhi blasts', *Hindustan Times*, 24 September 2008. Available at: https://www.hindustantimes.com/india/five-suspects-nabbed-for-serial-blasts/story-62wPBdQKLkc8WEGfe5AEAL.html.
4. PTI, '2006 Mumbai train blasts: IM co-founder and accused Sadiq Sheikh retracts confession', *India Today*, 6 April 2013. Available at: https://www.indiatoday.in/india/story/indian-mujahideen-sadiq-sheikh-2006-train-blast-case-india-terror-malegaon-blasts-2008-blasts-157963-2013-04-05.

5. Swati Deshpande and Rebecca Samervel, '2006 Mumbai train blasts: Death for 5 bombers, life term for 7', *Times of India*, 30 September 2015. Available at: https://timesofindia.indiatimes.com/city/mumbai/2006-mumbai-train-blasts-death-for-5-bombers-life-term-for-7/articleshow/49164388.cms.
6. Aaratrika Bhaumik, '"Grave error": Why Bombay HC acquitted all 12 convicted in 2006 Mumbai train blasts', *The Hindu*, 23 July 2025. Available at: https://www.thehindu.com/news/national/why-bombay-hc-acquitted-all-12-convicted-in-2006-mumbai-train-blasts/article69841319.ece.
7. 'India court pauses acquittal of 12 men in Mumbai train bombings case', *BBC*, 24 July 2025. Available at: https://bbc.com/news/articles/cy4n4yzpx07o.

30. Final Encounters

1. Deeptiman Tiwary, 'Explained: The case against BJP candidate Sadhvi Pragya Thakur', *Indian Express*, 18 April 2019. Available at: https://indianexpress.com/article/explained/sadhvi-pragya-thakur-digvijaya-singh-bjp-bhopal-lok-sabha-elections-malegaon-case-ajmer-dargah-blast-5681180/.
2. PTI, 'After court rap,state names Raghuvanshi as ATS chief', *Indian Express*, 12 June 2009. Available at: https://indianexpress.com/article/cities/mumbai/after-court-rap-state-names-raghuvanshi-as-ats-chief/.
3. PTI, 'Under fire Raghuvanshi removed as ATS chief; Maria to take over', *Hindustan Times*, updated 25 March 2010. Available at: https://www.hindustantimes.com/mumbai/under-fire-raghuvanshi-removed-as-ats-chief-maria-to-take-over/story-CuA44lt3rfbDXhyhmoqj4I_amp.html.

ACKNOWLEDGEMENTS

My utmost gratitude goes to K. P. Raghuvanshi, the protagonist of this story. The book is a product of the numerous coffee sessions I have shared with him at his office in Churchgate and his Thane residence. Our meetings started in September 2022 and I lost the count after thirty. Although he has retired from the police force, his life after superannuation is no less busy. He continues to work as a consultant for some private entities. Despite his busy schedule, which includes frequent travel, he generously spared time to share anecdotes from his life with me.

Some say that there is no 'thank you' in friendship, but the author in me cannot refrain from thanking Anish Chandy – my friend and the founder of Labyrinth Literary Agency – enough. I am grateful to him for not only agreeing to represent my work (based on merit, not friendship), but also shaping the book into its present form. It was on his suggestion that the theme of *Troubleshooter* was altered from Naxalism in Gadchiroli to the biography it is today.

I met Abhinav Deshmukh (IPS) when he was the SP of Gadchiroli in 2018, while I was shooting a documentary.

We spoke again in 2022 when he was transferred to Mumbai as a DCP. He helped me understand the role played by the C-60 commando force in weakening the Naxal movement in Gadchiroli. I am grateful to him for his time and all the inputs he offered for the book.

Another IPS officer who made a valuable contribution to this book is Neelotpal. It was due to his kind cooperation after we met in Gadchiroli in 2023 that I was able to access some surrendered Naxals and C-60 personnel. Although I have not been able to incorporate all the inputs received from the surrendered Naxals, since the theme of the book changed while it was being written, I am hopeful that such information will appear in my later work. My thanks to Neelotpal for all the help he extended to me in Gadchiroli.

I am grateful to C-60 personnel, Ashok Biswas and Kamala Alaam, for sharing interesting anecdotes from their policing careers with me.

My former colleague, Romit Tombarlawar, was my guide in Gadchiroli and accompanied me during my numerous visits to the district. He not only introduced me to valuable contacts but also arranged for my accommodation and transportation. I am thankful to Romit for all the help he provided during the research and writing process.

My gratitude to Pan Macmillan India for publishing this book. The editorial team has diligently and passionately made efforts to refine my work and make it as error-free as possible. Still, if you notice any mistakes, I am to be blamed for them. Thank you to Pujitha Krishnan, Shreya Ahlawat, Shreyoshee Bandyopadhyay and Udyotna Kumar for bringing this book to its present form. The intelligent queries you raised, the structural changes you made and the mistakes you corrected have added to the readability of this book. I look forward to working with you all again on future projects.

I am thankful to Sudhakar Solomonraj, who was my political science teacher at Wilson College, Mumbai, for encouraging me to write on contemporary issues. The staff of the Asiatic Society, Mumbai, also deserve my gratitude for making old newspaper clippings and reference books on the Maoist movement available to me.

Lastly, with thanks, I acknowledge the tolerance of my wife, Rimpi, and son, Vedaanta. I wrote this book by encroaching on time which was rightfully theirs. As a TV journalist, my life has been super busy. Like my previous books, I completed *Troubleshooter* by cutting down on our family time.

LIST OF ABBREVIATIONS

ACP: Assistant Commissioner of Police
AIG: Assistant Inspector General
ASP: Assistant Superintendent of Police
ATS: Anti-Terrorism Squad
BDDS: Bomb Detection and Disposal Squad
BJP: Bharatiya Janata Party
BMC: Brihanmumbai Municipal Corporation
BRO: Border Roads Organization
BSF: Border Security Force
CAG: Comptroller and Auditor General
CBI: Central Bureau of Investigation
CID: Crime Investigation Department
CM: Chief Minister
CP: Commissioner of Police
CRPF: Central Reserve Police Force
CSMT: Chhatrapati Shivaji Maharaj Terminus
DCP: Deputy Commissioner of Police
DG/DGP: Director General of Police
DIG: Deputy Inspector General of Police
FIR: First Information Report

FSL: Forensic Science Laboratory
GR: Government Resolution
IAS: Indian Administrative Service
IB: Intelligence Bureau
IED: Improvised Explosive Device
IFS: Indian Foreign Service
IG: Inspector General of Police
IPC: Indian Penal Code
IPS: Indian Police Service
ISI: Inter-Services Intelligence
LeT: Lashkar-e-Taiba
MCOCA: Maharashtra Control of Organised Crime Act
MLA: Member of Legislative Assembly
MP: Member of Parliament
MSF: Maharashtra Security Force
NCB: Narcotics Control Bureau
NSA: National Security Adviser
ONGC: Oil and Natural Gas Corporation
PIL: Public Interest Litigation
PWG: People's War Group
RAW: Research and Analysis Wing
SI: Sub-inspector
SIMI: Students' Islamic Movement of India
SOS: Special Operations Squad
SP: Superintendent of Police
SRP: State Reserve Police
STF: Special Task Force
SVPNPA: Sardar Vallabhbhai Patel National Police Academy
TADA: Terrorist and Disruptive Activities (Prevention) Act

UAPA: Unlawful Activities (Prevention) Act
UPSC: Union Public Service Commission
VHP: Vishva Hindu Parishad